KT-521-937

Educational Traditions Compared

Content, Teaching and Learning
in Industrialised Countries

Martin McLean

David Fulton Publishers

London

David Fulton Publishers Ltd
2 Barbon Close, London WC1N 3JX

First published in Great Britain by
David Fulton Publishers 1995

Note: The right of Martin McLean to be identified as the author of this work has been asserted by him in accordance with the Copyright, Designs and Patents Act 1988.

British Library Cataloguing in Publication Data

A catalogue record for this book is available from the British Library

ISBN 1–85346–356–6

Typeset by Textype Typesetters, Cambridge
Printed in Great Britain by The Cromwell Press Ltd., Melksham

Contents

Preface

In many countries education is becoming a burden on its participants, who are driven to perform at increasingly high levels, as much through fear of failure as by the excitement of anticipated reward. The weight is increased by the unwillingness of civic authorities and popular opinion to expand resources for public education while expecting, perversely, better measurable returns. This oppression occurs in a new world which has shed much of the totalitarianism of an ideologically stringent past and where economic, social and cultural opportunities for individuals and communities are still immense. Opportunities for the expression of diversity and individuality appear greater than before.

The challenge to education comes from a global economy that makes work more complex and more mercurial. It also deprives governments of traditional powers to protect their citizens from external threats. While globalization has revolutionized the economy and has made inroads into culture, through telecommunications, it leaves much social and personal life untouched. It is egalitarian in that it offers peoples of some, but not all, previously poor countries new opportunities for material benefit. It is libertarian in that it expects no obedience or even loyalty beyond the market place. So why is it associated with the education of Mr Grandgrind?

The problem is not in the story but in its telling. Politicians and employers have narrated a parable of imminent doom. Vast improvements in educational achievements are necessary to compete in a world economy which has no hiding places for the under-equipped. Much is correct in that account. But the supporting evidence is often spurious and the suggested strategies too limited. There are many ways to compete and even more strategies to prepare young people to be effective workers. Education is about much more than narrow or uniform vocational preparation and, ironically, the economy requires that this be the case. The best citizens, the most fulfilled persons and the most imaginative, resourceful students make the most effective workers in currently successful economies. The crucial element in the equation is motivation. Whole populations need to thirst after education. Education has to be attractive if it is to be so desired. In a world of shrill injunctions to improve performance, those in education have to dig deep in their cultural resources to fuel their inner drives. And these cultural riches are not only old but also often specific to particular countries.

This book is mainly about the variety of ways in which countries throughout the world, but mainly in its wealthier sector, respond to these challenges. It tries to account for success and failure in ways that relate to wider and older educational practices. It is meant as an antidote to crude international statistics and to attempts to erect particular national paragons of educational virtue – Germany or France for the British, Japan for Americans. The central argument is that each country has distinctive traditions of education, sometimes overlapping but ultimately unique. Educational improvement in each country needs to draw upon these traditions if its citizens are to be effectively motivated. Yet each tradition has strengths and weaknesses when confronted with contemporary global pressures. Successful adaptation requires appropriate, clever and wise selection from traditions.

Such selection needs understanding of the range of differences between national or regional educational traditions. Educational participants in each culture, like a football team, need to play in their own style but to be able to compete with the other contestants. The point of comparison is to allow members of each culture to know themselves better through contrasts with others. This purpose is especially relevant to education where historic shared values have a particular impact. Within education, valuations of knowledge and the personal attributes it may develop are specific to cultures yet crucial to global competition. Comparison will focus on these areas.

Yet knowledge and skills, teaching and learning are dependent on valuations about who should get education and who should decide its character. Values of access and opportunity, participation and control also differ between countries and affect the coherence of educational effort.

The early chapters analyze these elements of educational traditions. The effect of these broad values and the interactions between them can be observed in the ways of teaching, learning and assessment at each level and in each kind of education from early childhood to higher education. What happens at one level of education powerfully influences what occurs at another and these impacts can differ between national systems. The interaction between education, economy, society,culture and politics over the last century in various countries and at each level can give life to broad generalizations and explain the uniqueness of each system.

This task can hardly be applied to the whole world coherently in one book. Indeed the conceptual exercise would be beyond currently available intellectual schemes. Particular attention is given to a European trio of France, Germany and Britain with sidelong glances at the USA and Japan. These five countries, with the exception of Japan, have had educational influence throughout the world. Japan is a representative of a Confucian educational culture which promises or threatens to become the world standard in the near future. Each can make claims to have had, at some time and in some aspects, the best education in the world.

Europe is the main focus. France, Germany and Britain also provide a means to make sense of other important and distinctive European educational cultures in north and south as well as in the as yet unclear relationship between the West and an East.

There is not space – conceptual as well as physical – to deal with the great variety of other educational cultures, each of which has its own specific history and character. Hindu Vedic culture may be as important as those with Hellenic or Confucian roots. Islamic culture has an immensely rich educational tradition. African and Latin-American educational philosophies need fuller investigation and description. And within each of these traditions there is almost as much variation in each country as there is in the European national *mélange*. Examples are sometimes taken from outside the chosen five but these are incidental rather than systematic.

The point of a comparative anthropology of national education cultures is to help to make sense of the present and, perhaps, to make choices about the near future. There are always similar economic and often broader social forces which affect education systems throughout the world at roughly the same time. The pressures for change have much in common internationally. It is against these contemporary global developments that each national system can be judged, both in its recent manifestations and the heritage from which it can draw to compete.

The difficulty faced at the end of the twentieth century compared with mid-century and later nineteenth century isomorphisms is that one convergent and universal dynamic is not easy to detect. Jean-Jacques Rousseau's dilemma that education must prepare the citizen and 'man in nature' simultaneously applies more forcefully than ever in a contemporary world in which convergent and interdependent economies coexist with a fragmentation of values and personal aspirations. All education systems need to be judged on their capacity to develop areas of morality, rationality and personal–cultural authenticity. And these educational goals can be conflicting rather than complementary. The nature of the challenge will be sketched before the potential responses of the various national systems are examined.

1
The global educational challenge

Education is an intimate activity. The unique disposition of each student confronts the personal style of each teacher. Concordance comes from shared, long-established values about the desirable traits of individuals, society and knowledge which education should foster. From this standpoint, the proposition of a global challenge seems to be hyperbole.

The larger world of politics and economy has only recently intruded in the ancient activity of education. Mass state systems, in their loosest definition, are little more than 400 years old. Politicians and managers of educational institutions urge an unnatural uniformity in processes of learning and teaching which have a primeval diversity. Political demands change. Allegiances to new or reformed nation states was the prime aim in much of the early history of public education. Goals of social justice prevailed only from the mid-twentieth century. New economic and cultural issues have emerged since the early 1980s. It is understandable that changed national priorities are treated with scepticism by educators or are ignored in the hope that they will blow away.

Embellishment of recent global developments may be necessary to confront the innate conservatism of not only of pedagogues but also of the clients they serve. Education has become a component in a competitive international economy. Teaching and learning in one country are judged by comparison with achievements in other parts of the world especially in the development of cognitive, social and moral attributes upon which occupational competence is based. The peoples of diverse countries and regions have been set against each other. For many, in previously poor countries, the new global economy offers chances for individual self-improvement which can be realized through education. For others, accustomed to a place of relative comfort and status in the international order, improvement of educational achievement is needed to maintain the status quo ante.

Pressures to reduce the public costs of education have been equally powerful. The analogy is that countries, like business enterprises, gain competitiveness by reducing prices as well as by enhancing quality. Restraining government expenditure may be dictated by the global economy. The decline of the power and legitimacy of the nation state in the eyes of its citizens may also contribute.

Politicians and the media have measured educational competitiveness by international league tables of student attainment, rates of participation and cost-efficiency. International agencies provide composite lists (OECD, 1992a; UNESCO, 1993). While these indicators have rudimentary inadequacies, they suggest some rules for a competitive game which has to be played with deadly seriousness. The general economic and political context underlying apparently arbitrary and arcane criteria of educational success needs to be explored.

The difficulty in understanding comes from paradoxical movements in the contemporary world. Economic and technological convergence is accompanied by political, social and cultural centrifugalism. The boundaries of the previously monolithic state are being pushed back. Personal and community values are more diverse. The rationality of a high-technology economy is narrowly instrumental. Whole-life meaning is elusive for most its participants. Education has always been concerned with more than narrowly occupational aims. But the cultural and personal implications of a global economy are less satisfactorily defined.

The simple distinction between economic convergence and cultural diversity needs to be elaborated. What is the nature of work in a global economy? How has the role of the state changed? What is the nature of civil society? How have new relationships emerged and how do they differ between countries? How can the educational implications of these international developments be described effectively?

Global economy and society

Globalization is qualitatively different from the international movement of goods, people and ideas which has occurred for centuries. The global economy involves an unprecedented integration of production across countries especially through the operations of multinational companies. A global culture becomes possible through telecommunications and media. The hermetically sealed nation state is threatened and cannot insulate its citizens from international influences.

While globalization brings a technological world into the back yard of each individual, it does not necessarily overrun all cultural spaces. Instead, modern economic values coexist with a variety of traditional cultures. Concepts of transition from traditional to modern societies and of a world divided into a modern metropolis and traditional periphery, which have informed attitudes in the mid-twentieth century, are outmoded.

Three specific elements affect education. Changes in the character of work in the global economy have a particular impact on the education which prepares for employment. Globalization affects the capacity of national governments to provide and pay for public services including education. Yet the non-economic aspects of education may also gain more freedom. All need to be placed in the context of the changes in production from which they derive.

Changes in production – from national economies to global companies

The birth of global economy is usually dated in the mid-1970s. Its conception can be placed earlier in the three prongs of the twentieth century material revolution: automation, communications and the organization needed to exploit them. Machines replaced heavy, repetitive manual work in field, home and factory. Most people were then available for other productive activities. The world could become urban and industrial. (Kennnedy, 1988, 1993) Rural, agricultural populations became peripheral and, often tragically, redundant.

Communications were a product of automation. They allowed the transport of goods, people and information across localities, regions, countries and continents. Goods and services could be produced in one part of the globe and sold in almost any other. The catalyst was organization to produce the most efficient ordering of work. So, for instance, books could be conceived and financed in one country, written in another, typeset in a third, printed in a fourth using equipment produced in a fifth for sale in 100. New productive activities were provided, at first in East Asia then later central Asia, East Europe and Latin America. The impetus for international dispersal was that the costs for each element in the activity varied considerably between countries.

Globalization of production had three phases. The initial stage was the development of efficient agriculture, especially in grains and meat, in virgin lands of European settlement in the USA, Canada, Argentina, Australasia and Russia in the mid-nineteenth century. The development of railways, shipping and refrigeration allowed the export of this production and a competition which severely shook European agriculture (Orwin and Whetham, 1964: 258–88) This phase affected the 'traditional' area of European economies and merely intensified the movement to industrialization and urbanization. In the second stage in the mid-twentieth century, older manufacturing sectors of Europe and North America such as iron and steel, shipbuilding and especially textiles were undermined by Far Eastern competition based on low wages. The assumption was that competitive advantage would disappear over time as wages rose and that superior skills of workers in advanced countries would always give them advantage.

The third phase gave lie to this assumption. It was based on high-technology, multinational companies, financial deregulation and improved communications. The oil price hike of 1974 is seen as the trigger because Japan and Germany, the two dynamic manufacturing economies, were most disadvantaged by oil shortages. One response was to replace workers by machines notably in automobile and electronics production and to develop manufactures with a high added-value of scientific–technological sophistication such as pharmaceuticals. The scientific–technological drive, meant to counter rising energy and labour costs led to further globalization of trade in competing rather than complementary goods since transport costs, of high-value added manufactures – even across half the globe – were relatively low.

However, the main spurt to globalization of production came from financial liberalization and the development of telecommunications in the early 1980s. The currencies of most industrial countries, following the US dollar, were allowed to find their international market value rather than being restrained by national–political controls on exchange rates and currency transfers. The result was a stimulus for global circulation of investment and an international trade in stocks and shares. Telecommunications in the mid-1980s allowed instantaneous financial decisions across continents. As a result European, North American and Far Eastern companies set up operations in each others' countries. Overwhelmingly the movement was to concentrate investment in the most fruitful areas whose fecundity was measured at least in part by the quality and/or cost of labour.

Production was globalized by the late 1980s. Multinational companies began to split their operations so that, for instance, management, research and development were located in science rich countries while production – despite automation still often a relatively low-wage activity – could be situated elsewhere. Telecommunications could allow co-ordination of overall production across continents. Furthermore, the location of production could be unstable and ephemeral. Activities could be quite rapidly uprooted from one location and transferred to another in a different country or continent (Chesnais, 1993; Dunning, 1993). Company hierarchies of status could be split with various levels of workers located in different countries.

High levels of learning and demonstrable intellectual attainment are a *sine qua non* for skilled work in high technology or organizationally complex types of production. Learning is competitive between countries as much as within them. Enterprises are attracted to areas with capable labour forces. If workers are not highly skilled then they have to be cheap enough to be more efficient than machines. There are many countries in the world with cheap labour which removes the second option in most existing industrial nations.

Local and regional economies do survive especially where face-to-face contact between people is central. But the kinds of occupations which are immune from international competition are difficult to predict. Hairdressing, for instance, is not likely to be globalized. Yet shopping malls in the USA have security guards in Africa operating through satellite television. Even teaching, which relies on physical–biochemical reaction between people, can employ internationally standard communications programmes.

Many educational questions remain. There may be personal traits of workers, encouraged by education, about which it is possible to suggest international standards. Yet the means of comparing educational attainments across countries have a doubtful reliability. On the other hand, various kinds of workers in separate economic sectors require different capacities. Despite international economic competition, employers in disparate cultures have different culturally conditioned expectations of their employees.

Employment, training and education

The paradox that a highly integrated global economy can operate with workers who have different kinds of attributes may be explored in cultural–historical contexts. However, this variation is built upon a certain uniformity of occupational capacity. The standardization of skills may be examined first.

The apparent trade-off between quality and cost of labour can be illustrated by a taxonomy of worker abilities. Some kinds of production requires all workers to have high levels of skill for which they are well rewarded and other types still call for poorly paid workers who bring older qualities of industriousness, persistence, consistency of effort and time-discipline. While national labour markets are segmented in the kinds of work available and the rewards offered (Carnoy, Levin and King 1980), in high-technology economies the older kind of occupations that involved simple manual dexterity and a submissive reaction to machines are declining. Even low-paid, part-time workers operating computer keyboards or in service occupations, which deal with the interface of customers and complex organizations need some rational understanding of the overall framework and functions of their particular tasks.

The labour–skill needs of complex work are even more problematic. Refined communicative capacities in language and number as well as the ability to follow logical procedures and draw upon basic scientific principles seem to be fundamental to all skilled jobs. Businesses, however small, are complex systems and their activity is remote from the experience of those who have never worked. Sophisticated intellectual preparation – which includes developing capacities for abstraction, logical connection and systematization – is a necessary foundation for entry to this kind of work (Drucker, 1993).

Further specification is surprisingly difficult. The problem arises because skills are now company rather than occupation specific (Dore, 1985; Dore and Saki, 1989: ix–xiv, 76–113). Workers need to be able to learn the systems of a particular employer rather than to have a set of general capacities related to a craft or profession which are relevant across enterprises. Indeed, some companies have set up 'universities' to fulfil this purpose (Feldman, 1985). Capacities for learning, for decision-making and problem solving are important and feature strongly in job-descriptions. But they are so ill-defined, perhaps unavoidably, that they become little more than platitudes which are given real meaning only in the unarticulated ethos of recruitment and actual work. Furthermore there are other qualities of co-operativeness to engage in dynamic team-work, acceptance of individual responsibility for outcomes of work as well as, in some cases, capacity for divergent thinking, imagination and a set of professional ethics. Some qualities seem to be incompatible with others.

This raises a quandary for pre-work education. Broad intellectual preparation is needed in educational institutions for specific training that will occur in companies. A set of convergent, theoretical capacities need to be developed even though neither teachers nor students can have very clear ideas about how these will be specifically applied in work-centred training. But there is also a need to encourage divergent, individualist, self-reliant thinking and a variety of social and moral predispositions. Though educationists are aware that higher standards of achievement are needed among all students they cannot know exactly what and why. With the company-specific nature of work and its rapid change, employers are not very well placed to enlighten them.

These developments have thrown into doubt a whole generation's assumptions about the relationship between education and work. Much of this analysis was weak from the outset. When economists examined the relationship between education and economic growth in the 1950s and 1960s (Blaug, 1970; Schulz, 1977), they could not determine whether the former was the seed or the fruit of the latter. 'Manpower planning' approaches were more successful in some countries than in others (Youdi and Hinchcliffe, 1985). There were difficulties in persuading students to enter courses of study which were deemed to be more economically appropriate, in planning the provision of the right courses with the right number of students and in ensuring that graduates entered jobs for which they were qualified. There was no guarantee than students emerging from appropriate courses would have the qualities, especially of the personal and social kind, which were most needed by employers.

Employers operating in a global investment market began to perceive that some national education systems were apparently better than others and these perceptions could affect decisions to place investment in one country rather than another. How they were better was not particularly clear. In this confusion, some reliance was placed on levels of intellectual achievement in language, mathematics and science and about the proportions of students reaching certain standards. Such judgements do have a basic validity, if suitable measures of differential performance can be devised. However, beyond this level of prescription, the difficulty of measuring the relative performance of students in different education systems is inhibited by vagueness and, indeed, cultural specificity of desirable worker qualities.

Culture-specific elements of work in high technology economies

Economic convergence can coexist with cultural diversity even within work. Companies need to be organizationally complex to operate globally in high-technology areas. The ethos of the company becomes important as a unifying guide for workers. Such a company culture can be most soundly developed when it refers to social and political norms of the wider society.

This diversity is not new. British workers in early nineteenth century textile factories were largely women and children whose submissiveness was exploited. Large numbers of landless labourers, created by the eighteenth century agricultural enclosures, helped to swell an unskilled labour force. Craft workers in factories, having origins in pre-industrial occupations, remained a socially exclusive and isolated group (Pelling, 1963). Antagonistic governments did little for training. Unskilled workers predominated and training for skilled work was unregulated by the state (Landes, 1969: 151, 187).

In Germany industrialization in the nineteenth century was also regulated by the hostile government of a Prussian squirearchy which insisted upon the preservation of pre-industrial traditions, notably of the old crafts, controlled by the guilds with their religious, 'vocation' orientation. Unskilled work was professionalized so that most occupations required apprenticeship training. Nineteenth century government intervention also forced the creation of massive industrial cartels, whose size allowed them to adopt more general training and qualification standards (Clapham, 1961: 334; Pinson, 1966: 240-6). The predominance of the highly formal apprenticeship in contemporary Germany draws from these historical origins.

French interventionist and centralized government industrial policy drew upon traditions of Louis XIV and Napoleon. Government took over the control of apprenticeship training. The qualifications were awarded by the state and reflected an intellectualism associated with rational-enlightenment traditions of seventeenth and eighteenth century state-led modernization. The reference point was the vocational intellectual train ing of the élite cadre of engineers of Napoleon's system. The integration of general–academic and vocational education and qualification remains much stronger in France than in Britain or Germany.

The USA had mass unskilled labour traditions with the nineteenth century flood of poor immigrants and the survival of occupational structures associated with slavery even after abolition in 1864. The view of the worker as unthinking and amoral machine, systematized in F.H. Taylor's scientific management ideas in the 1920s, continued in American industrial psychology (Braverman, 1974). There were traditions also of the individualist aspirations of immigrants as well as the flexibility and co-operativeness produced by the pragmatic mind-set of frontier society. This lack of formalism served the American economy well up to the 1960s. Workers were willing to learn, to adapt, to co-operate and to offer great energy. By the 1970s, the lack of a more formal 'vocational' view of worker craft responsibility among significant groups of lower-skilled became a drag on further development.

In this context, the emergence of Far Eastern industrialism with different concepts of work was no surprise. East Asian commitment to learning as a moral activity and duty drew from Confucianism while unquestioning obedience and respect for elders which affected relations with managers may have had origins in traditional lord–vassal feudal relationships. In return the paternalist companies of Japan – unlike those of Britain, France and the USA – accepted a responsibility for providing training and life-time employment, as they did in Germany within a different tradition. Workers were vicarious siblings who cooperated rather than competed (Lipset, 1994; Vogel, 1987). There are differences between Far Eastern countries. The large company in Japan is the substitute authoritarian but benevolent father. In Taiwan and Korea it is the state reinforced by the family (Brandt, 1987; Winkler, 1987).

This historical–cultural account does not forecast the future. Changes in the world economy may marginalize the large, paternalist company of Japan or Germany. Smaller enterprises and emphasis on divergent creative worker skills may swing the balance back to more individualist cultures (though with the great social danger that only a minority of the population may be able to participate). Paternalist conceptions of lifetime employment may be unfeasible as more countries participate in the world economy and countries such as Germany and Japan can no longer insulate themselves from trade-cycles. The global economy is likely to make these swings more rapid and perhaps more violent than in the past. This cultural perspective does imply that each country needs to draw upon its own indigenous social–moral traditions to compete.

Responses to providing peculiar mixes of intellectual, social, moral and personal education for culturally authentic yet globally competitive work are complex. But there are also other drives behind politically expressed demands for reform of education. They are not only concerned with producing the best workers. They focus on reducing the public cost of education. These imperatives also have their origin in developments in the global economy.

Cost-efficiency, globalism and the retreat of the state

The demand from governments for higher standards of student achievement is matched or exceeded by their insistence on lower costs of teaching and learning in public institutions. There are international economic pressures on governments to reduce public spending despite the apparent conflict with the need to improve quality. The central issue may be the loss of legitimacy of national governments which has a less direct connection with economic globalization.

The retreat of the state is not a uniform. Privatization has been a slogan in Britain and the USA as well as in a number of poorer countries. The core of public education has survived. Instead the pressure has been for public educational institutions to provide services more cheaply. Note has been taken of the ability of some Far Eastern countries to provide aspects of efficient public education at lower cost – for instance through higher student–teacher ratios, shorter courses and lower infrastructural costs of, for instance, teacher training or buildings and equipment (England and Wales DES/HMI, 1991a).

Economic globalization encourages cuts in public expenditure. Global movement of investment is affected by comparative levels of taxation both on companies and on employees. Higher costs through taxation in one country act as a disincentive to movement of capital. So competitive tax cutting prevails as bids are made to attract more investment. If governments offer grants to foreign investors then less public finance is available for other activities including education.

The global economy has ended the capacity of governments to embark upon the autarkic, command economy policies which have been adopted since the First World War in Europe. The combination of high external tariffs, government subsidies to economic activities which were deemed to be in the 'national interest' and government financial support for the development of economic and social infrastructures including education have been undermined when self-sufficiency is no longer a feasible policy. The argument that the nineteenth century nation-state developed to secure larger markets needed by developing industry (Gellner, 1983) implies that when markets have expanded well beyond the state its rationale is undermined.

Other explanations of the decline of the state are less directly connected to globalism. The legitimation crisis has been seen as a loss of faith in government to provide effective welfare and infrastructural services based on a denial of its rationality, fairness and efficiency (Habermas, 1976). Rationality itself is no longer trusted as an avenue to organizing collective life in a meaningful way, though the critique is muddied by a division between moderately optimistic Germans and deeply pessimistic French (Connerton, 1976; Jay, 1973; Premfors, 1991). Governments lack the capacity to arbitrate fairly between competing interest groups or to handle the information on which it can make judgements. Public expenditure escalates as powerful interests are bought off. The consequence is spiralling government costs and taxation.

In specific cases, these arguments do not hold. Countries that find difficulties in remaining competitive in the world economy for other reasons tend to be most enthusiastic about rolling back the frontiers of the state. So the privatization movement has been most pronounced in the UK and the USA (Chubb and Moe, 1990; Lieberman, 1993). Countries which are already competitive – including Germany, Japan, Taiwan and Korea – have been under less pressure to privatize or cut costs with a result that there is a more state-dominated approach to the economy.

Anglo-Saxon liberalism makes it easier for the state to legitimate its withdrawal from a collectivist strategy by referring to established doctrines of utilitarianism of Jeremy Bentham or John Stuart Mill which have less influence in traditionally statist France or paternalist Russia and Japan. And, within states, there are debates centred on competing traditions of liberalism, federalism and collectivism. Despite the global pressures for cost-cutting, there can be differing degrees to which this is accepted in different areas of social welfare between countries.

Differing political traditions are linked to a variety of established practices of finance of public services. Local communities and, at the most, regions have financed schooling in the USA and, to a more limited extent in Britain while it has been a national responsibility in France. Employers accept an obligation to pay for training more easily in Germany and

Japan than in Britain or France (in the latter payment of a tax almost absolves them of responsibility). Britain has a tradition of short, efficient higher education courses which Germany has notoriously failed to match. English individual and experiential teaching methods have been cost-inefficient compared with whole class formalism of several other countries.

The role of the state is central in comparative study of education change. Against secular, universal movements need to be placed a variety of traditions of political action to which various countries historically subscribe. Then more sense can be made of the variety of educational reform options.

However, the decline of the state provides spaces in which a new privatism, individualism and communitarianism can flourish. This phenomenon is equally important in the comparative development of education. In effect the public domain no longer dominates education. The parameters of the private realm need to be explored to understand the range of educational demands across countries.

A new cultural diversity: individualism, privatism and communitarianism

Distinctions between state and civil society – for long so central in Anglo-Saxon political philosophy as indicated in the ideas of John Locke or Thomas Hobbes – are becoming more universally accepted. The grand collectivist vision has been undermined. The separation is more prosaically predictable with the decline of the power of the state. The more important question is what kind of 'private' values and identities will prevail with the demise of an older kind of collectivism.

The impact of globalism on these developments is not clear cut. Telecommunications – particularly when controlled by a few multinational companies (Smith 1991) – produce a world convergence of visual and linguistic culture encouraged by world trade in television programmes as well as satellite transmission and videos. Whether these global messages tend to produce a common global culture through the dominance of the use of the English language or through globally common forms of packaging and presenting visual images is uncertain (Rodwell, 1985). The range of telecommunications may also encourage individual choices of cultural menus as well as the emergence of esoteric, but possibly transnational, affiliations of ideology, taste and life-style (Toffler, 1980).

In contradiction, there is also the resurgence of a new localism and particularism. National identities can survive and even become stronger as world communications develop. The state may be dead but nationalism thrives. There are large questions about the nature of this new communitarianism – whether it enables a new philosophy of community based on cultural diversity or whether it is atavistic and tribalist (Bell, 1993; Gellner, 1994). The global economy may have weakened the state and has permitted culturally specific ways of organizing production. It does not seem to be able to inhibit demands for new communitarianism.

Indeed, globalism encourages a dichotomous culture. The modernization ideology no longer applies because globalism is neither monolithic nor holistic. The modernization ideology assumed that new kinds of work (industrial) would occur in new locations (cities) with new values of social stratification (social mobility and individual opportunities). Global, high-technology production is no longer modernist in a normative sense. Industrialization destroys the environment, it deprives work of personal meaning, its rationality is elusive, it can lead to deprivation of lack of work unpredictably and it does not satisfy emotional, spiritual drives as its prophets have admitted (Bell, 1976). So an economic life, which produces material benefits which most people want, has only an instrumental rationality which does not satisfy deeper drives.

There is much debate about the character of the new relativism, emotionalism and individualism – suggested by loose and catch-all concepts such as post-modernism. Much comes from cultural and media studies (McQuail, 1994; 31–60). The main issue, as far as education is concerned, is whether there is a rejection of optimistic rationality in favour of a hedonistic, narcissistic nihilism or a return to ancient often local values. Indeed, it has been argued that an educated, multi-role 'modular man' is sustaining romantic emotional attachments on the back of a rational understanding both in Europe and in Islamic fundamentalism (Gellner, 1994: 97–108).

Other demands may have a range of origins. There are national identities based on ethnicity, historical experience, language and religion. Societies in the global economy may be split into many ethnic groups with claims to separate identities. Some of the economically successful – Japan, Korea and Taiwan – have had a relatively high degree of cultural homogeneity. Others look to new relations between minorities, notably in the older industrial countries of Europe and North America. The barriers to such accommodation are not unsurmountable. It has been noted for a long time that diverse peoples can accept the common values of the market place while strenuously maintaining and defending minority cultures (Furnivall, 1948). However there are societies where these ethnic identities produce intolerance and competition – notably where one or more group claims a natural and historical right to dominance. Competition between cultural groups can spill into antagonisms which are genocidal. Old nationalisms can be suicidally destructive. The times are characterized as the new middle ages.

A number of educational issues are raised. Economic–vocational education requires high uniform standards and must also provide a degree of equality of opportunity to prevent some cultural–ethnic groups being damaged economically thus intensifying not only inequality but ultimately the social destruction of some groups which leads to the ethnic civil wars (including the wars of crime of the urban dispossessed). On the other hand, the deficiency of meaning endemic in instrumental economic training requires that other forms of education should be available. There are questions about whether this alternative education should be local, individualist and sub-cultural but so encouraging social fissure and disintegration. Or whether it should derive from old national identities which themselves may encourage social discrimination through association with old dominant classes and, incidentally, help to fuel xenophobia.

The choices are not entirely open. Just as some education systems have advantages in participating in a new world economic order so some educational traditions have been stronger in responding to different multicultural, communitarian and individualist demands. Despite the focus of politicians on internationally competitive 'economic' education, the global education agenda also involves examination of the strengths and weaknesses of cultural educational traditions which can be as strong and varied between countries as the economic and with similar inequalities but in terms of capacity to provide individual and communal self-fulfilment as well as intercultural tolerance and accommodation.

Comparative study of education and the global challenge

Cross-national study of education should help understanding of choices available in particular countries, regions, localities and institutions as well as for those individuals who have opportunities to be geographically mobile. One approach assumes movement towards global educational convergence so the curious look abroad to discover the future. Another conjecture is that education will always differ between countries, regions and localities because it is based on historical traditions and unique cultures. These cultural differences need to be elucidated. The third strategy, adopted most often by governments and their advisers, identifies desirable institutions and practices in other countries as blueprints for reform at home.

The competing interpretative stances often draw on different kinds of evidence. Some aspects of learning, teaching and the organization of education are common in almost all countries. Common developments in economy and society, like those described above, lead to similar government policies in the same time frame. Yet the reaction in each culture may be different because of historical values and institutions. The difference between the universalist and culture-specific approaches is largely in whether there is assumed to be an ideal universal educational solution or a range of culturally specific responses to similar global pressures and whether historic traditions are seen as obstacles to desired change or as its source and inspiration.

The conflict between description and action is endemic in all kinds of analysis of education. It is necessary to know and to understand to take action. But the impetus for understanding so often takes the inquirer away from practical concerns and into an interest in knowledge for its own sake. Action is easier to take on the basis of ignorance which removes so much of the complexity of decision-making. In comparative studies of education this so often means selection of educational practices from other countries without proper consideration of the differences between the contexts of donors and recipients which are likely to affect the outcome. Decisions need to be informed by more sophisticated understanding.

This has been the major problem in recent years. Governments have responded to international competitiveness by commissioning studies of foreign education systems though often very superficially through grand tours of ministers of education or leading officials. Results can resemble the indiscriminate collection of foreign curios which do not fit any coherent design plan on return home. Others involved in education do not have the means of evaluating these imports. Studies of foreign educational practices too easily become weapons of politicians and officials to be used against recalcitrant teachers.

One example may indicate this process. British national government education inspectors between 1986 and 1992 surveyed, among other subjects, methods of teaching in French primary schools, ways of assessing students in German secondary schools, school teaching practice in French teacher education, parental involvement in schools in the Netherlands and Denmark, vocational education in Germany and the cost-effectiveness of Japanese higher education. The stimulus came from ministers who wished to reform education in pre-determined ways. The conclusions were reached after brief visits. The constituency of educationists likely to be affected in Britain had little means of assessing the value of the recommendations (McLean, 1992: 16–24).

Surveys by other agencies can also be politically motivated. Again to use a British example, those of the political 'right' have favoured German models while those on the left have been more attracted to French or Swedish institutions. The supposedly impartial statistical surveys of international agencies such as OECD have been used selectively to support particular policy actions even though these statistics hide many cultural and historical determinants. Even greater difficulties appear with comparisons of student achievement where the relevance of tests, their compatibility with different prescribed curriculum content and the meaning of results have all been contested (McLean, 1992: 9–16).

Cross-national educational comparisons should be more accessible. All participants in education should be able to evaluate them. A number of ground rules do need to be followed. First are questions of why the comparison is being made. The practical policy orientation is legitimate. So comparisons may help to assess the magnitude of perceived problems in one country by putting them in a global context and they may identify superior educational achievements in other countries which are worthy of emulation. But these issues do need to be seen in a broader context of both global developments and of the cultures in which admired foreign practices have operated.

Secondly, foreign examples have to be used systematically. Countries have to be comparable in identified economic, social or political contexts and the most appropriate cases need to be chosen – which does create practical difficulties of width of knowledge about particular foreign cultures, including their institutions, history and languages. Thirdly, a clear scheme of investigation needs to be applied equally to all cases so that the results can be evaluated by the perceptive though not necessarily well-informed reader.

Comparative education studies, like other branches of inquiry, have various interpretative strands reflecting not only the kinds of research orientation of investigators but also their different cultural contexts. Each country has its own tradition of analysis of foreign education (Halls, 1990). The outcome is a field of investigation with wide parameters.

Comparative education inquiry

The issues of globalization and its educational implications may be examined from several comparative stances. Assumptions of the modernization ideology were that universally valid solutions could be found to problems by testing them in a sufficiently large number of cases throughout the world. This was consistent with basic conceptions of the purpose of comparison by nineteenth century positivists. Emile Durkheim's adage that social facts need testing in all contexts to have validity (Durkeim, 1983) reflected a widespread view of a unilinear development of society in all countries of the world.

This assumption supported a number of investigations. The approach of Pedro Rossello at the International Bureau of Education in the 1930s was to plot educational developments throughout the world to identify global trends. It could then be assumed that countries which failed to follow the identified trend needed to effect changes to conform to the norm (Rossello, 1960). Much comparative education work, from Jullien de Paris' scheme in 1819 to the activities of Unesco and OECD in the 1960s and 1970s, was concerned with refining the categories of educational provision across countries to allow such international trends to be posited, quantified and tested (Jullien, 1962; OECD, 1974, 1992b; Unesco, 1963).

More optimistic were proposals to test empirically hypotheses relating to educational efficiency cross-nationally. At a general level, economists have provided many studies of relationships between different kinds of educational provision and economic growth (Harbison and Myers, 1964). Specific interna of education were tested in this way in the International Educational Evaluation project (IEA) studies of the 1960s which attempted to obtain international evidence of the relationship between educational attainment in different countries and factors such as teacher training, centralization of administration or open and closed teaching (Husen, 1967).

Despite the revival of such approaches by the World Bank which wished to see whether it was spending its resources effectively by testing internationally the relative impact on attainment of, for instance, in-service teacher training or pupil textbooks (Lockheed and Hanuschek, 1988), the ambition was unrealistic. Politicians seized upon the international league tables of student attainment which came out of the IEA studies and those of other testing agencies (Foxman, 1992; Lapointe, Mead and Philips, 1988; Robitaille and Garden, 1989) to justify policies but reserved their options to apply whichever approaches were politically most congenial. Universalist approaches remained jammed in processes of identifying more and more complex indicators of performance (including not only comparisons of achievement in particular school subjects but of different topics within them). The social–contextual elements of the early surveys were increasingly abandoned.

Other universalists saw the world as composed of darker forces of oppression and exploitation. Marx had adopted a universalist scheme of historical development in which conflict and contradiction reigned. Concerns for the universal dimensions of oppression located in economic exploitation, ideological imperialism and dependency marked the work of others (Altbach and Kelly, 1986; Carnoy, 1974). A more detached universalism also emerged which eschewed both conflict and functionalist ideological preferences (Meyer, Kamens and Benavot, 1992).

The opposite extreme denied the possibility of a universal standard. Ethnographic studies started from the assumption that all educational activities were so context bound that any generalization violated the unique and individual nature of participants' perceptions. Such a view could not be reconciled with any kind of cross-cultural analysis (Paulston, 1990) but it had some reflection in views of leading comparative educationists in the 1930s and 1940s that the education of each nation and each society should be studied from the perspective of its historical uniqueness and that generalizations should be offered only after very careful consideration (Hans, 1958; Kandel, 1933).

There is an intermediate position which derives principally from Max Weber but which is reflected in much contemporary work in comparative politics, sociology and business organization (Weber, 1964). The assumption that there are differing values and institutions in various societies which constrain the possibility for action. However, the task is to describe these as parsimoniously as possible – through ideal typical models – with two possible purposes. It may allow the proposition of major differences – especially in values – which help to explain the relative success of some societies in achieving certain goals rather than others – as Weber himself did in relation to the protestant ethic and industrialization. Secondly, the ideal types are wider than nations. They spread across cultures so that countries can be grouped by similarities in particular issues. They may help to explain similarities across countries as well as their variations.

Such approaches have characterized much work in other fields of comparison outside education – but largely in areas where there are noted and puzzling differences such as political ideologies or behaviours of individuals in industrial organizations. In comparative education, as in comparative business studies, the starting-point is the common international pressures on each system. The next question is the roots of the differing behaviours in various countries which appear to benefit or disadvantage them responding to these pressures. The construction of ideal types – especially reflecting entrenched values – may help to explain these differences and also indicate the kind of changes that may be possible within each differing culture.

Construction and elaboration of the broad types will be the focus of the next three chapters with reference to major countries in the dominant economic blocs of Europe, North America and the Far East. The last three chapters will attempt to apply these broad types to very specific issues in different levels and types of education in these countries and beyond.

Issues for comparative education analysis

Running through all three dimensions is a concern with certain contemporary educational policy-issues. Prior identification of these at least gives a starting-point whichever investigative and interpretative perspective is taken. Three major educational issues arise out of the analysis suggested above. The first is about the content and style of learning and teaching. The common global concern is to reach levels of student attainment which will contribute to competitive economic success. There may be convergence towards a global norm which then acts as a standard against which educators in all countries judge their work. There may be such deep cultural variations that educationists in each country may best be advised to be true to their own values, whatever the consequences, and at most search their own traditions for those elements which are most appropriate to current global economic demands while seeking culturally authentic means of achieving meaningful non-economic education.

These traditional values of knowledge, teaching, learning and attainment have several dimensions. Some focus upon the education of the citizen, both in economic and political–cultural dimensions. Others are concerned with the individual and local community. Each culture has dominant citizen-oriented traditions of educational knowledge and those which serve interests of diversity and individualism. The two issues of vocational efficiency and of cultural autonomy discussed above can be explored through analysis of these traditions.

The second area of investigation is opportunity and access. For a long time, this was considered the central problem in education internationally. Attitudes have changed and there is less intense support for equality of opportunity as the first priority, largely because of disappointment in earlier efforts and a more widespread fatalism about social inequalities. However, questions of the quality of teaching and learning involve issues of access. Economic success depends upon the achievement of average and below average educational attainers in work.

Countries with a relatively large underclass, which cannot contribute in a major way to economic development, are in danger of losing economic competitiveness quite apart from threats to social harmony. Furthermore, there is the crucial question of popular motivation to raise educational standards which may be more important to overall educational achievement than any actions of governments or educators. Restricted access weakens the dynamic of improved standards. The national cultural dimension of this question has become more important as distinctions appear not only between cultures with open and closed norms of opportunity but also between ability and effort as the crucial markers of capacity to raise average attainments.

The third issue is participation. The initial question is about what kinds of involvement by what groups of people through what educational structures can improve the efficiency and the capacity for change in educational systems. The notorious conservatism of educational practice may be the product of a certain kinds of participation in decision-making and in the behaviours of particular groups of actors. However, there is also the issue of motivation to improve education among different groups of actors – including students, parents, teachers and employers – which various types of decision-making may engender.

Political cultures affect commitment and motivation. Boundaries between individual rights and duties not only differ between cultures but may affect overall levels of economic achievement as well as individual – community harmony and fulfilment. Questions about the importance of individualism and communitarianism in achieving economic development ran through the ideological foundations of the Cold War competition. They have re-emerged, in different guise, in analysis of western and eastern economic competitiveness.

There are still issues of how these grand, and often imprecise, concepts can be applied to analysis of educational questions in ways that can aid the discovery of most appropriate approaches to educational reform in each country and in each level and aspect of education.

From these broad typifications, most specific descriptions can be constructed about:

- the status of different subjects in the curriculum and differing aims of teaching it;
- the favoured styles of teaching;
- prevalent attitudes towards the assessment of students;
- the processes of admitting students to different kinds of levels of educational institution;
- and the parameters of power of students, teachers and parents over what should be taught in schools and how it should be assessed.

These last points will be examined in relation to different levels of education in the last three chapters.

PART 1
Educational Traditions

2
Views of knowledge

Contemporary global trends raise questions that may best be examined in the particularities of the past. Why is British education so strong in encouraging the divergent talents of some individual students but markedly weaker in catering for low achievers or in valuing abstract thought? What allows teaching in France to be precise, systematic and logical but prevents it from providing for any other aspirations than those of the state? Why has Germany been able to maintain such high standards of student achievement over a long period while remaining blind to the necessity of common secondary schooling? How did the USA overcome the division between education and life which still plagues Europeans yet fail to convince so many students that there is a life beyond recreation? Why do the peoples of Far Eastern cultures accept that learning is the moral duty of the individual yet bow to external pressures for extreme standardization?

The answers may be found in deeply imbued views about the most desirable kinds of knowledge, the best ways of transmitting it, and how to identify those who can benefit. These values are shared across a culture and are by no means confined to castes of educational professionals. Values may change over time, but in emphasis rather than essentials. New formulations may draw from even older ideas than those they replace, as in post-Soviet Eastern Europe.

The relevance is contemporary. The capacity to respond to contemporary pressures depends on a willingness to re-examine historical traditions to identify what is of greatest current value and to suppress what is not. Empathy with alien traditions provides the stimulus. And adjustments can be made at every level of decision-making from national governments to individual teachers and students.

The exercise has pitfalls. The study of the contemporary importance of entrenched historical values has for long been established in national studies in France, Britain and the USA (Bloom, 1987; Durkheim, 1977; Walsh, 1966). Comparative education analyses have been more tentative (Holmes and McLean, 1989; Lauwerys, 1959; McLean, 1990a) and face some scepticism. Counter-claims are made that collections of school subjects are prosaically standard through the world and differences within subjects are concentrated on culturally specific areas such as languages, history and arts. A number of projects have sought to discover what is common in curriculum content across countries rather than what is different (Council of Europe, 1968; Galton and Blyth, 1989).

Evidence of convergence can be reconciled with a cultural–historical view. Over the last two centuries a European humanist view of knowledge has predominated for long periods in many countries which aimed to inculcate moral behaviours among the élite on which stable government could be based which also permitted the extension of commercial and political imperialism. The European Enlightenment, followed by the 1789 French Revolution, offered the counter of a rational–scientific, materialist concept of worthwhile knowledge upon which public institutions, including planned economies, could be founded.

The rise of the USA in the twentieth century shook these Eurocentric conceptions. Pragmatism provided a dynamic and flexible approach to learning in a changing society. However, suggestions of an inevitable progression to a universal pragmatic view of knowledge were roughly shaken by the economic ascendency of Far Eastern countries whose traditions of worthwhile knowledge were founded on the archaic moralism of Confucianism. At the same time, the economic revival of Germany and France showed that older European rationalism and humanism were not completely lacking in contemporary economic relevance; while in the mid-century, the materialist educational views of planned societies and economies in Eastern Europe provided another alternative. Convergence reflects interaction between traditions rather than the development of one best system.

The second criticism is that the project is too difficult. The nature of knowledge has been the object of a vast philosophical enterprise for much of the twentieth century. Yet this did not deter earlier comparative surveys – notably Weber's analysis of Hellenic, Vedic and Confucian traditions (Weber, 1970a) – nor prevent later twentieth century comparisons of Islamic and Judaic values by anthropologists (Gellner, 1994). Indeed, twentieth century studies of knowledge may throw light on traditions. The despairing view that rationality is sterile and oppressive of Michel Foucault or Jacques Derrida may be symptomatic of the overwhelmingly rational culture of France. The more optimistic critique of rationality of Jurgen Habermas reveals that indestructible German belief that a final synthesis of understanding – in hermeneutics – can be attained and that it will incorporate a practical, earthy kind of perception which helps to explain Habermas' faith in American pragmatism (Habermas, 1984).

The remaining difficulty is of boundaries and classification. Cultural variations appear at different levels. The European tradition can be confronted with those of non-European areas. The rationalist and humanist strands of European civilization can be traced across a whole continent. Yet there are significant differences between French, German, Russian and English traditions just as there are between China and Japan within overarching macro-cultures. There are specific differences between France and Spain and between Germany and the Netherlands within otherwise cohesive sub-blocs. Furthermore, what is held to be typical of national educational cultures may reflect recent developments – the sharp contrast between French rationalist and English humanist education may be the product of restrictive interpretations of nineteenth century opinion formers such as Victor Cousin in France and Thomas Arnold in Britain (Zeldin, 1979: 209–10).

European humanism, rationalism and naturalism may be the starting-point followed by American pragmatism and Eastern Confucianism. National and sub-national variations within each tradition, its tensions and its capacity for change also need to be explored. To illuminate the contemporary relevance of the different knowledge traditions a number of subordinate questions have to be asked. The broad purposes of knowledge and aims of learning within each tradition link to the status of subjects in the curriculum and how they are interpreted. Types of teaching and expectations of student achievement are the next step. The kind of student access to education that each tradition permits is also crucial.

The European triad of humanism, rationalism and naturalism

The curriculum heritage can be mapped initially through typical writers whose ideas are recognized to embody the essence of a widely accepted tradition which can then be explored through evidence of historical and contemporary curriculum practice. The humanist *oeuvre* may start with Plato and move on to Erasmus but it has a variety of local and national expressions, including for instance, John Locke in England. The rationalist-encyclopaedic view has more diverse sources also including also those of Ancient Greece. The philosophy of René Descartes may have underwritten rationalism but its educational application can be explored more fully in influential educational thinkers such as John Amos Comenius, who predated Descartes. Naturalist views have universal expression in the ideas of Jean-Jacques Rousseau but many later proposals are specific to particular countries and cultures.

There is a significant difference between humanism and rationalism as élite, public traditions designed to develop citizens and those naturalist conceptions which have the person or the intimate community as the starting-point. Emile Durkheim, in the last two chapters of his major work on education, contrasted humanist concern for 'the extreme diversity of feelings which have stirred the human heart' and rationalist interest in 'procedures whereby human reason has progressively taken control of the world' (Durkheim, 1977: 339–40).

Naturalist views, in contrast, reject the submission of the individual to an external body of knowledge and seek understanding in the private, the concrete and the natural. The history of Western educational thought since the late eighteenth century can be seen as an attempt to make sense of Plato, from whom both humanism and rationalism derived, and the naturalism of Rousseau. Writers as diverse as Immanuel Kant and John Dewey took this starting-point (Bowen, 1981: 210–18; Dewey, 1961). The confrontation is still central to all western education.

Humanism

Humanist views start from the human character and its potential rather than the structure of the physical universe. The central aim is to develop qualities among the young, that will serve them in later life, through acquaintance with great achievements of individuals of past generations. The subject matter has focused upon history, literature and the philosophy with which to systematize this understanding. This human–moral motif has been central to all expressions through Plato and the Renaissance in Europe and in much Christian thought.

European humanist education can be dismissed as archaic. Plato's prescription of a moral education for a hereditary political élite has been held responsible for the social élitism and anti-industrial attitudes of later ages which deprived mass education of any real purpose. Respect for heroes of the past may lead to passive conservatism or 'other-worldliness'.

Re-evaluation is necessary. What unites the great knowledge traditions of the whole world is the humanist aim. Confucian, Vedic and Islamic educational values have been as moral as those of Plato yet those of Confucius, especially, have not proved as antithetical to late twentieth century utilitarian mass education as those of Europe. Rousseau's scheme of individualist, libertarian and naturalist education culminated in a humanist study of history in adulthood (Rousseau, 1993: 197–208). The critique of mid-twentieth century western modernism requires reconsideration of the education that it dismissed as traditional.

Aims and content

Among the many statements of desirable outcomes, J.H.Newman's is typical:

> 'Liberal education makes not the Christian, not the Catholic, but the gentleman. It is well to be a gentleman, it is well to have a cultivated intellect, a delicate taste, a candid, equitable, dispassionate mind, a noble and courteous bearing in the conduct of life.' (Newman, 1931:45)

These attributes were to be developed through the study of heroes in history and of moral choices in literature. The difficulty has been that for Plato the study of man in a moral dimension was the preserve of the ruling class and was unsuitable for manual workers and women. This was justified within the rigid class structure upon which his scheme of the *Republic* was based (Plato, 1953: 231–311). Humanism in nineteenth century European education became a means to organize and control people which was the function of the politician–manager.

Undoubtedly humanism provided a practical philosophy of élite education which had nineteenth political–economic relevance. English humanist education has been action orientated rather than encouraging a submissive respect for the past (Madariaga, 1970) which perhaps explains why it has survived more strongly than in France or other southern European countries. The predominance of humanist education in nineteenth century Britain can be explained by the nature of the imperialist mission. Large numbers of young people (almost always young men) were placed in situations in the far-flung empire of having to make decisions on human relations and people management without reference to higher authority. The archetype was the colonial district officer taking charge of a vast area with subject peoples whose customs and social institutions he barely understood. A sense of moral duty and a developed wisdom were of crucial importance.

Commercialism created circumstances in which a lower level élite would be expected to deal fairly and honourably with affairs of trade on a vast world. British commercial links, like those of the Netherlands, were vast over a longer period yet founded on trust and honour. Both countries have given emphasis to a humanist education which would be of practical value.

There are major differences between European humanist traditions. German universities followed William von Humboldt's prescription in the early nineteenth century that the Prussian bureaucrat class should have a classical humanist education (Hearnden, 1976: 20–4). But German *Allgemeinbildung* (general culture) is a spiritual search for the ultimate meaning, employing intellectual techniques but with moral outcomes (Lauwerys, 1965: 15). The political–administrative élite are those diverted from a life of scholarship into the practical business of managing people. Interesting contrasts emerge with non-European traditions. Hindu scholar castes have other-worldly orientations in the German mould. Chinese scholar-mandarins were much closer to the Platonic –English conception.

The humanist tradition has other elements. Erasmus insisted that the outcomes of learning should not only be fine moral judgement but an acute appreciation of beauty, especially in association with the Renaissance achievement, and, in a degraded form, with good manners and etiquette (Huizinga, 1952: 100–105). The aesthetic dimension has been largely lost in modern Europe yet it does provide a means to incorporate studies of the physical world within a humanist philosophy. There is an appreciation not only of the wonder of everyday things but also of the aesthetic totality of subjects which appear primarily rational and utilitarian. This justification for mathematics, science and music that they are simultaneously rational and beautiful, while not absent from the European tradition, is one aspect of the humanist approach where a Japanese world view is broader especially the belief that morality entails an acute understanding and respect for the beauty of the world.

Humanist aims do not guarantee morality. A perverse but also authentic expression was Niccolo Machiavelli's *Prince* based on a cynical appreciation of human conduct (Machiavelli, 1961: 90–102). For the revival of humanism in the Renaissance was associated with an individualism which could become egotistical and self-interested.

While humanism may open up that energetic, dynamic possibility for individual action which study of past achievements awaken, it can demand a passive, submissive respect. At the individualist extreme, in the French tradition, Blaise Pascal was associated with a seventeenth century piety which regarded knowledge as divine revelation. In a social context, for much of its history and educational application, humanism has been backward looking and stifling of individual initiative. For the humanist body of knowledge was seen as the means to inculcate a blind loyalty and patriotism by idolization of icons of a national culture.

Nineteenth and early- twentieth century elementary schools often had this purpose of political socialization. Meaning was not important but respect for the incomprehensible was. The classic official statement of the purposes of English elementary education in 1904 balanced a development of cognitive capacities with a necessary respect for a superior wisdom in which pupils could not hope to share:

'it will be the aim of the School to train the children carefully in habits of observation and clear reasoning, so that they may gain an intelligent acquaintance with some of the facts and laws of nature; to arouse in them a living interest in the ideals and achievements of mankind, and to bring them to some familiarity with the literature and history of their own country.' (England and Wales Board of Education, 1968: 154)

Nations, whose leaders took solace in past achievements but whose recent past and foreseeable future were bleak, emphasized this old culture – Greece, Ireland and, more recently Poland – in which ancient languages, literature and history were overbearing in national curricula. When a national curriculum was introduced in England and Wales after 1988, Shakespeare and English history of the sixteenth century were given a central role. Similar tensions have emerged in post-1988 Russia where humanism and individualism have been conflated in educational aims so that a romantic nostalgia contends with personal choice in the curriculum.

The subject of humanist study until the late nineteenth century was the literature, history and philosophy of classical Greece and Rome. By the end of the nineteenth century there was a move towards national literature and history. It was at this point that the humanist tradition was undermined in continental Europe. In France and Germany, the decline of the classics brought the rise of mathematics and science in élite secondary schools to a greater degree than in England, helped in France by specializations such as modern languages or Latin and Sciences (Prost, 1968: 252) and in Germany by the rise of non-classical schools (Sadler, 1898). In England, in contrast, the humanist ideal survived and indeed was reaffirmed after 1945.

The democratization of humanism has several hazards, notably in England where assumptions are made that the prior stages of cognitive, intellectual development can be skipped. This denied Plato's simile of the cave, of the prerequisite of grasping the logical intellectual apparatus before a true moral education could begin (Plato, 1953: 231–304). So English democratization has tended to offer study of literature and history without a requirement of prior proficiency in language, mathematics and other studies. Furthermore, while this early specialization was marked in the period after 1945, it was evident also 50 years earlier (Sadler, 1898: 120–32). Élite education lacked precision about the centrality of these cognitive logical studies. In effect, élite English education has obscured intellectual prerequisites through assumptions that the inherently intelligent will have no need for formal training.

This contrasts with a German scheme where a humanist education is only offered in universities after a thorough logical, cognitive education has been completed in secondary schools. So a moral commitment to learning for its own sake – including a commitment to acquiring the prior intellectual, cognitive foundations however unpalatable – can be part of a true humanist education.

The outcome in England was specialism based on personal taste of students or teachers which polarized the subject matter of education. Students could claim, even boast, that they were incompetent in some areas of knowledge and learning – often in mathematics or science or modern languages. Students were permitted choice with the justification, in the 1940s, that they had no need to struggle with studies for which they had no taste (England and Wales Board of Education, 1943: 60–62). This could be confused with likes or dislikes for particular teachers. The education of adolescents could become little more than indulgence in the emotional urges of a particular phase of maturation, with a predilection for soft areas such as literature or history. Subjects like mathematics and science, even modern languages shorn of their focus on literature, became more difficult to justify within this scheme of aims. Democratization of the humanist scheme has been discredited not only through archaic claims of a watering down of the pure milk of humanist high culture by its wider dissemination but also by the lack of attention to prerequisites of command of the intellectual equipment of logical–structural knowledge.

One puzzle, which may be relevant to the failure of democratized humanism in England to offer an intellectually demanding education, was the position of science in high culture. The English scientific flowering of the late seventeenth century, especially associated with Isaac Newton, provided the basis of a rationalist tradition. By the nineteenth century, while James Clerk Maxwell was at the educational centre in Cambridge, Charles Darwin led an isolated dilettante existence more typical of creative scientists. Science had become ideological. For the political establishment it had too strong a whiff of atheism or of the militant non-conformist attack on the traditional élite, notably by Thomas Huxley. After 1945, T.S. Eliot saw the science–humanities division as a threat to cohesiveness of high culture (Eliot, 1948: 95–109). Others, exemplified by F.R. Leavis, fought tenaciously to preserve a pure, literary humanism against technocracy (Walsh, 1966: 67–83). The potency of this division may be illustrated by Margaret Thatcher's assertion that it was more significant that she was the first scientist to become Prime Minister rather than the first woman. The problems of democratization may be traced to such weaknesses of the élite culture.

The English version of educational humanism has a rosier future than could have been thought possible in the 1970s if it can overcome problems of breadth of content and intellectual rigour. Individual creativity almost to the point of idiosyncrasy may be highly valued in new economic enterprises. Much economic development may also be underwritten by the seizure by individuals or small groups of opportunities and responsibilities. It is not only a question of making things – which may require individual inventiveness – but also of dealing with people. Unless the humanist creed can be genuinely opened to all then the danger is that only a minority of the population will be able to participate in these opportunities. Difficulties of democratization are also found in the extravagant and élitist ways the humanist knowledge is transmitted.

Teaching and learning

Active, individual learning and a teaching which it facilitates are central to the progressive element of humanism. Yet rejection of the standardization of content and its transmission can be very inefficient. Even more wasteful is the assumption, at least in the English humanist philosophy, that learning should be inductive and intuitive rather than deductive and transparent.

The inductive–heuristic, the standard–logical and the intuitive–revelatory approaches to learning and thus teaching exist separately from the humanist–rationalist–naturalist triad. Revelatory views, requiring submission and respect from learners for the content, have been associated with authoritarian humanism. Yet active, individualist versions and their association in the sixteenth century Renaissance with Protestantism, reinforced notions of the capacity of each person to learn for himself and herself. There are still differences between individual responsibility for learning and the adoption of an inductive–heuristic view of processes of learning. Calvinist and Japanese–Chinese Confucian schemes emphasized individual responsibility for learning without necessarily adopting heurism. English inductive approaches may be consistent with that action-orientated individualism which perversely allows a deeply conservative humanist tradition to survive.

English inductionism can be traced to Francis Bacon, as a practical scheme of learning, and to John Locke at a more philosophical level of the nature of human understanding. Locke provided the key to the reconciliation of a humanist education of the gentleman with the view that 'learning might be made a play and recreation to children' (Locke, 1968: 255) which stimulated Rousseau's development of a naturalist alternative. The heuristic–empirical view of phenomena can be reconciled easily with individualism and ultimately an individual moral responsibility.

The student is confronted with the material and makes his or her own selection and judgements about it. He or she observes and then constructs, tentatively, general rules about the phenomena. This scheme of learning developed in approaches to science teaching in the nineteenth century especially laboratory work which was not found to the same degree in other countries. It became associated not only with specialist studies in literature and history (and an emphasis upon starting from the primary evidence in history and the text in literature). It pervaded most of the school curriculum projects which emerged in the 1960s in Britain (Stenhouse, 1980).

While these methods could be associated at the highest levels with original scientific discovery, they could also be wasteful. So frequently they could be associated with discovering the obvious and well known in artificial exercises. Much inductive mathematics, science and, indeed, history actually presented students with concrete evidence – often in super-abundance – as a means to gaining understanding of scientific 'laws' which could be learned logically and theoretically much more quickly and efficiently.

As with other areas of the English tradition, the discovery-based approach originated in élite education and was transformed in its democratization. Latin and Greek together with mathematics were seen, in traditional formulations like that of A.N. Whitehead in 1930, as the means to training abstract thinking while science was to be learned inductively (Whitehead, 1962). The inductive–heuristic scheme, furthermore, could also be ingenuous. What often lay behind it were concepts of intuition which ultimately derived from a revelatory concept of learning.
The assumption was that a student would appreciate moral lessons by intuitive, indeed empathic, interaction with the material. And behind much of this assumption of learning was the social élitism that only the best and brightest would have that intuitive insight. Furthermore, intuition could hardly be trained. It was there or it was not. Inductive–empirical teaching merely became a field for the insightful to have scope to reveal their intuition.

Individualism and empiricism also straddled the standard high culture and popular naturalist aspects of education. In effect, ways of learning associated with the local, private, sub-cultural and personal were imported into processes public and universal knowledge transmission. A bridge between high and popular cultures of education may have been created but it also became a means by which a naturalist approach infiltrated higher levels.

This account has focused on England because, of all the industrial countries, humanism remains entrenched there, because it has a major impact still in schools whereas elsewhere the influence is mainly in higher education and because it has a vitality unmatched in other countries. But a humanist strand remains in many other countries, including non-Hellenic versions in much of Asia. The English example may serve to illuminate the implications of reviving or suppressing this component in other traditions.

Rationalism

The rationalist view of content, learning and teaching is associated with a systematic view of the physical world. Capacities for logic, deduction and abstraction together with systematization and synthesis should be developed to make sense of this universe and ultimately to change it. The medium is that group of subjects such as languages, mathematics and science through which these qualities can best be trained. But worthwhile knowledge is also external and standardized and the student should cover the encyclopaedic kaleidoscope of all legitimate areas for as long as possible. The private and irrational are rigorously excluded.

These attributes form almost a mirror-image of nineteenth and twentieth century English humanism. Rationalism is wider than its recent expressions. Its history, like that of humanism, goes back to ancient Greece. Plato saw rational thought as the necessary preliminary to the ultimate moral education. It permeated medieval education through Scholasticism. Yet its contemporary origins are revolutionary – in the seventeenth and eighteenth century Enlightenment and then in the 1789 French Revolution – stretching across an early nineteenth-century historical hiatus into post-1917 Socialist Revolutions. It may truly be seen to be the foundations of the technological revolution of the second half of the twentieth century. Yet this rationalism is also imperfect and does not offer true meaning and personal satisfaction. It may not even continue to serve future occupational economic needs.

In the revolutionary perspective, intelligence, rationality and calculation were means to construct a more perfect society. The human agents of this change needed the developed capacities to perceive the patterns upon which planned change could be based. Since change was to be collective, so the means of inculcating rationality would also be standard and explicit. The universal, collective, external and standard aspects of rational education were interlinked.

The high status subjects changed over time. As in other European countries, including England, classical languages were seen to be vehicles for teaching logic and abstraction. Their decay in nineteenth century France was accompanied by rise of the dual areas of rhetoric, in French and philosophy, as the seed beds of rational thought in upper secondary schools (Zeldin, 1979: 205–40). Rhetoric imbued precision and style in communication while philosophy encouraged easy manipulation of abstract concepts.

By the mid-twentieth century mathematics had become the new core subject, based especially on deductive Euclidian geometry. The criterion of high-status subjects was that they had the systematic–logical structures through which rationality could be developed. Mathematics had the added advantage of an avenue to the study of science and technology. Whatever the pinnacle subject, the general aim remained the same.

Rationality was concerned with synthesis as well as analysis. The study of history and literature – sometimes aided by 'sciences' such as psychology, anthropology, economics and sociology – sought general patterns which could be intellectually constructed rather than perceived through individual intuition. The broad sweep and understanding of major contours of historical development were encouraged (Durkheim, 1977: 338–40). The model could be the French historian Fernand Braudel with his majestic synthesis of the life of whole Mediterranean over a period of less than one century (Braudel, 1972).

There is always some tension between the rationalist and encyclopaedic elements of this view of education. On the one hand the 'intelligence' of the learner should be developed to provide general capacities to respond to unpredictable circumstances. On the other the learner should acquire all existing knowledge relevant to changing the world. The synthesis depended on abundant facts. Analysis was not diverted by problems of verification. Above all systematized facts, like logic, gave power. Durkheim approvingly quoted Rabelais:

> 'Let there be neither sea nor stream nor fountain with whose fish you are not familiar....Let there be nothing, neither all the birds in the air, all the trees, bushes and fruitful shrubs of the forest, all the plants of the earth, nothing of which you are ignorant.' (Durkheim, 1977: 213)

and justified in terms similar to those expressed more epigrammatically by Montaigne when as a youth he 'nibbled the outer crust of learning' and gained a proper respect for the richness of knowledge and humility in his own ignorance (Montaigne, 1958: 49).

Rationalism could reach the majority in ways which humanism could not match. The initial aim of revolutionaries, such as the Baron de Condorcet in 1792, was to develop the capacities of an élite, marked by its intelligence rather than a hereditary capacity for goodness – a career open to talents – which would lead social transformation (Barnard, 1969: 81–95). But it was also egalitarian in that explicit and external knowledge and intellectual principles could be accessible to all. This distinction between explicit rational education and implicit, undefined humanist achievement was central to late nineteenth and twentieth century educational theorists including Durkheim and Pierre Bourdieu (Bourdieu and Passeron, 1970).

This view of knowledge presents fewer obstacles to universal access. Logical-communicative subjects, especially language and mathematics, can be clarified to the point where they can be comprehended by all. Tests of attainment can be carefully pruned so that extraneous knowledge acquired unevenly from differences of cultural milieux of students can be excluded (Prost, 1968: 248). The French, together with the Americans, became the standard bearers of a twentieth-century movement to construct perfect means of testing students in the science of docimology (Pieron, 1969). A basic achievement level for all could be a realistic operating principle in teaching and learning (Zeldin, 1979: 209–20).

Of course not all students would reach the same levels. There is a separating device. When the apparent limits of rational educability of each student is reached, he or she is then diverted into utilitarian and vocational preparation where concrete practical skills are learned but each on the basis of the understanding of basic theoretical principles. This separation is justified by reference to the revolutionary ideal: that each person, whatever his or her capacities, has a role in the collective endeavour.

The greatest obstacle to open access is the student alienation which is an endemic response to the rationalist learning project. It is not only the pressure of study of so many subjects. Philosophy has been seen, even by the best students, as a meaningless game. For Claude Levi-Strauss it was a verbal exercise 'based on skill at making puns, which becomes a substitute for reflection, on assonances between terms, on homophony and ambiguity' (Zeldin, 1979: Vol. 2, 226). Rational-encyclopaedism ultimately is a means of enforcing an unreal and standardized conceptual system upon a real world of individuals and small-scale sub-cultures. The individual has to surrender his or her perception of the real practical world and of his or her emotional drives to this system.

Ironically, rationalism may have taken root in France because of the power of a residual and resisting individuality, irrationality and community in a country where, as E.L Woodward noted, the state tried 'to establish the sovereignty of the people without the cooperation of the people' (Thomson, 1958: 32).

Philosophical–logical games may even be individualist catharsis (Halls, 1976: 28). This stand-off has not survived into the later twentieth century. The target group for incorporation into rational study is now the underbelly of society – the lowest 20–30% of underachievers whose culture varies so much from that of the nation that they cannot accommodate the duality of external rationality and private cultures (Prost, 1990).

Rationalist views do not easily accept minority group familial cultures. Some aspects of distinct minority cultures can be accommodated into encyclopaedic universalism – languages of ethnic minorities such as Arabic or Portuguese in France can easily be accepted because they have logical–rational structures just as the study of non-French history and cultures, viewed anthropologically, can also be accepted. But minority identities based on apparent irrationality – especially religious beliefs as seen in French reactions to Islamic fundamentalism but also 'youth cultures' – are less easily negotiable.

Rational encyclopaedism may be digestible to highly motivated new entrants to education whose own familial cultures are strong enough to absorb this external and alienating body of knowledge because it offers occupational opportunities. When motivation declines as private cultures weaken so the encyclopaedist public culture may no longer be acceptable. Procedures of teaching and learning become all the more important.

Teaching and learning

The rational scheme has some contemporary attractions for educational policy makers on a global scale apart from the relevance of its cognitive thought to high-technology economies. There is the evenness of application and economy of transmission which are less attainable in other traditions. Standardization means that everyone is exposed to the same kind of knowledge content which is alluring to policy makers concerned with the uneven achievement of less controlled teaching. Rational encyclopaedism justifies a common externally determined curriculum. All schools and all grades or classes at the same level will follow the same broad courses. Comparability of effectiveness can be measured and the criteria of success made very explicit. The standardization of activity by which efficiency can be measured is underwritten by shared epistemological values of those engaging in the enterprise. There is no difficulty, in France, in getting widespread acceptance of the prescription of a universal syllabus for French language or mathematics or in the ways its learning should be assessed.

Engendering a common rationality requires an exposure of all students to the same process of thinking and learning. So teaching focuses on learning broad principles which can then be used to make sense of concrete evidence. This justifies not only those areas of study which are seen to be fundamental to other studies – especially language and mathematics – but also in the process of learning common rules before their relevance and applicability are touched upon.

Typical teaching within the rational encyclopaedic view concentrates upon exposition of rules to whole classes of students and the testing of their comprehension. The business of schools is about 'instruction' rather than 'education' (Halls, 1976: 24). This has applied not only in language and mathematics classes in elementary schools (England and Wales DES, 1991b) but also to science in secondary education where expensive laboratories are fewer and where the inefficient inductive, heuristic method is viewed with some scorn.

At all levels of schooling, there is a focus on analysis of an object, picture or text. It is at secondary, especially upper secondary level that the archetypical didactical technique appears. *Explication des textes* took root in the late nineteenth century (Prost, 1968: 248). It was a method of examining literary pieces which were analyzed in considerable detail for ideas and their development but also style and use of words. The analysis could be as long as the text itself (Zeldin, 1979: 233). It has been associated with the development of preciseness, economy and elegance of written style of its students.

The efficiency is without doubt. At its best, its outcomes are superior to English and American equivalents. But problems of motivation are as acute in teaching and learning as in content. Students are required to surrender themselves to the acquisition of remote and often alienating intellectual skills. The encyclopaedic element creates a heavy burden of learning, often memorization. Early twentieth century apostles of rational encyclopaedism – notably Alain – treated children as miniature adults who could be moulded without consideration of any personal autonomy or indeed resistance (Zeldin, 1977: Vol. 2, 214–16). Persuading children that it is necessary to learn obscure principles may become increasingly difficult.

Telecommunications and information technology may even make this basis of schooling redundant. Children have access to means of learning broad principles from the technology itself. Increasingly there may be unevenness in this out-of-school achievement. Much research has focused on the great variations in language capacities children bring to school from the outside world. The same kind of process is likely to intensify with technological methods of acquiring numerical and spatial capacities. The argument of E.P. Thompson that English working classes became literate without schools in the early nineteenth century (Thompson, 1968: 783) increasingly may apply to a wider range of logical–rational cognitive skills.

Rational encyclopaedic education in France and other parts of Europe had a basic design not dissimilar to that of Japan. France has the benefit of an broad ideology of progress which is consistent with this philosophy of education. But French rationalism, despite its obvious relevance to occupations in high-technology enterprises, is foundering on the rock of declining motivation in ways that Japan has not yet experienced.

Externality and alienation are not inevitably symptomatic of this tradition. In the sixteenth century, Montaigne advocated an education which started from the interests and observation of the child (Montaigne, 1958). More influential was Comenius (Jan Komensky) in the seventeenth century, who, from an individualist, Protestant perspective, suggested that while education 'should teach all things to all men' and should start from the natural world rather than man, the learner should be viewed as a developing person and knowledge would be acquired inductively (Piaget, 1967: 2–8). The reunification of Europe from the 1990s has led to proposals for a European educational synthesis around the ideas of Comenius which are not confined to his Czech homeland.

Comenius' encyclopaedic plan for education derived from a Protestant view of the educability of all ('men of all ages, all conditions, both sexes and all nations'; Comenius, 1967: 117) as a preliminary to each individual's ultimate answerability to God. Overall knowledge was a part of moral enlightenment and, in specific terms, literacy and control over language were essential to comprehend the texts upon which true religious faith was based. The scheme was built upon a personal motivation which never had a place in the French tradition.

The most ambitious of all encyclopaedic schemes were developed in the Soviet Union in the 1960s as part of a strategy of total social transformation, though it had its origins as much in the modernizing monarchy of Peter the Great in the seventeenth century as in Marxist–Leninism (Alston, 1969; Hans, 1931). Rationality was the guiding principle in the teaching of mathematics and science. Yet humanist, patriotic elements were added in the study of literature, art and music (Muckle, 1988). A vastly overloaded curriculum was enforced through external sanctions on students and their families. The outcome from 1988 were complaints about pressure of work and neglect of the health of children as well as their exclusion from participation (McLean and Voskresenskaya, 1992). Yet the system seems to have collapsed because of a general political–economic revolution rather than because of clearly identified inadequacies of the school system.

This account has focused on France because rationalism has most clearly and perfectly developed in her education tradition. Through French examples it may be possible to illuminate some general principles which are found in traditions throughout Europe and in further continents. The rational – encyclopaedic ideal is the most central in European education from Norway to Greece and from Portugal to Russia. Those countries which do not share fully in this tradition are disadvantaged, notably England even though Scotland retained its European rational connection.

The limits of reason may already be in sight, though it would be foolish to reject rational foundations for other kinds of learning. Much more adaptability, ingenuity, perhaps adventurism are needed for material success. Motivation is a major issue. More broadly there are questions about how far rationalist education can help people to be happy and fulfilled outside a narrow range of public functions.

Naturalist, private and sub-cultural views of knowledge

The terminology comes from Rousseau's differentiation between education of the citizen and that of 'man in nature'. Humanist and rational–encyclopaedic views are based on a knowledge external to the individual which has pretensions to be universal – to express the heights of understanding of the world and humanity in its richest expression over the whole of history. Another kind of intimate knowledge exists which is particular to the person which also serves real needs, emerging from an organic growth of the person and in the intimate community:

> 'The natural man lives for himself; he is the unit, the whole, dependent only on himself and on his like. The citizen is but the numerator of a fraction, whose value...depends on the whole....Two conflicting types of educational systems spring from these conflicting aims. One is public and common to many, the other is private and domestic.' (Rousseau, 1993: 7–8)

The imprecision of the distinction has been both a source of fertility when the public and private interact richly and an obstruction when the two become apparently irreconcilable. For some schemes of education have been successful or attractive because they have achieved an apparent fusion of public and private, as in American pragmatism, whereas others are important because the private is clearly distinguished from the public.

Naturalism has many orientations. One focuses upon the physiological and psychological drives of the person. Another assumes that the natural world is that of small-scale organic communities. There are also distinctions between the natural education of the child and that of the fully developed adult. Rousseau was unclear about whether nature meant personal instinctive drives or the natural environment and how far this milieu was social as well as physical. He was specific that his scheme of education was concerned with the child rather than the adult. But the fundamental distinction he made between the public and private entailed the possibility of a naturalist education beyond childhood.

Rousseau's paradigm shift created space for a whole range of different educational philosophies which took root unequally in different parts of Europe and beyond. Traditions differed from one country to another and educational philosophers whose ideas were predominant in one were almost unknown in another. Child-centred views assumed that children learned differently because of their patterns of physical–biological maturation.

Yet even these differed in their impact. Pestalozzi at the end of the eighteenth century stressed the need to give scope for the imagination of children (Bowen, 1981: 218–22) while Rudolf Steiner in the twentieth century stressed the importance of colour and touch in learning. Yet Pestalozzi has remained a distant figure in the history of education while Steiner's methods underwrite the aims of the majority of private schools in Germany which enrol 5% of the school population. Jean Piaget's early twentieth century scheme of cognitive development has had a wide impact while Ovid Decroly's near contemporaneous view that education should reduce anxiety among children by globalizing experience is influential in his native Belgium but peripheral elsewhere (Dubreucq-Choprix, 1985). Celestine Freinet, with his advocacy of an active, democratic, participatory learning and specific projects such as the pupil-produced newspaper is the most important influence on child-centred methods in France but has less impact elsewhere (Halls, 1976: 135–36). Peter Peterson's Jena Plan which stressed the breaking down of subject boundaries influences practice in northern Germany but has hardly spread beyond this location (Hearnden, 1976: 41).

A similar cultural specificity applies to naturalist ideas which focused on the community as opposed to child development. Frederich Froebel's ideas had little institutional basis in his native Germany. But his ideas of a learning co-operative of children had a major impact both in Britain and, through his influence on Dewey, in the USA (Hearnden, 1976: 26–28; Liebschner, 1991). N.F.S. Grundtwig remains a major influence in Denmark where, in the nineteenth century, he combined ideas of an education controlled by the local community which preserved its cultural heritage. Grundtwig expressed the aspirations of a particular localized, co-operative, egalitarian rural society of Denmark and so was culturally specific (McLean, 1990a: 89).

Yet similar movements can be seen in Britain in the community colleges in Cambridgeshire of Henry Morris in the 1920s (Ree, 1973) or even in nineteenth century ideas of a spiritual education in village co-operatives in Russia (Hans, 1931; Walicki, 1980) which remained submerged until the end of Soviet power. The idea of education for the collective in the USSR was Marxist in justification but associated with Anton Makerenko in the 1920s. Though he had been discredited in the 1930s his view of schools as co-operative groups of children running their own affairs and solving problems collectively was strongly held as an ideal among many Soviet teachers in the 1960s (Bronfenbrenner, 1970: 3–4).

These various movements were not only confined to some countries but were peripheral to mainstream education and were concentrated either in the private sector or in 'pilot' projects (as with Freinet methods in France), or affected only some parts of the country (as in Germany). What distinguished them also is that (apart from Grundtwig and Henry Morris) they were mainly concerned with children. They prepared for Rousseau's education of the citizen rather than offering a total alternative.

Naturalist movements which focused on adults or children in transition to adulthood were based on views of the nature of work rather than that of child development. Germany has a developed tradition of values about vocational education whose influence is not paralleled elsewhere. Soviet education developed polytechnicalism which also related education to work. The main questions are how and why these movements took root in particular circumstances.

The German tradition of vocational education is associated with Georg Kerschensteiner for whom education as occupation or work had a moral, religious and citizenship function. By being involved in manual activities, the creation of useful subjects and the social environment of work, the student would become more morally aware and develop values of duty, industriousness and co-operation. Craft gave a sense of wholeness and responsibility as well as releasing certain kinds of creativity (Simons, 1966). This emphasis on individual skill in both an aesthetic and moral dimension referred to a different kind of work – the crafts which William Morris (from whom Kerschensteiner drew (Gonon, 1993)) had been supported in England as the alternative to alienating urban industrialism. Yet this craft ethos was also central to German industrialism, in ways which were not paralleled in other countries, so that the craft orientation reflects the actual structure of labour relations in German industry and the values associated with a craft-based social status and the religious values which partly supported them. And the vocational orientation applied only to one sector of German education notably that of apprenticeship training and work-oriented courses in secondary schools.

Polytechnicalism grew out of an application of Marxism by Krupskaya, the wife of Lenin, that education should contribute to an understanding of productive processes as part of a wider aim that socialism should remove the alienation created by the distance of the worker from his work (Shapovalenko, 1963). All teaching was supposed to relate academic content to its productive applications. Largely the project failed through opposition of teachers holding to a rational–encyclopaedic frame. Yet post-Soviet educators still give it support perhaps because it also had older pre-revolutionary origins.

These various naturalist traditions suggest possibilities from which new alternative curricula can be constructed within established values. They are only examples. There are many other views and projects in Europe. Most, however, only provide a subsidiary education alongside that of the public citizen. For a naturalist educational tradition which conquered a culture it is necessary to look outside Europe.

The North American alternative: Universal and comprehensive naturalist education

Naturalism became a national concept of education in nineteenth century USA but, in so doing, was transformed into a holistic, mainstream approach which ultimately became instrumental and utilitarian. Its very success created problems. Pragmatism split into hard external utilitarian and soft co-operative wings. Its very ambition contributed to the crisis of the relationship between education and occupation from the late 1950s.

Pragmatism is one element in extraordinarily rich and diverse American education tradition. After the 1776 revolution, American education drew upon an earthy kind of rationalism derived from the French model and initiated by founding fathers such as Thomas Jefferson and Benjamin Franklin. Alexis de Tocqueville in the nineteenth century claimed that everyone in the USA was Cartesian though no one had read Descartes (Bloom, 1987: 378). There was also a residual English academic traditionalism which survived the revolution which was revived by the import of a German humanist research tradition from the late nineteenth century. This conservative tradition, entrenched in élite universities, periodically provided the attack on the excesses of pragmatism in a genealogy which included Irving Babbitt, Abraham Flexner, Robert Hutchins, James Conant and Allan Bloom.

Naturalism had a very specific American interpretation that drew from an optimism about the educability of the mass of the people, the social potential of individuals and small communities as well as the practicality of a new society without traditional class divisions and centralized control. The various strands include:

- a utilitarian expression of the French revolutionary rational idea;
- the commitment of administrator thinkers such as Horace Mann and

William Torrey Harris in the mid- and late nineteenth century who believed it was possible to create a genuinely mass system of education;
- theorists at the turn of the century, each of whom could be seen as the father of a separate approach which became important in the twentieth century, notably Willam James, Edward Thorndike and John Dewey (Cremin, 1962).

The dilemma which these various thinkers faced was between the individualism of Rousseau and various forms of collective improvement. Rousseau's belief in the innate goodness of the person and in active individual ways of learning was reflected in the educational writings of Granville Hall, in the 1880s (Cremin, 1962: 103). More central was the idea that through education society is restructured and developed and that educational aims are materialistic, concepts associated with the ideas of Herbert Spencer and the influence of Darwinist views of social progress. The key development in the American formulation was the philosophy of pragmatism summarized in a key sentence of William James, 'the truth of an idea is not a stagnant property inherent in it. Truth **happens** to an idea. It **becomes** true, is **made** true by events' (Cremin, 1962: 109). In its popular summary, knowledge is for its use rather than for its own sake. With this conceptualization it was possible to break away from the formalist and external view of worthwhile knowledge of the European humanist–rationalist tradition.

Pragmatism developed two strands which dominated debates throughout the twentieth century and which have not been reconciled satisfactorily. The 'soft', progressive view is associated, in intellectual origins, with John Dewey; and the 'hard' instrumental approach was given support by the psychometric formulations of Edward Thorndike. Dewey saw industrialism as a threat to the co-operative optimistic spirit of America. Industrialism created atomistic individuals who were controlled by industrial systems. The rural community should be retained within the school – as Dewey attempted to do in his Laboratory school in Chicago around the turn of the century. The community – represented by the students – achieved growth and progress by facing and solving problems co-operatively, and these problems could relate to earning a living or running the community's affairs co-operatively. Knowledge was viewed pragmatically. Existing knowledge was treated promiscuously. It was drawn upon where necessary to help to solve problems. But the learners sought solutions by starting from the problems and not from the acquisition of bodies of pre-packaged knowledge. A curriculum could not predetermine what knowledge was needed. Nothing had the right of inclusion or exclusion.

The process of learning was active and co-operative. The group set out to solve common problems co-operatively. They discussed approaches. They selected relevant knowledge. There were no superior authorities to which they needed to defer. Knowledge did not belong to any group. Indeed, Dewey's major synthetic work – *Democracy and Education* – was a sustained attack on the élitism of the Platonic view (Dewey, 1961). Yet Dewey, like other American pragmatists, also recoiled from the unrestrained individualism of Rousseau and the belief that educational growth was about the discovery by each person of his or her true nature and its place in the world. Dewey's naturalism was social. The group and its aims took precedence over the individual. And Dewey's school was for young children. It prepared for more conventional secondary education (Cremin, 1962: 135–42).

The strand of thinking identified with Thorndike took American pragmatism in a different direction. The psychology of learning predominated. Innate capacities of individuals were proposed, often through prior experiments with animals, and the stimuli needed to elicit certain, desirable responses were identified experimentally (Cremin, 1962: 110–15). The approach was pragmatic and naturalist in that the starting-point was not fixed and external bodies of knowledge but the capacities of the individual and the development of those already existing characteristics which were useful for him or her and the social group. But it was highly authoritarian because the aim of the psychology was to find the most efficient ways of manipulating the individual to achieve externally determined goals. In this way, Thorndike's psychology was the foundation of the hard pragmatic view which had so many supporters in early twentieth century America who were concerned to find the most efficient form of schooling for a new economy. Students were not treated as autonomous individuals but as passive machines whose maximum efficiency was to be developed by the educators. The advocates of this view often drew parallels with the industrial efficiency movement which also treated workers are manipulable machines. John Franklin Bobbitt, for instance, referred to schools as 'plant' and devised a scheme of 500 teaching objectives (Kleibard, 1987: 88–122).

This danger of external control, manipulation and passivity is a strong theme in certain naturalist approaches. It has been found in the English inductive, heuristic tradition also, notably in the curriculum of state controlled primary schools in the mid-nineteenth century. This orientation has reappeared at various times as in the Minimum Competency movement in the USA in the 1970s. Externality dominates but in relation to defined learning objectives rather than the attributes of a body of knowledge. Individual development and active, discovery learning with its varied and unpredictable outcomes are abandoned.

The American pragmatic approach excited wide interest throughout the world because it appeared to deal with social and economic needs and to be consistent with relatively egalitarian social views. Yet American pragmatism was the product of an expanding frontier society of immigrants in the nineteenth century in which suffocating traditions of élite knowledge and its controllers were defeated and in which small communities, freed by geographical isolation from external controls, could develop an education which was useful, co-operative and socially egalitarian if, almost self-consciously, philistine. Yet these historical conditions were not matched in other parts of the world and there are severe doubts about whether the educational proposals were transferable.

Furthermore, American pragmatic education suffered a problem in common with English individualism. The boundary between the private and domestic and the public and state-orientated was never clearly demarcated. Though Dewey's scheme was aimed at children, the strength of the pragmatic movement was that it could apply to all levels of education. The weakness, as critics from Flexner to Conant to Bloom have noted, is that a pragmatic education designed for children or the young workers of small-town nineteenth century society is not a sufficiently serious public education for adults in a sophisticated society. Yet, at the other extreme of pragmatism, hard utilitarianism ceases to cater for the needs of the individual or small group.

Non-Western challenges

Non-European epistemologies, from a western perspective, appear like distorted mirror images. Equivalences of humanism, rationalism and naturalism appear in other cultures. Confucian, Hindu, Islamic and, indeed, African traditions start from a moral concept of education. There are major variations between these traditions which produce quite different contemporary valuations. It is these variations rather than the communality which is of greatest interest.

Confucianism affected perhaps the largest number of people, though Hindu and Islamic traditions are not far behind numerically. The dynamic economies and education systems at the end of the twentieth century shared a Confucian tradition. Confucianism – as expressed in a number of works including the *Analects* but also as interpreted by major followers including Mencius and Hsun-tzu – emphasized education as a means of developing moral qualities such self-cultivation, propriety, frugality, sociability, loyalty and sincerity (Chen, 1990: 175–326). The curriculum stressed understanding of past achievements as a means to individual moral development.

The social function may have been to develop scholars who would become sages but the political–administrative dimension was that the Confucian system of education would identify a wise and loyal administrative–bureaucrat class – and in this way there were strong parallels with the European and especially English social purpose of moral education (Stone, 1970; Wilkinson, 1964). There were essential differences. Firstly, the moral aims were placed in a secular rather than divine context. Secondly, despite the use of the Confucian system to identify a small scholar–administrator class through a harshly competitive examination system, Confucianism did not preclude anyone from competing or becoming a scholar. There were no assumptions about some being genetically (Plato) or theologically (Calvinist) fit for superior education. Nor indeed were there ideas of naturally intelligent people. Effort predominates. This classless, meritocratic approach separates Confucius from Plato and indeed from much of the rest of the European tradition with the exception of radicals such as Comenius.

In contemporary context, this produced the valuation that educational success was based on effort rather than ability and that it was necessary to avoid shame rather than to win admiration. These concepts derive directly from Confucius whose many epigrams in the *Analects* include the memorable 'no force can steal the determination of even the humblest man' (Creel, 1951: 101). In effect, these elements of Confucianism have underwritten a drive for educational achievement among large numbers of people in ways that have eluded western societies. They help to explain why, also, educational achievement becomes a mass characteristic yet is based on individual responsibility. The Confucian ethos gives each individual responsibility to conform to standards of moral conduct rather than imposing them passively from above.

Confucian schemes lay down the kinds of knowledge that is to be acquired through education. While all knowledge is appropriate, particular attention is given to poetry and music. Yet poetry is also the medium through which rational systems of the material world are understood. Ultimately, it is not the nature of knowledge that matters but the attitude of the learner. Learning involves the application of moral qualities especially diligence and humility which then lead on to careful thought, concentration, reading and observation. Morality is the means to learn rather than its end. Rationality and intelligence have little place. According to Weber,'Chinese thought has remained rather stuck in the pictorial and descriptive. The power of *logos*, of defining and reasoning, has not been accessible to the Chinese' (Weber, 1970a: 431).

Confucian traditions have been associated with a lack of an individual, forward looking, active view of the world because of the great emphasis in conforming to the moral standards decreed in the classic texts and on qualities such as loyalty and filial obedience. The emphasis on effort and conformity has been seen to preclude imagination and creativity. These have been identified by the Japanese government as potential barriers to future economic development (Schoppa, 1991: 2). Similarly there are issues of alienation of young people in urban technological environments as in the west. However through a purely moral–aesthetic view of education, East Asian societies seem to be able to solve the problems of morality–rationality dichotomy and of uniform educational achievements of all students which have eluded western societies. In effect, an ancient conformist, backward-looking philosophy has been able to sustain a contemporary culture that all have a moral obligation to learn and all knowledge – however foreign – is worth acquiring. So the major conceptual leap was achieved that western civilization has never made – that it is the act of learning that counts rather than the worth of what is to be learned. In effect, Herbert Spencer's question – What knowledge is of most worth? – becomes redundant.

This itself has allowed a rejection of the holism of knowledge which has been central to western thinking. Twentieth century Chinese and Japanese educators sought to demarcate traditional and imported knowledge in distinctions between western science and eastern morals (Hiroike, 1996; Makiguchi, 1989). Educational reform proposals focused on a reconstruction of traditional moral education to give it a greater focus on individual responsibility rather than on blind conformity. Similarly, the rational deficiency which Weber noted could be compensated for in borrowing from other traditions.

The political–social dimensions of Japanese culture have produced the greatest unease among western observers. Loyalty is at a premium. Loyalty to family – indeed to ancestors – was central in the interpretations of Confucianism. This became the foundation of the absolute state in the twentieth century as in ancient times. Conformism to familiar authority then stretches to an unquestioning acceptance of the absolute authority of state-prescribed curricula, school principals and even teachers. Individuality and creativity are constrained.

Chinese–Japanese epistemologies differ also between themselves. Chinese Taoism, with as long a history as Confucianism, suggested an individualism as uncompromising as that of Rousseau. Japanese traditions have a strong animist element, drawn from pre-Confucian beliefs and invigorated by Buddhist influences, which allows for a naturalist view of education based upon conceptions of the ties between humans and the natural world of plants and animals. A pre-Second World War western commentator could write:

> 'Among Japanese of all classes is an instinctive awareness of beauty. Their habit of finding pleasure in common things, their quick appreciation of form and colour, their feeling for simple elegance are gifts which may well be envied... frugality is not the enemy of satisfaction... the characteristic attitude of Japanese towards moral and philosophical problems is their intuitive, emotional approach and their mistrust of logic and analysis.' (Sansom, 1987: v)

A naturalist view of education has strong bases which differ from the psychology of humanity of Rousseau and the western naturalist tradition. As in France, strong forces towards conformity in Japan are confronted by an inherent individualism and anarchic drives (Benedict, 1967: 2). Chinese culture may be less emotional, spontaneous as well as being very serious or indeed lugubrious (Sansom, 1987: 238–39) compared with that of Japan. Yet in China also there have been alternatives to Confucianism emphasizing also solidarity but with a future collective goal rather than a respect for the past as seen in Maoism.

Different configurations have emerged in other countries and cultures. Hindu educational philosophy, like that of China, predates its European equivalents. Its traditions appear to be dysfunctional to a technological and democratic society. The caste system restricts education to certain social groups and its education treats spirituality as an end in itself so that the brahmin caste is unconcerned with practical life and search for the meaning of that juncture between human moral behaviour and an after life or scheme of life beyond the mundane. Weber, indeed, argued that a magical element in the Vedic tradition discouraged openness and was distrustful of the written word (Weber, 1970a: 416–18).

At first sight, Hindu traditions are more archaic and unsuited to contemporary conditions than western Platonism. Knowledge is the property of a hereditary class who use it for contemplation and preparation for lives after death rather than the improvement of the earthly condition. The political-ruler and merchant castes have no right to knowledge. Yet, as in Germany where there are some parallels in other-worldliness, this absolute restriction can in some ways be liberating. Hinduism has had an open, accommodating view of other kinds of knowledge (Mayhew, 1926: 39–40). The non-Brahmin classes are free to adopt western and other knowledge for its practical purposes. India since 1945 especially has been at the forefront of developing western science and technology in institutions of advanced study. Furthermore, this movement had historical parallels in the development of mathematics and science in ancient Hindu schools as well as in the reception of Islamic ideas.

Islamic views of knowledge have been more difficult to analyze in contemporary conditions of rejection of western scientific modernization. Koranic injunctions emphasize the moral obligation to learn but the stress has been on the passive, unquestioning learning of Islamic moral precepts contained within the Koran and its subsequent interpretations. The core belief has been that each individual is responsible to God for his or her moral conduct and that, as a precondition, God's moral laws should be learned from holy texts. Despite this fundamentalism, however, there have been strong rational–scientific movements in ancient Islamic thought connected not only to mathematics and logic but the sociology of Ibn Khaldun in the fourteenth century (Gellner, 1994: 130–31) and in the place given to a rationally patterned art and architecture. Indeed, it is argued that modern fundamentalism is not a return to primitivism but the expression of an ascetic romanticism of a rationally educated class (Gellner, 1994: 15–29). Contemporary radical proposals seek both commitment to individual moral purification and the development of expertise to serve the nation (Mehran, 1990: 56).

The most difficult traditions to disentangle have been those of Africa and Latin-America. Much study of African educational traditions came from western scholars with a background in functionalist-anthropology (Fortes, 1938; Raum, 1940) who stressed the relevance of pre-colonial education to everyday material concerns for earning a living; though they suggested that this education was highly structured and based upon experience rather than words and texts. Perhaps as important was the moral obligation to learn as a form of social–historical survival. The African historic tradition was based upon the learning of the history of the group and the devising of ways – through poetry and song – by which this knowledge could be most economically and elegantly transmitted. African traditions – like those of China – emphasize the necessity of learning as a social activity. The bases were humanist as much as naturalist. Crucially there was commitment and motivation to learn to be an effective contributor to the maintenance of social solidarity. This motivational strength is one of Africa's greatest contemporary assets to overcome a resistance to western education seen by many as a cultural invasion.

Similar conceptions have appeared in Latin-America. Popular education is about developing social and emotional links and solidarity. It is oppositional in its rejection of public education. It is naturalist and egalitarian in the exchange relations between teachers and students which Freire advocated (Freire, 1972). It does not have a strong rationalist basis yet it does have a methodology of inquiry with rational elements as Freire developed.

Conclusion

Traditions are rich but contradictory. They overlap yet differ significantly. Some flower at particular moments to support dynamic educational systems. But they also imprison and support decay. World educational history is full of examples of stultifying traditions – the inwardness and passivity of Hindu education, the deadening conformity of the Confucian message, the irrationality of Islam, the élitism and the anti-industrialism of western humanism. Sometimes the conflicts are so intense that the possibilities of any reconciliation seem remote, as in the chasm of views of the educated person in Russia as exemplified in Fydor Dostoevsky's *Brothers Karamazov*. Yet within each tradition there are possibilities for educational revivals and especially to meet the twin demands of efficient public–rational education and a private individual naturalism.

In the contemporary world the more practical questions are about access and control. Philosophical traditions of knowledge and learning provide a start. But fuller analysis of other sources needs to be undertaken. Separate kinds of cultural tradition support attitudes about who should get access to knowledge and who should control its provision.

3
Norms of educational access

Teaching and learning in each national education system need to be judged by who gets access to them. The debates, across countries, focus on whether all groups have fair chances to participate and whether significant minorities are excluded. National priorities of utilizing the skills of the whole population are important as well as individual or social fairness. Variations in student opportunities between countries may come from national traditions of teaching and learning. Yet views about access may be independent and, indeed, may have an effect on the view of knowledge.

An abundance of evidence collected in many countries indicates that chances of students gaining access to selective types of education depends on familial social class, educational and occupational backgrounds or income grouping. Other research has concentrated on opportunities available to cultural or ethnic groups and to women. Though these inquiries have been conducted throughout the world, their results are rarely comparative. For comparison of societies and cultures is much more difficult than comparison of educational systems.

The focus in this chapter is on the established values in each society from which principles are drawn about which people should have access to different kinds of teaching and learning. The procedures of selection and their rationales are stressed. The comparison is between the ways that national education systems select students rather than on empirical evidence of the social justice of the selection procedure.

A number of comparative models have been proposed to account for differences between residual values of selection across countries. These concentrate on historic social norms – sponsored and contest, individualist and collectivist, credentialist and communitarian. They have been applied to the selection of small élite groups. The incorporation or exclusion of underclasses has been less satisfactorily covered. The relationship between values of selection and views of knowledge has not been explored very fully. It is with these areas that this chapter is concerned.

International studies of social mobility, social contexts and education, though peripheral to this inquiry, may help to clarify comparative study of traditions, largely to determine how the social conditions interact with residual educational values.

Student background and education opportunity

Received wisdom on educational access since the 1950s has been that educational opportunities, across nations and cultures, are dependent on the familial origins of students. The weight of evidence seemed overwhelming. The connection survives whatever kind of society is investigated – rich or poor, egalitarian or socially divided. Furthermore, the possibilities of action to change these relationships, except in marginal cases, seemed more remote, the firmer the results of research became.

Comparative surveys do not show which countries are more egalitarian than others. Countries are not comparable in their social structures. It is not possible to compare, easily, the relative chances of children from lower social class groups of entering or surviving in the mainstream education system or its élite sectors when social class structures differ. A skilled manual worker in Germany in the same 'trade' as a British equivalent may have a higher social–economic status and superior education.

Income levels are a slightly better guide. But countries do differ in the distribution of incomes. The poor were poorer in the USA, Britain and France in the 1980s where the lowest 20% had only 4.7, 5.8, and 6.3% respectively of the total household income compared with 8.0% and 8.7% respectively in Sweden and Japan (World Bank, 1991: 263). The wealthier have more opportunities for their children in countries where expensive private education is well established than where élite schools are concentrated in the state sector. So it is not clear whether the stronger relationship between educational achievement and parental income in Britain and the USA compared with Japan (Ishida, 1993: 242–43) is the product of differing social or educational divisions.

Students with better educated parents, internationally, have superior opportunities. Yet the processes by which that happens are not clear comparatively. This benefit is more likely to apply in some national traditions of worthwhile knowledge than others, and indeed to be affected by whether competence in the national language, literature or mathematics is the key to selection. Furthermore, the link between familial educational background and student achievement is weaker where educational provision has expanded rapidly and thus a relatively few students have well-educated parents, as seen most recently in South Korea (Sorensen, 1994).

More difficult comparative questions arise over differences in popular motivation. Cross-national studies have tried to explain different levels of economic growth by reference to differing degrees of popular motivation (McClelland, 1961). Other studies have suggested that the bases of popular motivation can be individualist in some societies and orientated to group aims in others (McClelland, 1987). But little is known about the differing strengths of popular motivation in various countries even though it is frequently invoked to account for educational achievement in the Far East.

The paradox of the consistent relationship between social background and educational achievement applying in all countries, yet the most disadvantaged performing better in some countries than others, became clear in the earliest comparative studies. The IEA project in the early 1960s indicated that in all countries studied there was a relationship between fathers' occupation together with parental education and student test scores in mathematics. Yet the most socially disadvantaged groups in some countries did markedly better than their equivalents elsewhere (Husen, 1967: Vol. 2, 253–55). It was also clear in these and subsequent surveys that the spread of test scores was much greater in, for instance, Britain and the USA (indicating larger groups of serious underachievers) than in Japan (Inkeles, 1979).

The issues of educational access and opportunity have changed since the 1960s. The initial concern was with the chances of children from less favoured backgrounds gaining access to educational institutions which provided openings to occupations at the apex of the social status pyramid. Over time, it became clear that the chances of those in the poorest 10 – 30% of the population escaping from the underclass was as important. Indeed, while aims of creating an egalitarian society without major social differences were rejected in almost every state in the world, those with larger underclasses than others aimed to reduce the size of these disadvantaged groups substantially. The comparisons that mattered seemed to be that Germany and Japan had educational failure rates of less than 10% of the population, which corresponded to the proportions who failed to get sufficiently skilled and adequately rewarded jobs. In Britain and the USA the underclass associated with educational failure was as high as 30 or 40%. Even in the successful countries, there were fears that occupational change and lack of educational–social response would swell underclasses that had been previously insignificant.

The shift of focus onto disadvantaged minorities occurred when it became clear that the certain groups never entered fully into the competition for social selection through education. The stimulus came from American studies, notably that of James Coleman in the USA in the 1960s (Coleman, 1966). American blacks and other groups identified by ethnicity or culture formed an educational–occupational underclass. Questions then arose about whether underachievement arose from racial discrimination based upon atavistic attitudes, views of history or established economic roles. For Gunnar Myrdal, discrimination sprung from the coexistence in individuals of higher valuations which corresponded to the overt ideals of the society (including equality of opportunity) and lower valuations of unarticulated often unadmitted prejudices revealed in action rather than verbal statement, like a Freudian id. Racism was the product of lower valuations (Myrdal, 1944).

Alternative explanations included an historical folk-memory of racial superiority which was drawn upon by the metropolitan inhabitants of imperialist powers such as Britain which was then used to justify denial of equal rights to immigrants from former colonial territories (Banton, 1977). There were also theories which suggested that racial–cultural discrimination was functional to the economic system since it kept cultural minorities in the menial and occupationally marginal positions they had under slavery in the USA (Cox, 1943) or, with immigrants in the 1960s in western Europe, to maintain the marginality of the position which they had first acquired on arrival (Castles and Kosack, 1973). Similar kinds of psychological, historical and economic explanations were offered for the denial of social opportunities for women.

These arguments did not apply as easily across cultures. Cultural divisions differed substantially between countries, with cultural–ethnic underclasses relatively underrepresented in countries such as Japan and old cultural cleavages very strong as in the Netherlands. Even explanations in terms of race could be given a cultural relative dimension with the claim that Protestant Calvinist cultures such as the USA and Britain were more racist than certain Catholic countries (Genovese, 1971: 23-52). Indeed the same typification could be applied to egalitarian Islam and stratified Hindu societies.

The main universalist argument was that of modernism; that there would be a global convergence towards ideals and practice of individual social mobility (Inkeles and Smith, 1975). The critical equivalent was that a global capitalist economy would force education systems everywhere to select students in response to the stratification of the industrial workforce (and unemployed reserve army) (Bowles and Gintis, 1976).

The issue changed again in the 1980s to the stages at which access was provided or denied. There had been a focus on access to secondary and, to a lesser extent, to higher education. Common secondary schools shifted concerns upwards to post-compulsory phases of education and to differentiation between kinds of courses rather than to the numerical level of participation in a stage of education. Attention was given also to the extent to which failure to gain proper opportunities at the ages of 16 or 18 was the product of educational experiences at much earlier ages – indeed from the pre-school phase onwards – which raised issues of the dividing line between school and family. Access to higher education has socially and culturally different implications when entrants were adults rather than children. With this widening of the field of analysis, so differences between countries and the more specific processes of selection across an age range from 2 to 22 became more important.

As governments attempted to reduce educational expenditure in the face of international competition the less scope there seemed to be to counteract the capacity of parents, based on wealth and on educational experience, to provide superior educational opportunities for their children at every level of the education system. Quite apart from difficulties of legislating for the cultural effects of family background, it became increasingly difficult to prevent the more affluent changing residence, even across national frontiers, enhancing the opportunities of their children in state systems or, ultimately, buying superior chances through private education.

Analysis of residual values on access allow education systems in their entire range to be examined. But they need to be modified by attention to traditional social divisions which themselves are imprinted on values. The consumers of education – students, their parents and even employers – have greater chance to influence decisions over access than over kinds of knowledge. Issues of differences of motivation within and between countries and of the lower valuations which operate are important.

Educational traditions and comparative norms of social selection

At a simple level, there is an apparent link between views of knowledge and concepts of social and occupational mobility. In the western tradition, 'humanism' provided education for an élite which had been separated and identified at an early age. Rational encyclopaedism seemed more egalitarian because it provided for a collective improvement of the whole population and, where élites were created, for the privileges of the chosen few to be justified by the benefit they could contribute to the majority. In contrast, naturalist views disdained any serious consideration of education as a means of social mobility.

There is a need for analysis of other sets of traditional values which relate to views of social structure and opportunities for social mobility. Contrasts were drawn in the 1950s between the survival of aristocratic values in western Europe, which could support the early and irreversible selection of a small minority via élite secondary schools, and the meritocratic norms of North America and the Soviet Union, which rejected any notion of a genetic élite, and provided a form of competition which allowed any individual to compete at any stage without an irreversible and final act of allocation (Turner, 1971). Further analyses of Europe and North America suggested a distinction between countries where selection was made on the basis of individual worth (both aristocratic England and meritocratic North America) and those where future élites were given opportunities on the basis of the contribution they could make to the collective good, which covered paternalist France and the communistic USSR (Hopper, 1971). Neither typology was as useful when applied to Far Eastern cultures in which competition and co-operation coexisted in a peculiar combination and ancient traditions did not seem to be a barrier to individual opportunity.

European aristocratic traditions

For Plato, true humane education was reserved for an hereditary caste of philosopher kings. Other social groups, including women and practitioners of manual crafts, were unworthy of such a moral education. This aristocratic association of humanism has continued beyond its rebirth in the European Renaissance and plagues its contemporary exhibition. The difficulty with democratization is that the major social benefits of a humanist education have been the qualities of leadership it bestows on those who imbibe it. The humanism of John Locke and its practical application by nineteenth century educational leaders in England such as Thomas Arnold or Benjamin Jowett was intended to create wise leaders who took inspiration from the heroes of literature and history they had studied.

Was education rigidly stratified by social class because the prevailing humanist tradition of knowledge demanded it or did humanism simply reinforce the social stratification of educational access which appeared independently? The power of the independent aristocratic values may be as important as interpretations of the humanist creed. Ralf Turner's distinction between sponsorship and contest norms of social mobility through education may offer an entry.

Turner claimed that sponsorship norms involved assumptions about the inherent worthiness of a minority for élite membership and that the existing élite believed it could identify such people at a young age without making their criteria of selection explicit. He associated such procedures with western Europe in contrast to the open contest which typified educational selection in both North America and the Soviet Union in the 1950s:

'Under **sponsored** mobility élite recruits are chosen by the established élites or their agents, and élite status is **given** on the basis of some criterion of supposed merit and cannot be **taken** by any amount of effort or strategy....Ultimately [they] grant or deny upward mobility on the basis of whether they judge the candidate to have those qualities they wish to see in fellow members.' (Turner, 1971: 72)

Turner identified this norm with traditional aristocratic societies and especially with England where he saw that industrialism had failed to change values but simply led to changes 'in the rates, the specific means, and the rules of mobility' (Turner, 1971: 76). More doubtfully, he suggested that it might apply in highly centralized, bureaucratic systems – industrial companies as well as nation states.

The evidence in England which Turner offered in support of his argument was a tripartite system of secondary education though this had only been formalized after 1944. There was early selection at the age of 11 mainly to grammar schools of about 25% of the age group, on the basis of a test of general ability – mainly linguistic and numerical. This selection provided access to the secondary school examinations at 16 then 18 which were the routes to higher education as well as to a high proportion of non-manual occupations. Relatively irreversible selection seemed to fit the sponsorship model.

By 1965, however, there was a movement against selection at 11 and by the end of the 1970s over 80% of children were attending common lower secondary schools. Turner's élite selection process was transferred to the age of 14 when 20–40% of pupils were allocated to selective streams of comprehensive schools leading to the unaltered secondary school examinations at 16 and 18. The barrier at 14 was reduced from 1986 when the examination at 16 was made more or less common to all and from 1991 attempts began to move towards a more open high education entry. The old sponsorship norm seemed only to apply in higher education where élite universities were able to admit students on the basis of their own judgements.

The apparent rapid decline of the sponsorship selection process in England after 1960 did not necessarily remove the norms associated with it especially in the values held by teachers or other social groups and the actions derived from these values. There continued to be assumptions that many children were fundamentally unequipped for higher levels of study and these judgements about the ineducability of large numbers of students continued to horrify observers from other countries (Maeroff, 1991). Teachers may have assumed that they knew which students were inherently worthy of selection for higher levels and to give them particular individual help. However, this may have reflected also what happened in universities where individual teachers' rights to admit the students they wanted did lead to a reciprocal commitment to help these selected students to complete courses. These behaviours were consistent with assumptions about inherent capacities for intuition in the humanist view of knowledge. However, there may have been also in selection of recruits to jobs an assumption that employers also could apply implicit criteria of selection.

Turner's analysis may have then reflected one moment of time in English history. While he underestimated the speed of change in reducing selective barriers at the age of 11, he may have also underestimated the strength of an earlier aristocratic tradition in which selection was purely on social class grounds. As late as 1861 the Newcastle Commission assumed that there would be different kinds of schools offering education up to the ages of 12 or 16 or 18 in which membership would relate overwhelmingly to social class origins of pupils, with only a tiny minority allocated on the basis of intellectual capacity.

The proportions of the age group in independent schools which, unlike those of other industrial countries, were typified by the wealth of parents, remained at around 8% and still provided half the entrants to the élite universities of Oxford and Cambridge in the 1990s. There was a clear survival of a system of educational stratification based on an archaic class structure without regard for achievement even though by the 1960s the élite independent schools and universities had stopped admitting students with inferior academic records. Rights to education remained patrimonial in some submerged valuations.

There was a separate strand of selection logic. The Northcote–Trevelyan reforms of public service in 1853 had attacked the procedures of admitting young men to positions in government adminstration purely on the basis of family influence (or indeed the purchase of positions, especially in the army). The arguments were made in terms of the efficiency of administration rather than individual fairness (Woodward, 1962: 621–22). In effect it was in the interests of the public good that certain positions in public life should be filled by the most capable – chosen by examination – rather than on the basis of social origin or wealth. The emergence of selective examinations in education can be seen in terms of the reform of the Civil Service. The main debate was whether those chosen on the basis of intellectual achievement in a written examination would also have the moral qualities of a gentleman (Briggs, 1965: 168–69).

This strand was compatible with another powerful though newer value system. The utilitarian movement stretching from Adam Smith through Jeremy Bentham to John Stuart Mill attacked waste and corruption in public life. The introduction of examinations for entry to public service coincided with utilitarian reform of the ancient universities and, indeed, was followed by the application of principles of efficiency to the financing of elementary schooling. The reforms of 1853 created the basis of examinations in schools as well as in public life.

It is questionable whether those who were denied social mobility through education actively sought it or themselves associated higher levels of educational achievement with betrayal of their social class origins and so were resigned to the aristocratic ethos. A study of 88 educationally successful working-class children in the early 1960s suggested that all were exceptional, belonging to the sunken middle class or a working class aristocracy of labour and religious leaders (Jackson and Marsden, 1966) while studies of the denial of pupil opportunities within schools by teachers showed no great protest by parents or students (Hargreaves, 1967; Willis, 1977).

Indeed, the conflict over denial of opportunities to children of ethnic minority background and to girls in the 1980s (England and Wales DES, 1981) may have been as much an expression of conflict between authorities regarding these groups as a passive, resigned working class when in fact they had strong motivations for social mobility (and the emergence of a new upwardly mobile working class in the 1970s may have been associated with new government demands for higher basic standards; England and Wales DES, 1977). But there still remained a strand of desire for the collective upgrading of the working class rather than individual mobility – reflected in R.H.Tawney's demands for better material facilities for schools for the poor and less attention to social mobility (Tawney, 1964: 141–47) but also having origins as old as the seventeenth century parliamentary revolution and perhaps earlier.

These different strands raise questions about aristocratic survivals and meritocracy, concepts of individual worth and innate capacities but also the professional autonomy of those who select. On the one hand a strongly individualist element survives – defined by Hopper as 'the right of the selected to privilege as a reward for their talents' (Hopper, 1971: 100). On the other hand, there is also an assumption of social class representation derived from old values but translated into ideas – as with Tawney – that the working class should have representatives, almost delegates, in the élite: a concept later revived from a different standpoint by John Rawls. This strand was consistent with Turner's view that élite status was inalienable in the sponsorship norm and which was later used by minorities – cultural, ethnic, gender – to defend their acquired positions. Finally there was the pluralist conception that the selective process was rightly under the control of certain independent professional groups – especially teachers but, at the level of employment, by employers or even professional associations.

The sponsorship model applied to other European countries. Selection between the ages of 10 and 12 for separate academic secondary schools prevailed throughout most of western Europe in the 1960s. Only Sweden had moved – since 1947 – to a common secondary school (Marklund and Soderberg, 1967). Yet by 1975 only Germany, the Netherlands, Austria and Switzerland in western Europe had retained a largely segregated system. Particular conditions applied in these countries. Social class divisions had remained strong enough for parents to accept the classification into occupational futures at the age of 10–12. But they were hardly aristocratic in the English mould. Élite private schools were rare. State selective schools catered for an urban middle class (like English grammar schools) (Ringer, 1979).

This modification of humanistic selection may reflect different class structures. The aristocratic traditions of Germany or the commercial history of the Netherlands did not demean the social position of other groups. The craftsman, small business entrepreneur, the minor professional had established positions in the class structure. An educational selection system emerged which gave recognition to their social standing with the importance of second-rank selective secondary schools such the *Realschule* in Germany. The protected social position of the craftsman also gave a meaning to the unselective secondary school. Above all, in Germany, the traditional élite had been weakened in the twentieth century and a more materialist even philistine set of values emerged. In contrast, in Britain, a traditional élite survived nineteenth- and twentieth-century economic and political change yet, perhaps more significantly, the traditional crafts were destroyed by nineteenth century industrialism leaving a mass of workers rooted in traditions of unskilled landless labourers.

Turner contrasted the English sponsorship norm with the open competition of the American contest model. However, the distinction between Britain and France as archetypical European extremes, drawing from the model of Hopper, is a more fruitful comparison.

The collectivist tradition in Europe

The rationalist view of knowledge does not support the assumptions of the innate moral worth of some persons upon which the Platonic vision is based. It can distinguish between an intellectual élite, marked by its developed intelligence, and the masses. But the externality and standardization of the rational-encyclopaedic curriculum may leave behind a significant minority of underachievers.

The collectivist view of access, which reached its greatest influence in socialist regimes in the mid-twentieth century, has two elements, both of which have links with the rational view of knowledge. One is that an intellectual élite is chosen to serve the masses and owes its position entirely to that social mission rather than to any innate individual worth. The second aspect is that a basic core of knowledge can and should be acquired by all. This second view also has a long European history and has roots in Protestantism as well as demonstration in twentieth-century socialist regimes.

The distinction of Hopper was that, with collectivist norms, 'selection is justified by the society's need ... to be led by the most suitable people' rather than that individuals to be rewarded for success (Hopper, 1971: 100). The claim that an élite chosen by education serves the masses perhaps was most influentially made by Condorcet following the 1789 French Revolution.

However, Hopper's claim that there was a difference between paternalist and aristocratic versions of collectivism does not stand up as well. In both French and Soviet values in the twentieth century there is an assumption that all should acquire a basic education in the collective interest. The difference was one of intensity of the drive for achievement.

The Soviet school was based on the belief that all citizens had an obligation to reach certain standards of attainment and that there were no inherent differences between students which would prevent these minimum standards being met. The Soviet common school up to the age of 15 or 16 attempted to ensure that all reached a minimum standard by the application of a range of sanctions on students and their parents. In contrast, French schools and those of other European countries required minimum and uniform achievement standards but simply failed those who did not reach them. Citizenship in both systems required the achievement of certain educational standards. The French assumed that collectivism could not be taken as far as forcing recalcitrant members of French society to reach these standards. The French state could not engage in the attempted conquest of French society in the ways that were possible in the USSR and other communist regimes.

The origin of this mass collectivism in Europe came as much from religious drives as from secular modernization. Comenius' demand that all things should be taught to all men and women of every class and nation was based on a theology that each person was answerable to God. Each person had a duty and obligation to use his or her talents to the fullest. It was not a question of individual reward but of individual duty to use talents to the maximum – a religious concept that was given expression in Karl Marx's aphorism 'from each according to his ability, to each according to his need' (Marx, 1963: 263).

The drive for minimum attainments for all was in the religious Protestant view that every person should be able to read and understand the

Bible as the fount of religious understanding. This underlay the egalitarianism of Comenius. It was also underscored by the success of Calvinist or Lutheran theocracies of Scotland or parts of Germany in achieving mass involvement in education at an early date. There were differences. In sixteenth-century Germany, state education was a response of both Protestant and Catholic states to a dangerous unregulated spread of literacy among a population with a radical interpretation of Lutheranism (Gawthrop, 1987: 31–32) whereas in seventeenth-century Scotland, the Calvinist authorities attempted to secure their control over an unenthusiastic population by universal schooling (Houston, 1987: 51–52).

The emphasis was inclusionist. But the sanctions were abhorrence of individual lack of commitment, energy, industriousness. These sanctions applied in the secular ideology in the USSR in specific terms in the ways that underachievers were dealt with in schools and within concepts of religious duties elsewhere. An individual sense of loyalty and duty was important but the framework had to be the universally available school without serious differentiation in content, teaching or organization.

The crucial distinction is when the aim shifts from ensuring minimum standards for all to deciding how to separate élites. For Condorcet, only elementary schooling would be universal and that view prevailed in France into the twentieth century. The principle of universal secondary education was only accepted in 1947 and began to be implemented after 1959 (McLean, 1985a: 65). By 1989 it was decided that France needed 80% of its young people to reach university entrance standards. At this stage the élitist and mass elements began to merge.

The indicators of this collectivist view can be seen at various levels of education. Pre-school education in France was developed in the early 1970s in order to reduce failures in the first grade of elementary schooling. Yet this high-grade repetition rate is also an indication that all must reach minimum standards as a public duty. Where France differs from the old USSR is in the lack of sanctions to enforce attainment of minimum standards and a willingness to abandon a group of students whose possibilities of achieving full symbolic citizenship are restricted from the age of 7.

The state–collectivist rationale for selection, allocation and incorporation is seen in the organization of lower secondary schools. The first two grades of the common lower secondary school (termed the *observation* cycle) are followed by two grades of *orientation* and, in the upper secondary level, a cycle of *determination*. The terms indicate that pupils are progressively allocated to appropriate careers, which correspond with national interests. Indeed, curriculum subjects in 1985 were linked in official guidelines with the kind of occupations to which they could give access even in the lower secondary school (McLean, 1990a: 125). Similarly, those leaving school at 16 are energetically recruited into vocational programmes, much more systematically than in Britain (Wolf and Rapiau, 1993). Yet there is an ambiguity at this level since pre-vocational courses, from the equivalent of the third grade of the lower secondary school which absorb grade repeaters and other underachievers, also imply a rejection with its implications of denial of full citizenship.

Certification of student attainment for courses at every level, with the main diplomas issued by the state is also a symbolic bestowal of citizenship. The difficulty in legitimation of this procedure in the popular view is that only the *baccalauréat* is seen as a true mark of citizenship, which allowed toleration of a high drop-out and failure rate in universities among *baccalauréat* holders. French education policy in the 1980s responded by widening access to the *baccalauréat*.

Examinations become crucial in the collectivist system. There is a carefully graduated system which extends to academic tests which give a professional standing, notably the *agrégation* for entry to élite secondary school or higher education teaching. Yet standard examinations have also been central to appointments in public service including school principals and inspectors. The fundamental difference with examinations in England is that the French diploma is a mark of public status which is carried round by its holder for the whole of his or her life.

There are exclusionist elements in collectivist selection even if these only operate informally. Notoriously, Muslim girls have been excluded from French schools from the late 1980s on the grounds that they refuse to observe the secular ideals of the school (Hollifield, 1992). Private Catholic schools, though enrolling around 15% of pupils and receiving state aid, have never fully been accepted as part of the state system. The students only become incorporated by taking state examinations. Only those who accept the values of a national lay system can hope for selection to higher positions through it. The persistently high failure rate in most courses from primary school to university (though not *grandes écoles*) suggest the survival of a view that the embattled state has never completed its pacification of the troublesome French people.

The contrast with the USSR is interesting. Exclusion was not possible, though differentiation of students in the public interest began from the end of the common school at the age of 15 or 16 when vocational schools separated from the general school (and there had been special élite schools for a small minority with particular gifts in music, ballet, mathematics, languages to offer to the collective interest). Grade repeating was abhorrent (Bereday *et al.*, 1960). Yet it was highly doubtful that achievement rates were the same over the country or even that compulsory school was completed everywhere. Where deviations existed, these were justified – as in the case of cultural minorities – by reference to stages of development of exceptional groups before they could be assimilated (Bromley, 1979).

Collectivist philosophies of individual submission to the general will produce cynical reactions when confronted with the evidence of individual selfish motivations in socialist regimes (Dobson, 1977). The response is that the state ideology has not been properly internalized by individuals which meets counter-responses that individual selfishness will always prevail. French parents seek to maintain social distance by maximizing the chances of their children. Soviet intelligentsia or political élite cadres sought educational means to turn themselves into hereditary castes. Yet the overt, manifest collectivist ideology is not challenged and that survival does have an impact on the opportunities available to students in ways that are not comparable with outcomes in say Britain or the USA.

The collectivist view has different manifestations in other parts of western Europe. Despite the sponsorship of a tripartite secondary school system in Germany, there are expectations of minimum standards of achievement to meet not so much state plans as the needs of employers who, since 1945, have formed a triad with government and trade unions to represent national economic interest. Trade Unions support this emphasis. As in France and other European countries, the final secondary school certificate, the *Abitur*, retained a symbolic function as a state mark of achievement giving automatic rights of entry to higher education. Yet there are clearly deeper roots to German achievement, in view of its long history as nineteenth century observers noted (Arnold, 1984). That pride in the status of occupation and religious commitment may have been as much a product of the individual determination of students as of a set of state-determined signposts as in France.

Yet Germany has its own type of exclusion. While French traditions exclude those who reject the secular modernizing mission of republican schools, German concepts of nationality have been ethno-cultural. Foreigners, defined by lack of historic German birthright, have been denied equal rights in residence, employment, and even education. The children of immigrant workers were isolated in their own schools in Bavaria (Castles and Kosack, 1973). The exclusion of non-Germans has become more intense since the late 1980s and has advocates within mainstream political parties (Faist, 1994).

Elsewhere in Europe the collectivist norm of selection operated in ways similar to France but in some cases within the context of a history of a modernist state vainly attempting the transformation of a backward society. Spain had a history of high repetition and drop-out rates in school so that government intervention in student assessment in 1981 was designed to limit teacher tendencies to fail students (McNair, 1984: 52–54). In Italy, repetition rates remained high at all levels of education (Monasta, 1994: 181) in a country where the gulf between central government and the people was more extreme than in France. The ultimate expression of such a state–society separation is found in rationalist–collectivist regimes in Latin-America where modernist education consigned the majority of the people to a culture of silence (Freire, 1972).

Collectivist rationales for selection are clearly consistent with the explicit and standardized view of knowledge. There would be difficulty in reconciling it with any other. But collectivist states face contemporary challenges to their legitimacy. This does not necessarily mean the end of collectivist views of access, but requires an accommodation with naturalist approaches.

Naturalist traditions and educational access

Rousseau almost contemptuously rejected any function of his education for man in nature to provide avenues for social mobility (Rousseau, 1993: 9–10). Education for man in nature has no place for unnaturally removing him from his social and natural milieu in which his nature can fruitfully develop. This was the position taken by so many advocates of naturalist education. It was the root of segregation of naturalist education from the education of the citizen. The dichotomy of public and private education was founded on the failure of the former to provide meaning and of the latter to offer opportunity for social mobility.

The tensions arose in that failure to integrate public and private. They were seen as opposed rather than complementary. Yet the character of this connection does vary between cultures and does relate to different traditions which have differing contemporary outcomes. At one extreme, private education is purely the function of the family so that any form of public education is inevitably a process of alienation. At the other, community education is an alternative to public institutions which are repudiated. Various kinds of compromises have been made between the two extremes.

The simplest division is offered by the family responsibility for private education and an exclusive public function of the school. This was broadly the tradition of nineteenth-century European countries. The assumption was that morality, folk culture, local languages and tactile experience would be provided in the home and thus had no place in the state school. French state elementary schools of the nineteenth century were founded on the basis that private cultures were provided for elsewhere. Indeed where private cultures were identified with a morality which was ordered locally by the Catholic church then these mores were a challenge to the state school mission. Elsewhere in Europe, the relationship was more accommodating. State schools in Germany and Scandinavia remain morning-only activities so that familial education continues to find space in a crowded day in ways that are not replicated in France, Britain, the USA or Japan. The pressures to attain in public spheres do not seem to have challenged this division, despite American claims that the length of the school day and school year affects national average performances.

The challenge has come instead from the failure of the family to be able to offer a complete private education. Naturalist education was provided to fill the gaps. Yet the character of this provision has varied between countries with substantial implications for the achievement of both minimum standards in public education and the fairness of provision of opportunities for social mobility through education. England of all the countries which achieved near-universal elementary education in the nineteenth century most ruthlessly nationalized familial education. For Britain was the most urbanized society of that period and state education was intended to civilize the urban masses by providing a familial morality in elementary schools. Compulsory schooling began earlier – at 5 – than in other countries where 6 (or 7 in the familial cultures of Scandinavia) was the norm. The English school offered a familial environment, notably in the infant section (5–7 year olds) but also in the parent-substitute role of the teacher. The family was deemed incompetent at providing moral and private education and the school aimed to compensate.

There were other elements in this tradition. The aristocracy – and in the nineteenth century the new commercial and industrial middle classes – almost uniquely were educated away from the family in boarding schools which also had primarily a moral, family substitute function (Bamford, 1967). State schools for the masses in the nineteenth century in many ways aped those of the social élite. The Public School domination of élite preparation in independent moral communities prevented the emergence of a state-created educational élite as in France and Germany.

The community function of schools was never totally lost. The introduction of common secondary schools in the mid-twentieth century raised debates about how far the aim was to provide equal opportunities for social mobility on an individualist basis and how far their function was to create social harmony among urban communities through having socially (and later culturally) balanced communities. Yet the assumption of a naturalist function by state schools – initially the elementary schools and later the secondary sector – had to face the social class basis of schooling. Community schools in effect were seen as serving particular social class communities in ways that denied opportunities for social mobility. Distinctions were drawn between high culture and folk culture (Bantock, 1968) which were associated with different occupational –social futures.

The relationship between public and private education differed in other cultures. The community was identified on more strictly geographical lines in other cultures. Scandinavian folk schools – at least in Denmark and to a degree in Norway – were expressions of community identity of based on the village (Lauglo, 1990: 28). The Danish folk school is controlled by the community and is an extension of the village economic co-operative. It stresses co-operative values and, following Grundtwig, the teaching of local folk historic culture. It is helped by the weakness of social class divisions and, perhaps, the lack of religious, ethnic, linguistic divides. Community schools do not become those designed to keep the lower classes in their place as in Britain.

Instead the conflict emerges when rites of passage from private to public education are undergone. The Danish gymnasium is a thoroughly national, public and intellectual institution. Danish community philosophies allowed the transition period to be pushed back by unifying a new common lower secondary school in the 1970s with the elementary school. But the transition at the age of 16 or 17 proved difficult and increasingly the alienating public curriculum penetrated the community orientated *folkeskole*. Even the *folkeskole* was too national for many tastes. The state-subsidized 'little' schools are run by parents and provide a content and ethos reflecting the conservatism of rural communities or the ideological preferences of urban radicals. In the early 1990s they accounted for over 10% of enrolments (Winther-Jensen, 1994: 50).

Tensions existed between community schools which were initiatives of parents and local groups and those which emerged out of public policy. Throughout the world separate and often private education provides for the development of local cultural values for which the public system does not cater. These schools may be supplementary, providing for separate religious, linguistic and literary–aesthetic–historical education of cultural minorities. They may be classes provided outside and additional to public education (McLean, 1985b; Wong, 1992). They may be private alternatives to public schooling. In some cases they may be crammers designed to offer mainstream education in an environment which is culturally more secure for cultural minorities.

Naturalist, community education may eschew individual or collectivist aims of social mobility. It provides for a kind of education for which there is a persisting demand. However, there have been difficulties in reconciling it with reasonable demands for the achievement levels in public education upon which individual and collective material improvement depends. The USA appeared for long to provide a particular kind of reconciliation which, in recent years, appears to have lost its effectiveness.

American community and competition

The American case is interesting because rationality was modified by pragmatism and communalism. But the nineteenth century common school was to provide universal opportunities without any distinction of streams or types of learning. The contest model rejected any kind of formal, institutional barriers. The American common school was as egalitarian in aims and structure as that of the Soviet Union in the mid-twentieth century as Turner indicated. Yet its egalitarianism and communality came not from standardization, centralism or abstract rationality. It was founded instead on a protestant concept of duty made secular by Thomas Jefferson by the substitution of religious piety by civic responsibility. Its rationality was expressed in a plastic utilitarianism rather than a crystalline logic.

But this coincided with an individualism of Anglo-Saxon secular origin which urged each to compete with his or her fellows at the same time as co-operating in civic matters. Unrestrained individualism – later legitimated by appeal to Darwinist analogies – seemed to undermine communalism and equal opportunities. Indeed, the common school – reinforced by anti-discrimination measures of the 1960s and 1970s – seemed to legitimate inequalities of outcomes in terms of individual wealth on the basis that all had chances and those who failed would have to accept failure as a personal responsibility.

Turner's typification of the contest norm of social mobility derived from this peculiar American compromise:

> 'Contest is ... fair only if all players compete on an equal footing. Victory by a person of moderate intelligence accomplished through the use of common sense, craft, enterprise, daring and successful risk taking is more appreciated than victory by the most intelligent or the best educated.' (Turner, 1971: 74)

Individual effort was the key. But there were to be no hurdles. Schools were common and without streams, grade repeating or external assessment. And the competition was conducted over the whole span of the education system so that even those entering a Community College after High School could end up eventually in the most prestigious university.

The qualities needed for success were those associated by Turner with the early phases of industrialization. They were also the idealized qualities of the Frontier. Yet they could hardly have been given weight unless competition was built onto the community school with its naturalist curriculum and its wider objective of encouraging a co-operative community spirit which was antithetical to individualist effort. Indeed, over the history of American education, co-operation has taken priority over competition. The community ethos of the elementary school was transferred to the High School and then to Community College and university. The recreational and vocational curriculum spread to higher levels together with that peculiar social studies programme which encapsulated the co-operative aims of the progressive elementary school. The link with the community was a significant element of the university from the time of the Land Grant Acts of the 1860s.

The academic, intellectual public curriculum was only pre-eminent in a smaller number of high schools in prosperous areas and then especially in the private and high-ranking public universities. But a new kind of separation emerged. The essence of the community school is that parents and children identify with it socially. Parents, through property purchase, created geographical communities of their own income and occupational group. These could just as well espouse soft community and private values but attainments were high because of motivation and other aids provided by privileged parents. The obverse was the neighbourhood community school of the disadvantaged without this capacity to achieve highly by occupational standards. So by the 1980s there were calls to end the hypocrisy and to replace vastly different public community schools by private alternatives which were more responsive to parent aspirations (Chubb and Moe, 1990; Coleman and Hoffer, 1987).

What is less easy to explain in the USA, for Americans as much as outsiders, is the loss of a common commitment to minimum standards and of a fear of and shame at failure which a Comenian philosophy should engender. Educational achievements of the majority have been claimed to be in decline since the 1950s (Conant, 1959). Yet the school has no inbuilt drive to improve apart from competition with other community schools and by reference to the various attempts to apply state or federal standards especially since the 1970s.

It is within this context that ideas of fairness associated with John Rawls gained currency. The proposal was the opportunities could be deemed to be fair if individuals who failed to take advantage of them admitted their fairness or if candidates for success were prepared to admit the fairness of the scheme even though they failed (Rawls, 1972). While the philosophy derived from utilitarian concepts of the primacy of the greatest individual happiness of the greatest number, its effect was to create a pluralist-collectivism. Individuals were representatives of their sub-culture. Their individual advancement was on behalf of this group. It was thus an attempt to reconcile small-scale community and the wider public interest but conceiving of a larger nation as a collectivity of separate cultural interests, not unlike that of the Netherlands.

Though American educational expansion offered an example for the rest of the world, the American tradition of educational access and social mobility, like the American curriculum, is very peculiar to that country. The model does not transfer easily. Ironically, the national systems in Asia which seemed to offer the greatest threat to American traditional practices also shared rather similar starting-points of a tension between individual and community, co-operation and competition but reached a different kind of accommodation.

Eastern alternatives

In Confucian cultures, views of equality of opportunity which are stronger than those of most western societies coexist with a greater competitiveness. Commitment to uniform standards of achievement is maintained alongside an individualist view of social opportunity and mobility. Confucian moralism and concepts of a gentlemanly education can be reconciled to ideas that all must achieve minimum standards and that none can be excluded from competition. Yet there are also strong pressures for a naturalist education which ignore issues of social mobility.

Confucian concepts of education on the one hand focused on the selection of an élite bureaucrat class which would provide good government. This group had not only power but social and material privilege. The processes of selection were rigorous and highly competitive. Yet the competition was open to all and Confucius emphasized that any person, from any social background, through his or her determination, had the capacity to succeed. To fail was no disgrace but not to try was shameful.

In the twentieth century Japanese schools, both before and after the American occupation of 1945, were comprehensive and egalitarian. By the 1980s, the numbers completing secondary education were the highest in the world. Comprehensive schooling was achieved on American lines. Furthermore intense pressures – drawing on negative emotions of shame which Confucianism legitimated – prevented the emergence of a class of underachievers.

Yet competition was intense to enter the best schools and universities. All secondary schools – both junior and senior – were notionally equal and relatively few schools denied basic educational quality. Yet those which were seen to offer the best chances for progress to the best universities or to occupation at 18 were able to impose selective examinations. A similar process occurred with universities. The best schools and best universities offered opportunities of work in the great corporations.

Yet parents could not easily buy advantage through change of residence to socially exclusive districts or by patronizing élite private schools or universities. Selection has been savage but within a relatively egalitarian education system. To maximize individual advantage parents have to resort to cram schools, yet even those do not discriminate through high fees. There is a form of selection through the designation of vocational schools for about 25% of 16–18 years olds who tend to enter less prestigious and, previously, less secure jobs in small companies. But basic educational standards remain high even in the vocational schools (Prais, 1986). The clearest form of discrimination was at higher education level where 2-year community colleges in effect prepared young women for marriage and housewively duties. Yet, since the 1990s, even these institutions have declined and in many cases have closed.

The highly competitive yet egalitarian Japanese system of selection supported by norms that are both competitive and co-operative may have been made possible by the survival of discrimination by age rather than deep social divisions. Early nineteenth century Japan had strict feudal class divisions. Yet schools for the *samurai* warrior class were noted for individual competitiveness (Dore, 1984). Individual effort was tolerated, even encouraged, within particular age groups. Japanese companies are noted for a sibling-like co-operation between workers and unchallenged acceptance of paternalist managers, promotion by seniority and commitment to the organization. Competitiveness is within the framework of ideals of communal rules and conformity. Despite typification of American values as individualist and competitive and Japanese as co-operative and conformist (Lipset 1994), Japanese 'shame' at disgracing the family may be a greater spur to individual effort than American 'guilt' at not fulfilling personal aims.

Japan has been egalitarian at least in opening the competition to all within a moral–humanist set of Confucian values whose western equivalents have stressed social stratification and genetic – or at least socially transmitted – concepts of fitness for improvement. There are questions about whether other Confucian societies achieve the same kind of balance. China after the egalitarianism of Mao Zedong's Cultural Revolution (1966–74) has moved to a new competitiveness in line with participation in the global economy. Competitiveness does appear to be open but it is savage in its application, notably in the selection for keynote schools and universities. Values and goals appear to be materialist, as in Hong Kong, Singapore and Taiwan. Each of these countries or territories experienced political ruptures which prevented the development of a modernist yet nationalist dynamic and thus public adherence to traditional national values. The success of individuals contributes to the success and prestige of the family, especially in Taiwan (Winckler, 1987). In Korea, the collective shame of a colonized past provides an incentive (Brandt, 1987). Such drives may be as powerful in competition as a simple egotism.

Of the other great civilizations, Hinduism faces apparently a traditional view of social stratification more extreme than that of western societies. Not only has the brahmin caste a monopoly of higher learning but 'scheduled' castes and tribes faced hostility and violence when attempting to enter education. Indian government positive discrimination laws since 1947 attempted to allocate a proportion of places to scheduled castes and tribes but again faced a violence when they were enacted (Mahar, 1972). Even in Japan the children of those pioneering groups who take jobs abroad suffer discrimination on the basis of their non-Japaneseness (Goodman, 1990). The other cases of positive discrimination include Malaysia where economic and possibly family structures give Chinese advantages over Malays.

Yet apparently fixed and archaic traditions can be breached or challenged. Hindu civilization has long traditions of absorption and accommodation, partly through the impact firstly of Islamic Mogul rule and then that of Britain. Opportunistic values can prevail towards the acceptance of foreign knowledge – reflected in the post-1947 policy of creating centres of excellence in higher education. Yet, like Germany, the traditional cultured class was not strong enough to resist these incursions. Unlike the Platonic British scheme the cultured élite had lost real political and economic power; indeed in the Hindu caste culture they were more priestly and other worldly and lacked the political leadership function of Plato's philosopher kings.

In contrast in Islamic societies, ancient class structures based on economic and political power have created barriers which may not be justified by egalitarian religious ideas where each person has been answerable individually to his or her god and where political magnates have not been able as easily to claim divine rights. The obstruction to the opportunities for women has also been challenged with reference to Islam so that women may demand economic–occupational rights while adhering to traditional cultural concepts of the separate social–familial position of women. The educational segregation of women may be used as much as a basis for claiming equal occupational rights as accepting a socially depressed and disengaged status.

Conclusion

The issue of access and opportunity now has both maximalist and minimalist parameters. Concern up to the 1980s was with maximalist concepts – to allow a minority from the masses to enter the élite through education. Concepts of leadership groups, their intellectual and moral qualities and the extent to which these qualities were inherent or could be given chances to flower through educational provision created the context of policy debate. Yet in some ways these debates have become sterile. There is little that can be done to prevent the rich and powerful giving advantages to their children and interventionist policies foundered when it became difficult to identify representatives of social or cultural groups who could be admitted to élite classes on condition they would help those they represented.

Some cultures do have a greater openness than others but still only minorities can benefit. Furthermore, there is uncertainty about what kinds of qualities future élites will have – wisdom, prudence, consistency and self-sacrifice have to be balanced against intelligence and reason. Yet other kinds of qualities need also to be considered such as energy, risk-taking, dynamism on the one hand and creativity even eccentricity on the other. Various analysts from Wilfredo Pareto to T.S. Eliot have bemoaned the disaggregation of élites as the first stage in political–cultural anarchy. Yet this multiplicity of élites may be the product of a diverse global economy. In some ways this complexity and unpredictability of élite requirements has done as much to undermine the maximalist case for educational access as the survival of self-interest and traditional views.

The minimalist dimension has become more important. Deep social fissures based on the growth of large underclasses become more threatening in richer countries as a generally desirable erosion of distinction between rich and poor countries occurs (even though the extreme poor in the poorest and most unstable countries are as badly off as ever). Underclasses threaten social stability and are irreconcilable with democracies. Education has a prime role in reducing underclasses. Yet their apparent abolition in some societies such as Japan or, relatively, Germany may be linked to traditional mores and economic institutions which cannot survive the competitiveness and unpredictability of a contemporary economy. The levels of attainment required in high technology societies are increasing so rapidly that the traditional social institutions which helped to maintain them such as the paternalist company or, in some countries, government simply have no longer the resources to continue to operate in this way. And a technology which requires not only high levels of communicative–rational skill but also individual creativeness, small group loyalty and effort has no in-built bases for securing the future of the majority.

The position of naturalist, familial, private and personal development becomes even more important even though such identities – while possibly economically rewarding – need to be developed without reference to future public rewards. Naturalist identities and naturalist education have no function in social mobility. Occupational success fails to provide meaning and personal–cultural satisfaction. Private alternatives need to be developed and fostered.

But the reconciliation of public and private both in their occupational and ultimately epistemological dimensions is a matter for polities. Political arrangements and political cultures become important both to safeguard types of knowledge transmission and to maintain a proper boundary and articulation between private and public. And political cultures differ between civilizations and countries as much as views of knowledge and views of social mobility.

4

Political cultures and the control of education

Teaching and learning have always been about the interaction between the individuals. The relationship between Socrates and his acolytes or between Confucius and his followers is as much a practical ideal now as it was over 2000 years ago. External control is artificial. It is volatile, reacting to economic and political changes. The control of teaching and learning, however, reflects the historic political cultures of each country. Even when faced with common pressures for change, the responses can differ significantly between countries.

Peculiar convolutions have occurred over the last 20 years. Demand for international comparability of educational standards has strengthened central authority. Other forces encourage autonomy of institutions and even the individual accountability of each teacher and student. Power over educational decisions is devolved downwards just as it is gathered in centrally. The national state, while asserting a strong surveillant role, has begun to privatize public education. In some ways the relationship that Socrates and Confucius had with their students is being reasserted.

The reactions to these centripetal and centrifugal forces have differed between countries. The construction of authentic pictures of each system is the key to the understanding of diverse reactions. Typologies taken from the study of comparative politics may be useful but they do not go far enough. Contemporary issues are about managerial efficiency as well as political legitimacy. Each country has to reinterpret its own political–administrative traditions to respond effectively.

This chapter is concerned with the relationship between national political cultures and the control of educational content, teaching and learning. To put this in context, description may start from convergent global pressures for change. The position of various groups of educational decision-makers in different countries needs also to be considered.

Contemporary issues in educational control: Managerialism and political legitimacy

Contemporary demands are to find the most efficient form of management. In a longer perspective, shifts in decision making have been determined by administrative, political and ideological rationales – the first concerned with the most efficient ways of organizing education, the second with changes in the relative power of various groups of people and the third with broad views of the most desirable kind of education, culture and society (McLean and Lauglo, 1985: 9–16).

The organizational perspective has been prominent even in the earliest comparative analyses of educational control. While Isaac Kandel in the 1930s started from a distinction between centralized–authoritarian and localist–democratic systems, he went on the explore their implications for efficiency. Centralization seemed to be associated with more equal geographical distribution of resources and with uniform, though slow, implementation of reform. Localism was linked to geographical inequalities, a greater range of quality of institutions but with dynamic changes in teaching (Kandel, 1933).

These organizational propositions can be explained by older concepts. Centralization is justified by economies of scale which Adam Smith described in the late eighteenth century. One million textbooks cost much less per book to produce than 5000. Centralism can allow for the most able people to make decisions and for a consistent, rational ethos to pervade an education system (Weber, 1970b). Specialist services – whether diagnosis of children with special needs or reputable student examinations – are better provided centrally in large systems.

Some activities can be stable and programmable like national examinations while others are intensely unpredictable like the inspiration that one student may get from one teacher. The examples of industrial management are sometimes invoked but these styles can vary between the extremities of standardization and localization both between different kinds of enterprise and over time within the same type of production (McLean and Lauglo, 1985: 19–27).

From a purely managerial perspective, contemporary ambiguities of educational administration are not surprising. Standardization of curriculum and student assessment are responses to international economic competition and popular aspirations. Education in any one country needs to be as good as that of others and all young people must be educated to basic standards without marked failures among particular groups. Yet there is also diversification of occupational futures of students and in their cultural or personal aspirations for which standard measures cannot easily provide.

Resources must be used most efficiently. Comparisons between schools, colleges and universities are made by national criteria. It may be best to make each institution and, indeed, each teacher individually responsible for achieving greatest efficiency. Some controls are best exercised from above. Others may be best left to the immediate consumers – students, parents or employers – who have direct knowledge of and interest in the work of an institution.

One consideration is the impact of different schemes on the motivation of participants. Are the best results achieved by encouraging teachers and students to identify with national systems, local communities or their own individual drives? The answers to these questions, even in objective organizational theory, are not immutable.

One approach is to consider the nature of educational activities. Teachers may perform best if left to decide their own teaching methods but they may need the security of belonging to a national teaching force with uniform qualifications, pay and conditions of work. The content of curriculum in some subjects may benefit from the crystallization of the wealth of experience of a whole country (and indeed from international expertise) while others areas of knowledge inevitably have local, even individual, variations. Principals may be given more power to achieve a corporate identity of teachers and students in their schools and to liaise with local external groups. But leadership in matters of what is taught and how it is taught might better be left to national specialists.

Organizational priorities seem to follow secular global trends. In the period after 1945 most national governments centralized control over the distribution of the material resources of education:

- the 50 states of the USA took over much financial responsibility from 16,000 or more school districts;
- central government in England and Wales by the 1970s paid for more than half the educational spending of over 100 local authorities;
- federal government in West Germany after 1964 pushed, with some success, for harmonization of the educational practices of 11 states;
- national government in countries such as France or Japan, which had long enjoyed a monopoly of power, gained more influence through the substantial expansion of the system of public education.

The key was the drive for equalization of provision of education, and larger authorities were better able to provide the resources.

Since the late 1970s, the movement has been towards national rule-making and local responsibility for implementation. The introduction of a national curriculum may have been a particularly British phenomenon after 1988 which the USA failed to emulate and which Germany sought stealthily through co-operation between states. But France, with a long-established national curriculum, introduced national testing of school students from 1989 while in the USA testing and evaluation expanded at state, inter-state and national level. Everywhere, governments scrutinized both expenditure and student achievements very closely.

In most countries also there was a devolution of management, whether to regions as in France or to individual schools as in Britain. Even more pronounced throughout the industrial world was a reduction of government aid for some educational activities, especially in higher education whether in support for students or for institutions. Governments signalled an end to constantly expanding public expenditure.

The source of these changes was international competitive cuts in expenditure. Denmark, with almost 8% of gross national product (GNP) devoted to public education in 1988, could not maintain this level when the industrial country norm was around 5%. Nor could Britain keep educational expenditure at the same proportion of GNP as Japan (4.7%) when the quantitative and qualitative results from similar proportional spending seemed much poorer than differences in overall national wealth could explain (OECD, 1992b: 111). The drive for reduction of expenditure was a product of the unwillingness of citizens to pay higher taxes to governments in which they had lost confidence as well as of global competitive pressures to attract investment or reduce production costs.

The movement was not uniform. East Asian countries did not relax central controls as much as those of the west. This difference may have arisen because economic success in the east reduced the pressure for reform. In the west, the economically most successful country, Germany, resisted the most dramatic changes of educational administration of other countries. If this is the case, then the global trend may be short term and may change again quite rapidly in response to new economic and social imperatives.

These changes also had political and ideological elements. The ideology of privatization, which held sway in the USA and Britain, assumed that progress could come by removing restraints on individual initiative (Friedman and Friedman, 1980). The political dimension was to transfer power away from professionals and towards the consumers at local level, both parents and students. In the Far East, these ideological and political movements were much weaker. Even measures driven by apparently objective organization theory could be resisted if their ideological and political implications were unpalatable.

While the new global economy has encouraged similar movements in educational administration in many countries, politics and government reflect very particular national traditions which are only partly affected by economic change. To make sense of the great variety of political cultures, which are affected also by enormous differences in size and population between states, some stark polarities may be used. Distinctions between centralism–collectivism and localism–pluralism are most frequently the starting-point in the kind of comparative analysis begun with Alexis de Tocqueville's early nineteenth century comparison of France and the USA (Almond and Verba, 1963; Blondel, 1990; Schmitter, 1974; Tocqueville, 1956). It has been refined into a number of explanatory spectrums.

National political cultures have historical as well as comparative dimensions. There may be patterns of historical evolution as in Weber's scheme of development from traditional to legal–rational justifications for power with interludes of charismatic authority at times of disruption (Weber, 1964: 328). Historical change may leave behind latent values so that, in some countries, caesarism, feudal clientism or cynical Machiavellianism may also form powerful underground strata of political culture. These latent values may operate in the running of schools and other educational institutions. Individual institutions may be microcosms of larger political systems both of an antediluvian past and a Utopian future.

There are specific educational dimensions in government. There are explanations which focus upon the power of particular groups. How do the status, identity and power of 'producers' from politicians and officials to inspectors, teachers and academics and 'consumers' such as students, parents and wider communities affect educational decisions?

Interest groups may have similarities across countries but they also behave differently in various political cultures. There is also a link with cultures of knowledge and access discussed in the previous chapters. Conceptions of knowledge and of access to education are the product of political–administrative cultures as well as the other value systems analyzed above. Each of these interactions may be explored through the broad typology of political culture.

Political cultures and educational control

The commonest distinction is between collectivist and pluralist political cultures. This duality may have different meanings in Europe, North America and East Asia.

European collectivist cultures

State collectivism has its origins and justifications, in Europe, in a lineage which stretches from the Enlightenment and the 1789 French Revolution. Central government became the vanguard of economic and social change. The central state was identified with progress. So the modern–traditional dichotomy has its origins in a concept of state power and of modernist state policy invading a backward civil society.

Education was part of that state transformation. Its agents – the teachers, inspectors, officials and academics – were employees and representatives of the state rather than independent social groups. The school was a fortification defending state values in a sometimes truculent society. Jules Ferry's black-coated army of elementary school teachers in late nineteenth century France were missionaries of a central state devoted to converting heathen provinces (Singer, 1983).

One characteristic of collectivism is central control. In France as in Spain, Italy, Portugal, Greece as well as in most of eastern Europe educational power, at least until the 1960s, was centralized. Finance was raised and spent centrally. Schools were located according to central plans. Teachers were employed by central government which placed them where they were needed. A highly prescriptive national curriculum was in force and examinations led to certificates which had the imprint of the state.

A more authentic expression of collectivism is state monopoly. Educational institutions are state organs as much as the army. Programmes, typically, are framed as quasi-constitutions which begin with grand general aims before the details for implementation are elaborated. Teachers are state officials with as strong an obligation to serve the aims of the administration as the officials in ministries. Certificates of attainment are a *sine qua non* of the practice of an occupation and imply full citizenship. A representative school council is as much an organ of state as a national parliament. Universities are part of a unified state system as well as schools.

This state monopoly still prevails in France, Italy, Spain, Portugal, Greece and Sweden. It used to apply, rigorously, in eastern Europe before 1989 where the strength of the statist legacy is now unclear. Some, but not all, elements operate in Germany, Belgium, the Netherlands, Denmark and Norway. State monopoly has been relaxed in some ways in most states in recent years. The most crucial point is that the monopolistic state view of education is still deeply imprinted in the minds of teachers and students, parents and employers. It is hardly likely to disappear in the face of temporary shifts in the winds of fashion.

Collectivism has had significant variants. Extreme state monopoly has been associated with corporatism (Panitch, 1980; Schmitter, 1974 Stepan, 1978). The state tolerates no rivals in provision of any kind of public service. Twentieth century examples have included fascist regimes in Italy, Germany and Argentina where the state was the sole upholder of national values to the extent that organizations such as political parties, industrial companies and trade unions were absorbed where they could not be abolished.

Corporatist tendencies are not completely absent even in the prevailing pluralist versions of collectivism in western Europe. There have been a succession of political crises in France since 1959 over proposals to give more state aid to Catholic private schools which provide for over 15% of all pupils. Even in Germany, with much stronger pluralist institutions than France, there can be powerful informal pressures for employers and trade unions to join in a concordat with government over education, training and employment which has produced a much admired system of training. Yet the origins of this concordat lay in the corporatist policies of Bismarck in the 1880s and its link to the extreme corporatism of the Nazi regime is still uncomfortable for many Germans.

Monism has been used to describe twentieth century totalitarianism where acceptable social values and beliefs are dictated by a single political party (Schmitter, 1974). The boundary between public and private life was abolished. The goal of Soviet education was upbringing (*vospitane*) and the creation of a new socialist man. Its institutional expression was the development of youth organizations like the Young Pioneers and *Komsomol* and the domination of political education and history in schools by teachers who were members of the Communist Party. Indeed, the collapse of the youth organizations after 1990, which had provided social, recreational and extra-curricular activities in the afternoons and vacations, created one of the more severe immediate problems for education in the new Russia (Jones, 1994).

Monism, of course, can exist at local level in other political cultures where pressures to adhere to one set of beliefs has been strong in Calvinist cultures including historically Scotland, parts of Germany and, indeed, the USA. One irony of the Cold War was that the USA has had, in various educational movements from Creationism to Political Correctness, a monist streak not shared by most of her allies.

Collectivist regimes in western Europe since 1945 are democratic. Though Rousseau's formulation of the idea of the General Will in his *Social Contract* was ultimately totalitarian, in practice political divergence has become acceptable in collectivist systems. Indeed, pluralism has a strong justification in French political culture through the influence of ideas of Montesquieu and Tocqueville (Aron, 1965). Teachers can be members of teacher unions, split into factions, in conflict with an unsympathetic government and often linked to opposition political parties while simultaneously perceiving themselves as the agents of state-led modernization.

A collectivist ethos can survive decentralization. In France, the movement was towards more power for 25 regional decision-making bodies in the 1970s, which by 1991 controlled 20% of expenditure (Robert, 1993: 172). In Sweden local educational management units covering three or four schools each from 1979 gained considerable autonomy (Ekholm, 1987). Yet the national collectivist identities of teachers and officials have been sufficient to maintain collectivist educational cultures. Parents have been given more influence in France through school councils yet these bodies have been seen as integral to the state system. They are not viewed as vehicles for local opposition.

Despite these developments France, together with Sweden, is still at one end of the western European collectivist continuum – with only Greece and Portugal surpassing them in educational statism. The centralist tendency of Spain, modified even under authoritarian governments by the special educational rights of Catholic schools, has been undermined by the 1978 Constitution which gave a degree of autonomy to regions such as Catalonia, the Basque Country and Galicia. In Italy, central government has had collectivist ambitions which have not been realized through the power of regional allegiances and the emergence of city governments as alternative educational providers.

In contrast, Germany, the Netherlands, Denmark, Norway and, with exceptions, Belgium maintained a collectivist view of the state as the motor of progress and of state cadres of teachers and schools as its instruments. But each allowed local variations – in Germany in a federal system where each of 16 *Lander* (after 1990) is constitutionally independent and follows its own policies; in the Netherlands and Belgium church and state schools coexist (Catholic and State in Belgium; Catholic, Protestant and State in the Netherlands). In Denmark and Norway, elementary education has been the jealously guarded function of local communities while upper secondary and higher education belonged to the nation.

Collectivism survives despite the threats to state power posed by global economic developments. The explanation may lie in residual attachments of participants to the state, authority and national identity. Kandel depicted centralism as both autocratic and administratively cumbersome. Yet both weaknesses have been tackled without losing a collectivist ethos. So, in France, consultative bodies at central level have long existed with a representation including teachers, employers and trade unions without reducing central power. They were extended in 1984 to include a National Curriculum Council. When parents were admitted to consultation through school councils from 1968, they organized national federations (both left and right orientated) to express their views through national politics (Beattie, 1978).

Instead, within a collectivist system, all groups comprise an integral unit. Consumers are participants rather than customers. There may be confrontational interactions between parents and teachers in class and school councils but it is within a cohesive framework. Individual upper secondary schools could be judged by parents and students by the publication of their *baccalauréat* results from 1992 (*Le Monde de l'Education*, 1995). But when national testing of pupils at the ages of 9, 12 and 15 was introduced in France in 1989 it was stressed that this was to provide information for teachers and parents to allow more fruitful discussion between them (Thelot, 1993).

The problems of collectivist states come mainly through the survival of atavistic attitudes. Parents may become passive, even submissive, in neglect of their rights of participation as they become more self-interested. Producers can retreat into conservatism. Teachers, inspectors and principals are less willing to deviate from a national pattern of school organization even when invited to do so by law as in the 1975 Haby Law (McLean, 1985a). Teachers protect themselves by appealing to traditional practice.

In these conditions pre-rational forms of authority may reappear. School principals in late nineteenth century France responded to an influx of better qualified young teachers by becoming their landlords and exerting a paternal moral censure (Ouzof and Ouzof, 1992). More widespread is clientism. This is institutionalized in eastern European cultures which include Greece as well as Russia (Legg, 1973) where supplicants pledge loyalty to politically powerful individuals in return for favours. School principals in the new Russia with wider powers to construct curricula and solicit local private funding may become autocratic Czars.

Collectivism may now have a specific context. It may be, in effect, a coherent political culture only in homogenous societies or those where a unifying ideology is accepted. Suggestions of the demise of European collectivism may be challenged by the limited nature of the pluralist movement in several countries. And they can be confronted with the rude good health of a different kind of collectivism in the Far East.

Pluralism in Europe and North America

Pluralist value systems are based on the principle that absolute power must be balanced by secure rights for other organizations. Pluralism has modified collectivism in most European countries rather than replacing it. More deeply pluralist cultures have been confined to Britain and the USA but in these cases the political culture differs in significant ways and in neither country is the collectivist urge completely absent. Even the ideal expressed in John Stuart Mill's principle of 'the greatest dissemination of power consistent with efficiency' (Mill, 1967: 115) is Anglo-Saxon.

Three broad types have educational expressions. First is localism and regionalism together with recognition of non-geographical cultural affiliations. Second is an individualism based on private and entrepreneurial rights of action without reference to a wider administrative system. Third is a concept of interest groups which extends to include social, ideological, economic and professional bodies.

Communalism, regionalism and bi-culturalism

Localism, regionalism and bi-culturalism in most European states assume that any person can be a national patriot and simultaneously have other loyalties. There is some confusion with the idea that democracy and participation can only operate at a local level – the rationale of the city state of Plato or Aristotle. In Britain there has been uncertainty about whether local education authorities reflect cohesive geographical cultures or whether their rationale is to permit ground-level democratic decision.

Some countries do give weight to distinct local cultures. Scandinavian 'villages' are social–cultural entities where communities are also economic co-operatives. The school therefore prepares students for entry to the local economy based on social–personal ties and obligations. The community may be monocultural in religion, language and historic folk memory which reinforces economic cohesion (Lauglo, 1994). This kind of co-operative economic geographical culture has been the basis of many 'community' school proposals. Its political–administrative bases are that the whole local community rather than teachers and parents should control education. Lay interests predominate.

Local community control over schools may be associated with parochialism and philistinism and refusal to modify values in response to economic and social change. It has rarely been able to accommodate higher and more sophisticated levels of education – partly through the logistic difficulty of obtaining specialist teaching and services but also, at the level of values, in accepting that education also prepares for a modern world. So community ideals, though applied in adult education as well as in schools, rarely gains a strong foothold in upper secondary or higher education.

Community control survives mainly in geographically remote areas. It cannot easily accommodate the cultural diversity of cities. Ideals, however, survive longer than their practicability. Community control is still advocated in multicultural areas though multiculturalism is incompatible with traditional geographical communalism. Cultural diversity requires schools which are not linked to localities but form national or international networks whether they are based on long established European ethnic, linguistic or religious identities or on newer groupings including those of acquired belief as well as of inherited culture.

Cultural diversity has been accommodated in regional or bi-cultural arrangements. Frequently the bases for separation are religion, language or historic identity. Within Europe, such federal arrangements are the basis of educational provision in Germany, the Netherlands, Belgium and Switzerland. There are pressures also to accommodate such diversity on a regional basis on a modified scale in Spain, Britain and Russia and even in the older unitary states such as France.

In Germany, a federal arrangement accommodates a historic multiculturalism based partly on regional identity and partly on religion. The north is broadly Lutheran and the south broadly Catholic. There are also political–ideological differences with northern states having a left-of-centre political tradition and those in the south with a conservative political domination. So common secondary schools have been introduced in northern states (and accounted for 20% of all enrolments in West Berlin before unification) but do not exist in conservative Bavaria; and child-centred, active teaching methods have more encouragement in northern states than in the south.

Bi-culturalism coexists with regionalism in Germany. Private religious schools are rare because state schools have, individually, an identified Protestant or Catholic character. Independent schools based on a divergent educational philosophy have generous public financial support (Weiss, 1986). Provision is made for the languages and religions of children of more recent immigrants to be taught in public schools but under the control of the representatives of these cultural groups – a pluralism which has been rejected in France and Britain. On the other hand, separate schools for recent immigrant cultural groups, though consistent with German pluralist traditions, have been rightly regarded as discriminatory.

Elsewhere the divisions are of a different kind. The cantons of Switzerland are also totally autonomous and divided by language. In Belgium there is a double split between the geographically demarcated Dutch and French speaking areas and the State–Catholic school distinction which crosses language boundaries. Catholic schools, which have full state support, often reflect politically and educationally conservative interests (Vanderhoven, 1991). In the Netherlands the three groups of Protestants, Catholics and Secularists have roughly equal numbers of schools and students. In Britain and France the pressure for regional separation has been in geographical peripheries – Scotland, Wales and Northern Ireland; Brittany and Corsica.

It is not the type of regional–cultural variation which is crucial but the relations between regional or bi-cultural affiliations and the state. Collectivist–Jacobin traditions survive in Germany, the Netherlands, Belgium and Spain. In the Netherlands the aim is to try to ensure equal rights for each community through political accommodation. In Germany it is a little stronger – to move towards common standards, especially in courses and examinations, across the Federation. In Belgium political tensions between language – but not religious – groups have been so acute that a *de facto* federal state emerged in the 1980s but there is a residue of collectivism expressed in broadly common curricula and assessment standards which removes the system of education from the linguistic conflict.

Conflicts are reduced as individuals have the opportunity to migrate to achieve an education in accordance with their wishes. More important is the separation between public and private, local and national in different spheres which permits coexistence. Tensions that do exist can occur through applying older political attitudes to newer cultural groups, as in Germany. Dutch pillars also tend to identify ethnic minorities with a particular social class and occupational grouping though on the other hand the established politics of accommodation tends to encourage acceptance of cultural rights of minorities (Bagley, 1973).

The style of politics, in European pluralist regimes, is based on consensus. It was sustained even during the radical changes in the 1980s – in contrast with Britain and the USA. Conflict and confrontation threatens political stability. German political calm in educational matters in the 1970s and 1980s has been attributed to the safety valve of regionalism (Weiler, 1989). Yet the political cement for consensus may have come from residues of collectivist values which remain in most continental European countries.

Privatism

The privatist–individualist political culture has its strongest expression in Britain. Its political theory is based on the ideas attaining characteristic expression in John Stuart Mill. The foundation is the inalienable freedom of individuals which is necessary for improvement of human life:

> 'originality is a valuable element in human affairs. There is always a need of persons not only to discover new truths, and point out when what were truths are true no longer, but also to commence new practices, and set the example of more enlightened conduct, and better taste and sense in human life.' (Mill, 1956: 110–11)

Any form of restriction on this freedom, which Mill thought was the inevitable consequence of almost any established form of government, was a threat to human welfare. From a more narrowly economic viewpoint Adam Smith suggested that:

'every individual...neither intends to promote the public interest nor knows how much he is promoting it....By pursuing his own interest he frequently promotes that of the society more effectively than when he really intends to promote it.' (Smith, 1956: 25)

However, late eighteenth and nineteenth century utilitarianism was built upon earlier concepts especially of Thomas Hobbes and Locke. Hobbes, despite the apparent endorsement of absolute state power, founded his analysis on the assumption on a natural and inevitable individualism, the excesses of which government needed to check (Hobbes, 1914: 112). Locke also placed restrictions on this liberty by giving emphasis to the place of property which would give individuals a stake in maintaining the status quo. This ultimately justified the provision of education by corporations, especially universities but also schools, which were separate from the state and free from serious state intervention. And the utilitarians, following Jeremy Bentham, were aware of the dangers of untrammelled individualism, especially of the corrupt and self-interested, and required a central legal authority to check against corruption and inefficiency of quasi-public agencies including those in education.

Private education, developed through entrepreneurial initiative, was consistent with utilitarianism. The private schools in Britain, in sharp contrast to almost all other industrial countries set the tone for the rest of the education system. All universities in Britain, again unlike most other countries, were independent corporations rather than organs of regional or national government. So when public education developed it had its private roots. Teachers and school heads saw themselves as independent professionals and entrepreneurs who had little community responsibility, who knew best what was good for children, who often held parents in contempt and who rejected any idea of being state officials. A public system was based on private yet entrepreneurial values.

Recent changes in Britain have occurred within this framework. Parents and (in higher education) students have been given rights as customers which predominate over their responsibilities as participants. Governments have acted in authoritarian ways to support the rights of consumers by insisting on measures to define the quality of education. In ways which are fully consistent with Locke and Bentham, central regulation is exercised on the basis of the individual freedom of schools and teachers. Recent extensions of central government control can be traced to the efficiency drive of utilitarianism. Central assessment of students in schools as well as an edifice of quality control are as much a part of the utilitarian tradition as the payment by results system of the mid-nineteenth century or the 1834 Poor Law reform which inspired it.

Rival views exist in Britain. A collectivist drift was pronounced for 100 years after 1870. The rationales were not of a French modernist type but sprang from a paternalist traditionalism evident in the criticisms of early nineteenth century utilitarianism in, for instance, the novels of Charles Dickens.

American localism, communalism and privatism

American political–administrative pluralism arises from the localism of a country with a strong community orientation which became highly industrialized and mobile. Privatism is strong and the USA was also the birthplace of highly developed educational interest group politics.

Tocqueville in 1835 argued that American democracy was based on the township which behaved as an independent nation (Toqueville, 1956: 58). The state emerged later as the dominant force in domestic affairs including education while federal institutions only intervened in education after 1945. The educational equivalent of the township – the School District – with its elected School Boards provided schools. The state exercised legislative power, determined textbooks and organized universities. When federal government intervened, especially after 1958, to help the poor and sponsor curriculum projects the initiatives were permissive and federal finance usually had to be balanced by state or local resources (Spring, 1978: 91-165).

There has always also been a strong private element in American education. Religious (mainly Catholic) schools provide for around 10% of enrolments but, unlike European equivalents, receive no public funding. Élite universities have been private, again with no significant European parallels. This private strand interacted with a very powerful communalism of a public school system which required daily saluting of the flag and the exclusion of all religious teaching.

As school districts weakened in their capacity to provide full education and to maintain financial support, so the state took over a greater responsibility for schooling. The school, especially High Schools, became autonomous in what was taught. But powerful interests – including the major teacher unions, the National Education Association (NEA) and the American Federation of Teachers – became organized interests which negotiated with state governments throughout the country. Private agencies also were able to take advantage of the privatist strand of American education to run national examinations, especially the Scholastic Aptitude (later Attainment) Tests since the 1920s. It was out of this unclear division of power that interest groups became powerful. Their influence depended on their organizational, manipulative and presentational capacities (Dahl, 1982: 40–54).

American collectivism only began to appear in the 1930s with federal economic intervention in the 'New Deal'. Its educational equivalent had to wait until the 1950s. Its expression is usually seen to be the federal laws of the 1960s which allowed federal government to help states and districts to provide resources for the education of the disadvantaged. But the values which underlie it are quite different from those of Britain and, indeed, may be closer to those of France. American collectivism is founded on the 1776 Constitution. The Constitution guarantees certain rights to all citizens which are then interpreted in specific cases by the Supreme Court. The 1954 Brown v. Topeka judgement which declared racial segregation of schools to be unconstitutional provided the basis for later federal financial aid. Later less egalitarian decisions by the Supreme Court permitted a *laissez-faire* federal policy in the 1980s.

Political cultures and education outside the western tradition

One puzzle for a world-wide comparative study of contemporary education is that the West has responded to a global economy by reining in the power of the state while the East – Japan and Taiwan, South Korea and Singapore and China – has reacted by strengthening state intervention.

Explanations refer to the eastern state as the father and, however rebellious and individualistic the children, ultimately they must submit to his authority based on tradition, age and wisdom. Eastern political philosophies have not been concerned with problems of how to reconcile the power of government with the individual or small group aspirations of its people. It has been about how to establish government in natural conditions of anarchy. It has responded to the background of violence, greed and oppression of warlordism. Thomas Hobbes' phrase about a natural anarchy of human existence producing 'the life of man, solitary, poor, nasty, brutish and short' has particular eastern parallels. Confucius had a similar premise but came up with a rather different solution.

The starting-point of this eastern political philosophy therefore was the unfortunate necessity of strong government and the civilizing of its brutality through the influence of moral values inculcated through education; the search for calm, serenity and harmony as the social aims of life; and the identification of family as the possible source of these benign characteristics which could then be transferred to political relations. Politics were not the highest goal of social life as they were for Aristotle but an unavoidable necessity.

The absolute power of central government to determine the content of education should be placed against the background of a natural individualism and self-interest. So powerful central authority does not preclude the existence of private education seized by the initiative of individuals in Japan or, more recently, in China.

Central government – under Confucian precepts – depended upon wise and learned administrators who would civilize its natural barbarity. Central authority thus had a right to exert absolute control over that education of a bureaucrat class which was necessary to produce good government. From this position a highly centralized education system in contemporary Japan, where other groups are not incorporated in the decision-making process, can be justified. Central control of education is necessary not simply to ensure that the right moral lessons are taught but also to regulate the relations with the West which was seen as a threat to social and political stability. While there are local education authorities in Japan their powers are weak. Not only are Japanese schools organs of the state but teachers are state employees accepting tight control from central government. The Japanese teacher unions after 1945 responded by acting as a rebellious faction demanding worker rights and linking their struggle to attempts to undermine government (Schoppa, 1991: 150–62).

However, a paternalism based on the family has deeper and more diverse roots. The family is a model for the unstable through all-powerful state, for the family is the only reliable agency of stability. For Confucius the state was 'the father and mother of the people' (Creel, 1951: 137). Even in this view paternalism was not despotic. The traditional authority of the father was not challenged but each subordinate member had a recognized individuality and rights. The father could not rule without the ultimate consent of other family members. So 'the Chinese family seems always to have been monarchic in theory and democratic in practice'. While among the family members 'there was subordination among them but each had his place, his functions and his dignity'. So Confucius insisted that 'men of all classes possessed worth in themselves, and must be treated not merely as the means **by** which the state accomplished its purposes, but as the ends **for** which the state existed' (Creel, 1951: 138).

The essential difference was that the dynastic concepts of traditional authority of Europe where rulers had god-given right to control land which they owned (and thus owned its incidental human inhabitants) did not exist in eastern traditions where governments controlled people rather than territory. A kind of authority could thus survive in eastern societies which had ceased to be acceptable in the western tradition.

However, all political cultures need to be seen in the context of the actual behaviours and rights of particular participants in educational decision-making. This kind of classification may stretch across all educational systems in the contemporary world.

Education politics and spheres of legitimate action

Another angle to questions of who determines what students should learn
and how they should do it is to examine the power of groups of actors
across countries and to identify the differing impact they have on certain
areas of educational activity.

Producers, consumers and public interest

The commercial analogy of educational 'producers' and 'consumers' has
been widely used. Yet government is allocated a role of arbitration above
the transaction. Political action may see producers and consumers allying
against other producers (for instance teachers and parents against educational officials). An older, more bureaucratic, distinction links government
and immediate producers through a group of officials. Talcott Parsons'
scheme of public interest, managerial and technical (worker) groups
leaves teachers in a relatively passive, subordinate role (Parsons, 1958).
It may more truly reflect actual decision-making where hierarchy counts
more than an often mythical enterprise culture.

Politicians operate at several levels – national, regional, local, institutional – and may have conflicting interests (especially where different
parties are in power at the different levels). Furthermore there are distinctions between those in power and those out of it and between educational ministers and those representing others interests (finance, economic development, employment, health). In some countries, the
politicization of education reaches a long way down into the decision-
making process through election of local officials such as School District
education superintendents in the USA. School councils in most countries
are public interest agencies which represent special groups such as parents, students and teachers of a school rather than the community at large.

Interest groups are also divided between the official and non-official
(Kogan, 1975) according to whether they are incorporated into official
consultative bodies or not. So teacher unions – or teachers selected individually by government – in most countries are represented on committees charged with advising on the curriculum but not in other areas of
educational policy.

Interest groups are often politicized, especially in collectivist cultures
where they ally with political parties. So in France or other centralist,
collectivist systems such as Greece different teacher and parents unions
have left or right (and sometimes religious) affiliations. Catholic teachers
and parents link with the right in France, most others with the left except
for teachers in selective, élitist institutions who everywhere tend to iden-

tify with the political right or centre. Politicians may manipulate these permanent alliances as in the passage of the liberal–radical 1975 Haby Law by a right of centre government in France (Coombs, 1978).

In more developed interest group cultures, especially in pluralist systems, the interests maintain a greater distance from political parties (as in Britain or the USA). Indeed, in the USA, the major teacher union – the NEA – acted as a national organization which negotiated with the 50 state governments of different political complexions and has strength both from its national spread and non-partizan political stance (Spring, 1978: 169–77).

When teachers are involved officially in curriculum and assessment decision-making, their professional capacity is not challenged. What is more likely to happen is that teachers (or indeed inspectors or academics) are seen to represent views about curriculum which politicians may wish to support or oppose and will give influence to one group rather than another at particular times. In France in the early 1970s and in Britain from 1988, government tried to weaken established interests (in France the inspectors, in Britain the teachers) by bringing in outsiders to lead major curriculum reform committees.

These distinctions also apply at other levels. Traditionally the officials in most systems have had an educational background and have experience in teaching rather than general management. A consensus could emerge between officials and teachers over issues of content or, as in England and Wales after 1945, teacher unions could be allowed to take the lead in curriculum matters (Manzer, 1970). Managerialism penetrated national management in France since the 1970s (Broadfoot, 1985) and has infected perceptions of the expertise even of school principals in a number of countries in the movement to school autonomy in the 1990s.

Other groups which influence the curriculum have a varying impact in various countries at different times. University academics are influential in some countries but peripheral in others. Their influence may come from alliances with school teachers or from links with government. Certain grades of inspectors have the predominant impact on content and teaching in France but inspectors are weak in Germany (and do not exist in Norway). Employers may be a dominant group in the official determination of a vocational curriculum in some countries but are peripheral elsewhere. Parents have believed they have a right to intervene in curriculum in the USA but not in Britain. Everywhere parents are more confident in expressing their views on the teaching of sex education than on the teaching of mathematics or on primary rather than upper secondary education.

Yet the influence of each group in each country can vary both in relation to the particular historic position it has had and in relation to the overall political culture. Yet there can also be international movements in the relative power and position of certain groups, notably teachers and parents. A number of groups should be examined more fully.

Curriculum actors – inspectors and academics, teachers, parents and employers

The central issue is which groups have expertise in the content of education and approaches to teaching and learning. Experts may be expected to win battles with lay interests. But this power may corrupt. Ancient practices may survive simply because they support the power of particular groups. Differing curriculum traditions may be powerful in various countries because of their defence by certain organized groups as well as because of the strength of values across a culture.

Three wider groups are the centre of attention. First are those who form a superstructure of decision-making about the content of education and its transmission – inspectors, academics, teacher trainers and educational researchers. Secondly, there are the teachers of various levels whose power, authority and status are now problematic – about whom much has been written but for whom a sustained comparative analysis is still lacking. Thirdly there are the consumers – students, parents, employers and a hazier and shifting conception of a community constituency.

The superstructure of educational knowledge is not easily defined nor is the power or, indeed, the expertise of the various groups of people involved in its construction despite considerable analysis in the sociology of knowledge. One academic may be a specialist in mathematics but not on how the subject can be taught to average attaining 12 year olds. Educational researchers and teacher trainers know much about debates on teaching methods and their contexts but do not have practical skills in teaching particular groups of children. Inspectors have a broad overview of current practice but cannot rival the school teacher's understanding of specific students in one institution. Claims to expertise of various groups depend for their credibility not only of the general social standing of the group but also on how their segment of the overall process of teaching and learning is valued.

The balance between inspectors and academics differs between countries. At one extreme – in France – the inspectorate has been a very powerful controlling body, much more important than the academics. This group has held power to define the subjects of the curriculum and how they shall be taught. The origin of this power is in the view of a revolutionary, intellectual cadre. Inspectors have been an intellectual élite whose expertise in subject areas is less easily challenged by academics because inspectors are chosen for their intellectual capacities through tests and through possession of the peculiar French qualification of the *agrégation*. But it is helped also by the separation of higher education as a teaching activity, which is subject to centrally determined curricula, from research carried out in specialized institutes.

The inspectorate in France is not unchallenged. As elsewhere they can be defenders of lost causes, notably redundant subjects such as classical languages. But inspectors also divide into national cadres concerned with broad policies including the content of education and those with local responsibilities of assessing teachers or arbitrating between teachers, school principals and parents. Local inspectors may identify more with cross-disciplinary subject areas and a more adjustive relationship with teachers to the extent of representing teachers' views rather than those of government. Yet their power ultimately depends on a centralist–collectivist administration and a rational standardized conception of school knowledge.

In other countries with a rational–collectivist tradition the inspectors are weaker. In the federal system of Germany, a residual and constitutionally ratified independence for teachers reduces inspectoral powers. The English model of inspector traditionally followed the conception of the wise and moral gentleman without necessarily much experience of schooling, derived from a partly utilitarian and partly aristocratic view of control of the mid-nineteenth century public elementary schools (Lawton and Gordon, 1987). Inspectors, outside hierarchical, collectivist regimes can find their power taken over by academics or by school principals.

Academics have a residual power because they can claim to have superior expert knowledge of the content of school subjects, especially at secondary levels. Furthermore they can exert influence on teachers at lower levels because they themselves provided these teachers with their subject knowledge. They can also aid teachers through the subject associations which have been described in England (Goodson and Medway, 1990) but which also exist in most other countries.

The USSR presented an interesting exception where understanding of the processes of transmission was considered more important than the content. An encyclopaedic view of knowledge was subordinate to the social objective of creating a new socialist man. The Academy of Pedagogical Sciences was divorced from the higher education system yet had a dual role of research into educational sciences and methods, their testing in schools and the design of curriculum. Its definition was so limited that it could not easily survive the radical changes in educational aims of 1988 onwards (Nikandrov, 1989; Rudman, 1967: 213–30; Simon and Simon 1963: 3–18,).

A weak parallel may be offered in France with the use of professors of education – Antoine Prost, Pierre Bourdieu and Henri Legrand – by government in the 1980s as education advisers who produced public policy statements. In contrast, the federal agencies of the USA after 1958 called on academics outside education areas such as Jerome Bruner or Benjamin Bloom to design new approaches to the curriculum. In Germany, educational researchers have marginal influence but one group of academics was instrumental in forcing the adoption of a larger core curriculum for upper secondary education in the late 1970s (Fuhr, 1989).

School principals provide an interesting and indicative case for analysis of culturally variable and temporally changing relationships in the politics of education. Collectivist traditions have been for the principal to be only a bureaucrat who ensures that national rules and values prevail in every school. Communalist cultures assume that he or she shall be a local figure with a specific role in community leadership.

Privatist culture – exemplified by the nineteenth century English Public School head such as Thomas Arnold (Bamford, 1970) – gave an independent, entrepreneurial role to principals. In practice they interpreted it in the 1960s and 1970s in terms of educational philosophy so that head teachers became almost prophets of curriculum innovation (Bernbaum, 1973). Pressures for institutional autonomy and accountability of schools have forced these heads to seek an organizational even financial entrepreneurial role.

The position of teachers is much more varied. On the one hand distinctions can be made between privatist–communalist and collectivist definitions. In privatist systems – notably England – teachers aim to be independent professionals based on their distance from a national bureaucracy. There is a tradition that they are appointed to specific schools and are only distantly linked to the state. They act as if they are independent. They have internal school hierarchies of knowledge leaders – school principals and heads of departments – and of differing philosophies from school to school. They emphasize an expertise based on knowledge of students and the best ways of arranging knowledge to meet needs and capacities of these students. The various analyses of teacher roles in England tends to reflect these conceptions (Hoyle, 1969).

There has been overlap between this approach and that of communalist systems. Communalism gives other groups at local level a greater say in content including local business as well as parents. But, as in the USA, teachers use academics and unions to protect their independence which, as in England, may derive from older conceptions of the teacher as priest or shaman – or even independent craftsman or woman. At the extreme of the communalist model the special expertise of the teacher is denied – as in the Freire model of teacher and student constantly interchanging roles

– or the idea of teachers as those working in the community rather than a separate caste (Illich, 1973a).

Within the collectivist model the teacher gains status as member of the public administration. Being a public functionary – for which competitive entry examinations are held after qualification as a teacher in Spain and Italy – is the root of status in political cultures where public administration is a progressive and highly respected activity. Teachers accept and defend the national curriculum. But the tradition has been also that as a public functionary the teacher has the right and capacity to assess students and can be trusted to apply national standards.

There are variations within the collectivist model. Older conceptions of a teacher as a professional with a respected craft have peculiar survivals in Germany which makes it difficult for outsiders to challenge this authority (so assessment of teaching is usually by other teachers) (England and Wales DES/HMI, 1986). The constitutional defence of teachers' pedagogical freedom in the 1949 Basic Law, while having origins in anti-Nazi guarantees, also reflected much older traditions.

There is also a tradition of teachers being a member of an intellectual caste (Jean-Paul Satre, Simone de Beauvoir and Alain in France) and defending social status on this basis – a tradition also powerful in the USSR. But the reverse of this was a hierarchically divided profession based upon levels of initial education of teachers. In most of Europe there is a formal distinction between pay, qualifications and status of primary and secondary school teachers (Neave, 1992) which is only being eroded slowly, notably in France since 1982 (France, 1982). Yet where teachers are of one grade in one school they act collectively rather than through internal school hierarchies as in England where there are no distinctions between basic grades but a superstructure of those in higher grades reflecting additional responsibilities.

Producer interests, in both collectivist and pluralist traditions, can coalesce into self-interested protection of expertise. American–British conceptions of profession give much stress to possession of esoteric knowledge (Lieberman, 1956) but even elsewhere – as in France – teachers aspire to being intellectuals and subject specialists. There is a tendency for views of content and assessment to be protected by these interests so that knowledge professions actually damage the broader community as Ivan Illich powerfully suggested (Illich, 1973b). Yet their actual views can vary. In collectivist cultures they support encyclopaedic or other standardized views of curriculum in which they see themselves as the specialists whereas in pluralist systems they may emphasize experience of organizing content to meet the great diversity of students. In both cases there is a tendency towards monopoly and to exclude others in defining knowledge.

There are common movements towards proletarianization of teachers. As early as 1953, Robert King Hall suggested an inexorable decline in teacher status based on the increasing commonness of teacher subject knowledge as the overall level of educational experience of the population rose and on the low status of teachers' position as the social status of the pupils fell with the democratization of educational access (King Hall, 1953). The tragedy was that as teachers' work became more difficult and demanding the regard in which society at large held them declined. This process has also occurred in collectivist countries (Huberman, 1993). The pincer attack on teacher status of lowered equivalences compared with other occupations (signalled in collectivist cultures by attempts to discouple them from older public service equivalent grades) and of demands for highly quantifiable measures of output through student or teacher test scores as in the minimum competency movement in the USA (Kerr, 1983) has been worldwide.

Employers are both producers and consumers of education. Their passive, consumer role has been most pronounced in the extremes of collectivism and of privatism. Centrally planned economies – whether of the old Eastern European bloc or France – organized educational provision in such a way that government determined the relationship between economic needs and educational provision and the education system was supposed to deliver these identified requirements. In the privatist culture of Britain, pedagogues and employers were distanced by mutual contempt. Education, for educationists, provided for a higher plane of social and personal usefulness; employment required skills that were learnt on the job and education was best forgotten. All that it provided was a form of initial selection of potentially capable employees at different levels.

Employers have differing national roles. In Germany and Britain they have had a major place in determining the content of vocational education but a weaker one in affecting that of the school. In the USA employers are able directly to influence local schools because of the particular history of school boards in small autonomous communities – and frequently use this influence to support schools in ways that, for instance, were not replicated in Britain when attempts were made to establish City Technology Colleges.

Parent participation is culturally specific. In the older traditions of the collectivist state, parents often represented the backward mass of superstition of traditional society. They were forbidden to interfere with processes of modernization of the school. The extreme examples could be found in the old USSR where parents were harassed and indeed subject to political–industrial sanctions if they did not obey the demands of the school. In the democratic–participatory version of collectivism parents are represented at every level of decision-making on condition that they accept the broad modernizing ideology. Within this definition, they can therefore become allies of teachers in attempts to exert pressures through an integral state system.

Yet there is also a demarcation of roles which allows parents to determine moral–social education (below the level of national political socialization) and schools to look after the intellectual, occupational and national dimensions. In the USSR the state took over many of the functions of upbringing. In contrast, the time during the day for familial education was strongly defended in Germany and but less fully in France.

In communalist–localist cultures parents control schooling – through School Boards and parent teacher associations in the USA or school councils in Denmark. Parents are involved in curriculum construction in primary schools in the Netherlands (England and Wales DES/HMI, 1987b). This is justified because the school also performs some of the parental educational duties in social and moral education. But in the privatist culture of England, schools displace parents and take on the role of *in loco parentis* on the assumption that parents are incompetent or neglectful. Assumptions underlying the reformed independent schools of the nineteenth century were taken on by the mass system. As much as in monist systems parents were the enemy and schools made up for their incompetence.

Within this context, parents as distant consumers made some sense in both monist and privatist systems. It was an extraneous development elsewhere signalling the growth of individualism and lack of communal – or even state – loyalties. So parents became disengaged consumers in proportion to their exclusion from the decision-making process – largely at their own instigation in some societies, notably the USA, but enforced upon them in others. But where collectivist–participatory and communalist cultures survive there are counter pressures for a more participatory consensual parental involvement. Ironically, in England and Russia the reduced status or autonomy of teachers has made it in their interest to seek alliances with parents – whatever the historical distrust on both sides – while parents as consumers increasingly are driven into a participatory role to secure full consumer rights.

Conclusion

The politics and administration of education are defined by constantly changed agendas which the external world creates. The dynamic of these changes has come not only from change in economies and politics but also changed possibilities for greater efficiency at either central or local levels. Simply administrative criteria can determine the movements backwards and forwards to localism and centralism in education as it does in the organization of business.

However, despite these universal secular movements, traditional political cultures survive and determine the ways in which these universal secularist forces are met. The greatest force for their preservation is the sense of identity and social function which they give to various participants which are not surrendered lightly. Traditional political cultures, when applied to education, are consistent with conceptions of what knowledge should be transmitted and who should be educated. These traditional values will change little. For they also operate on the ways that the various participants in the politics of education also see their status, obligations and rights.

Yet the problem for all these analyses over space and time in this and the three preceding chapters, is that education systems are assumed to have a unity. The major problem with this approach is that education always has had a longitudinal dimension. It covers growth from infancy to adulthood. It moves from the family to the nation and the world over time. It shifts from being intimate to being public. It can be very different things at different stages. The broad lines of analysis of the last three chapters thus need to be tested against the different and distinct phases of education in the next three chapters.

PART 2
Contemporary Responses: Content, Teaching and Learning

5

Schooling 2–16

Basic schooling is a nineteenth-century idea which took a century to achieve. The common phase begins with children being wrenched from their families to learn language and number with other parents' children. It ends in institutions which aim at universal undifferentiated education. Some differences between countries are only the battle scars of the twentieth-century struggles to replace stratified systems with common schooling. In most industrial countries, communality of content has now been agreed up to the age of 14. Some countries have moved the boundary of basic education up to the age of 16 while others, including the USA for most of the twentieth century, have had 18 as the target age for the end of truly common education. Eighteen may become the universal watershed in the near future.

Significant differences remain between major industrial countries. Pre-school education is almost universal in some states but caters for less than half the age group in others. Elementary schools survive in most countries but elsewhere one institution serves all ages up to 16. The common lower secondary school has been widely adopted since the 1960s but a few countries continue to differentiate between students at the ages of 10–12 according to anticipated occupational futures. The content in some countries serves the public interest while elsewhere it mirrors familial environments or starts from the interests of the individual child. How teachers relate to children in different countries can diverge greatly.

These differences may be explored separately in each bloc of nations – the collectivist and pluralist countries of Europe and then the states beyond Europe. Within each group, matters of access and structure provide the context for exploration of questions of content, teaching and assessment. Differences may be explained by the traditional values of the participants.

Traditions and change in regions and nations

France and collectivist southern Europe

In collectivist traditions the school is an agency of the national state from the moment that children enter it. They learn for the nation and if they perform well enough they gain full symbolic citizenship. French approaches most perfectly exemplify collectivism. Variations in other collectivist countries may suggest a greater range of responses to contemporary pressures.

France

The contemporary principle of access in the basic phase is that children should be schooled as young as possible and that any differentiation should be delayed to the age of 14 and ideally 16. While pre-school education has expanded and lower secondary education has been common since the 1960s, elementary schooling has changed little since universal, free, compulsory state education was proposed in 1833 and implemented in the 1880s. Archaic primary education aims influence both the newer forms of pre-school and lower secondary education.

French governments reacted to stagnant population growth since the mid-nineteenth century with generous state maternity benefits (Ardagh, 1973: 428–29). By 1970, almost all 4-year-old children and 55% of 3 year olds were in pre-schools (Woodhead, 1979: 4). In 1989, parents gained the legal right to a place for 3 year olds producing universal participation by 1993 when 35% of 2 year olds were in school. Almost all places were state provided and were staffed by teachers who had had equality of training and status with primary school teachers (France, 1993a: 4,10).

Universal pre-school education is also a response to repetition rates of around 10% in the first grade of primary education (ages 6–7). Failure in elementary school has had administrative–historical origins. Primary school was completed at the age of 13 (before 1936) by the rigorous examination for the certificate of primary education, success in which gave access to local salaried official positions (Halls, 1976: 81). In contrast, in late nineteenth century England 12 year olds who passed an examination were permitted to leave school 2 years early to start work.

Minimum standards in the lower secondary school and grade repetition for failures also had nineteenth-century origins where higher primary schools provided entrance to teacher training and similar opportunities. From 1959 short secondary schools (like English secondary modern schools) were established alongside traditional *lycées* but were quickly replaced (from 1963) by a common *collège* covering the four grades corresponding to ages 11–15 for those who did not repeat any years. The *lycée* became an upper secondary school.

Initially, stratification was maintained through three *filières*, the highest of which offered classical and second modern languages taught by teachers trained for the *lycées* and the lowest failed even to cover the standard curriculum. After the Haby Law of 1975, a genuine national curriculum emerged which offered all the chance to cover each mainstream subject. The outcome was standardization with failures restricted to about 20% of the age group which even extra measures like special educational priority zones failed to reduce in the 1980s.

A proto-rationalism dominates the elementary curriculum and enters the *école maternelle*. The Ministry of Education stated that 'the predominant activity in the nursery school is play and games, which does not however preclude the importance of rigour and effort' (France, 1993: 8). There is a specific programme of work which includes science and technology; oral and written expression. This was the balance advocated by Pauline Kergomard, who led the nursery school movement in France at the end of the nineteenth century (Prost, 1968: 284–89). *École maternelles* are to ensure that all children can read and count to long-established standards by the end of the first grade of elementary schooling.

The rational–encyclopaedic tradition in the twentieth century has had language at the core of the elementary school and mathematics as the central axis in lower secondary education. Language is seen as a logical structure whose universal rules have to be comprehended. Initial stages of teaching reading can be peremptory. Syllabic techniques, which concentrate on the learning of the alphabet and upon sounds of letter combinations, can fail to relate sounds to the meaning of words. It is claimed that this approach, which prevailed from the mid-nineteenth century (Prost, 1968: 120–21) still predominates in the 1990s (Bedarida, 1991: 61). Neither the view of Nicholas Adams in the late nineteenth century that reading should start from children's existing vocabulary nor that of Freinet that reading comes through self-generated pupil activity have had expression beyond the fringes of the standard pedagogy (*Le Monde de l'Éducation*, 1993: 34–35).

The spelling and combination of words is the basis of proper education. Six year olds in the first grade of elementary schools quickly move onto the structures of sentences – subjects and objects, recognition of nouns, pronouns, adjectives and verbs and the rules of agreement that govern them (Sharpe, 1993: 265–67). The written work of pupils, throughout the school system, is penalized for mistakes in spelling and grammar more consistently than any other kind of individual achievement is rewarded. Above all, 'French schools have a reputation for starting children with difficult subjects at an early age and forcing them, through memorization and repetition, to learn them' (Hollen, 1994: 80).

Conventional elementary school teaching methods present a picture, object or blackboard construction. Pupils observe. Teachers expound. Students are questioned over time periods that would seem excessively long to the British. Then there may be some short written exercise (England and Wales, 1991c). In practice, teachers may excite or inspire by their choice of materials and presentation. Student voices may appear to predominate over those of the teacher. But student responses are kept very much to the topic and its logical, systematic development.

Liberalization has focused upon subjects other than French and Mathematics. The *activités d'éveil* (curiosity awakening subjects) of the 1970s lumped together all other subjects in the elementary curriculum and it was suggested they could be pursued through topics and pupil activities. The distinct subjects were restored in 1985 in the name of rigour. The 1990 aims of the elementary school curriculum maintained the hard core:

> 'Elementary school education is to ensure the acquisition of the basic elements and tools of knowledge: oral and written expression, reading and arithmetic. It stimulates the ...improvement of a child's intelligence, emotional development, artistic sensibility, manual and physical skills. It promotes a child's perception of time, space, and material objects in the world around him, as well as that of his own body. It ensures progressive acquisition of methodological fields of knowledge and gives him adequate preparation for secondary school.' (France, 1993a: 18)

The elements of the nineteenth-century curriculum designed to create loyal citizens have been diminished. History, geography and civics became adjuncts to the teaching of French just as science and technology were added to mathematics (France, 1993a: 21). The major addition has been spaces for a modern language for the last three grades, experimentally since 1989 and universally from 1994.

The *collège* curriculum is made up of ten discrete subjects expanding to 11 when physics–chemistry is added in the third year to biology. The legacy of the élite system is a compulsory option chosen from Latin, Greek, a second foreign language or reinforcement classes in the first foreign language (France, 1993c: 16–18). In the third year, technology as a subject has a vocational orientation and some low attaining students leave for vocational institutions. Some schools may have musical, sporting or foreign language orientations. Otherwise, in all schools, differences in teaching relate only to the pace of progression through the core subjects.

Mathematics becomes the core of lower secondary education school curriculum. Algebra, geometry, trigonometry as well as sets are introduced. French in the lower secondary school is concerned with expansion of vocabulary and refinement of style. Social studies, artistic and physical education areas struggle for status. Literature and social studies focus on synthesis and pattern construction. Literature is pared down so that students are expected to have appreciation of the historical development of French literature. History–geography emphasizes the construction of patterns of time and space.

Teaching and assessment do not change dramatically between primary and lower secondary education despite the replacement of one class teacher by subject teachers. Rationalist philosophies, allied to standardization, are associated with a teaching which groups students in rows or circles facing the teacher who orchestrates the discourse. The teacher determines the content and order and has a sequence of logically ordered concepts to present.

The view of knowledge permits a range of relationships between teachers and students. At the extreme lies a simple lecture – the teacher transmits content in the correct sequence without concern about what has been learned. It is the student's responsibility to learn. Socratic methods are equally valid. The teacher questions pupils in such a way that the development of ideas is maintained but comes through the responses of pupils. The teacher accepts a prime responsibility for persuading the children to learn. In both approaches the students are held together in a group as the major part of the 45-or 50-minute lesson. Individual or small group activity of students is rare.

External, standardized bodies of knowledge can be linked to standardized conceptions of assessment. Tests are held every week with a common grading scheme. Their cumulative results are used to decide whether pupils have reached the levels associated with their grade. While the emphasis is on what the students do not know rather than what they know, children are not tested on knowledge which they could not reasonably have expected to learn in school. What is more important is the frequency of testing so that children are aware of their attainment.

Testing is a matter for teachers. Their skill and their position as state officials gives them the right to make such judgements. Teachers collectively discuss end-of-year assessments of students in French primary and lower secondary schools. So the examination at the end of lower secondary education, the *brevet de collège*, while externally controlled matters little for most students. The majority progress to the upper secondary level on the basis of cumulative teacher assessment.

Basic education in France is faced with severe challenges. Alienation of students leads to violence and vandalism in suburban Parisian *collèges* (France, 1993b: 108–9). Passive rejection occurs more generally. For this education gives little status to non-intellectual activities and very little space for personal inclinations. It demands total submission from students of non-French cultures. The continued motivation of students cannot be assured.

This crisis has produced an irony that traditionally regimented France joined formerly permissive Britain in national evaluation of students and the transfer of responsibility for outcomes to each institution. Systematic evaluation of student achievement by the Ministry of Education began in the late 1970s and France joined Britain in the late 1980s in introducing national testing (Le Guen, 1994). School autonomy has meant more financial responsibility and the headteacher changing from being a bureaucratic go-between for the school and the Ministry to being a co-ordinator of educational initiatives (France, 1993c: 11–12). As in Britain, the differences in achievement of different schools are becoming crucial.

Teachers are the most important actors. The variety and the communality of methods may arise from the teacher's view of himself or herself. This may be personal. The French teacher has the ideal of being an intellectual. It is also public and professional. Teachers in France see themselves as national public servants. So the curriculum content is the equivalent of a law which the teacher has the obligation to obey (Broadfoot and Osborne, 1992). Intellectual status gives teachers an informal responsibility to transmit the material with the greatest intellectual poise.

While the inspectors have great power over teachers' transfer between schools, their impact on methods may not be great. Communality may come from initial training and education. There are no internal hierarchies of teachers within schools, beyond the principal and deputy, so that co-operation between teachers is largely informal and democratic.

Teachers have formed both a unified ideological cadre and deeply fissured factions. The unity of a national functionary class was reinforced by training in which all were, for a least part of the time, salaried cadets rather than rootless students. This made the old *écoles normales* for primary school teachers (*instituteurs*) attractive to able students from poor families. The two grades of *lycée* teachers, the *professeurs certifiés* and *agrégés*, also received sponsored training either in post-graduate teacher training or in the *grande école* preparation most often enjoyed by the latter. Furthermore, the tests for entry to training and, to some extent, qualification were largely intellectual.

The fissures came from the gulfs in pay and conditions between different grades. The *instituteurs* were trained and employed in a region, the other two nationally. The caste characteristics of each grade posed major problems in the creation of the comprehensive *collège* in which all three grades were employed (though relatively few *agrégés* in practice). Unions were split according to grades. While teachers could co-operate within a grade they were sharply divided between them.

The unification of grades was made possible only after 1989 with a common pattern of post-graduate professional training for primary and secondary school teachers (Blondel, 1991). By then, however, teachers were faced with the decline in status of public service occupations. They were better placed than their equivalents in other countries because of the competitive teacher-training entry system. But appeal to status on the dual bases of being a functionary and an intellectual was wearing thin. Alternative strategies of elevating the craft of pedagogy, encouraged through specialist teacher networks, and of forging alliances with parents began to have more appeal.

Parents were involved systematically in schools from the formation of school councils in the 1960s. Class councils followed in which parents and students were represented as well as parents and which decided student grades. The overall direction was towards giving the school a social–educative as well as an instructional function. But in a centralized system, the local community was defined arbitrarily as the school catchment area and the natural links between consumers and producers did not emerge as in countries with organic communities.

French basic education, with its rigidly intellectual aims and standardization, does still provide a model for Rousseau's education of the citizen. It still has great contemporary relevance. Its weakness is its lack of real provision for the education of 'man in nature' with the enormous contemporary diversity of conceptions of man and of 'in nature'. Even its strengths depend on the survival of archaic views of the state and of the teacher which may have no chances of resurrection on other societies. Above all it needs well-motivated and loyal citizens.

Other South European countries

French practice has strong echoes in Spain, Portugal, Italy, Greece and Belgium. Each of these other countries has centralist–collectivist traditions of educational direction. Yet they have been modified in significant ways in Italy, Belgium and Spain. Basic schooling has become common up to 14 or 16 in all, with some variation in Belgium. None has matched the dynamic, modernist egalitarianism of French educational change in the second half of the twentieth century.

Provision of pre-school education illustrates the similarities.

Belgium,which had almost 90% of 3 year olds in nursery education in 1970, has had higher participation rates than France (Woodhead, 1979: 4). Spain had rapidly expanded in the 1980s to reach over 90% of 4 year olds in school by 1990 (OECD, 1992b: 92) and Italy also had high enrolments. Relatively low economic development helps to explain low participation in Greece and in Portugal where even universal elementary schooling is far from secure.

Italy and Portugal make education compulsory to the age of 14 while it is 15 in Greece. It was 14 up to 1990 in Spain. Basic education corresponded to the old extended primary school until recently in each country, except Belgium, even though the last phase has been in separate lower secondary schools in Italy since 1962. The other countries moved towards common lower secondary schools in the 1970s and 1980s. Belgium still has a variety of selective and common secondary schools for children after the age of 12 but, in the German and Dutch mode, has enforced a common programme in the first 2 years of all schools.

Programmes in all countries have followed a common pattern of a national curriculum, centrally determined, which contains the same range of subjects – including a modern language – as in equivalent French schools, except that all include religious education (with possibilities for pupil withdrawal and, in Belgium, for substitution by moral education). The national language(s) and mathematics predominate and develop in ways not dissimilar to France.

There are variations. The humanist tradition was powerful in Spain, Italy and Greece in lower secondary education until the 1970s. History and literature (including the Classics in Italy and Greece) encouraged a passive respect for a national identity which lasted even longer in Spain and Greece where dictatorial regimes were ousted only in the mid-1970s. But conservative nationalism did not prevent a continued emphasis on a standard encyclopaedic curriculum (McLean, 1990a: 52–63, 107–9).

In some countries, naturalist elements entered the official curriculum. In Italy, vastly ambitious curriculum aims in practice provided spaces for teacher choice. According to the 1985 elementary school regulations, the teaching of Italian should 'articulate rational experience and individual feelings' while mathematics should be practical and encourage intuition, imagination, hypothesizing, deduction and verification (Lombardi, 1987: 530, 542). In Spain, the 1970 Education Law created a basic school which had programmes based on areas of experience rather than subjects. Belgian primary schools were influenced by the child-centred ideas of Decroly with a result that official injunctions suggested that teaching should always be concerned with the emotional and psychological development of children (McLean, 1990a: 64).

Italy, Spain and Belgium experience greater cultural division than

France which influences the curriculum. In Italy, this is expressed in a failure of central government with corporatist ambitions ever to impose itself on the regional identities of an imperfectly unified country. Regional and city administrations provided alternative education since the 1970s. Spain recognized regional autonomy in the 1978 Constitution so that local languages and cultures are taught in schools in Catalonia, the Basque country and elsewhere while private Catholic schools still provide over 30% of places (Boyd-Barrett, 1990: 292). Belgium, since the end of the nineteenth century, has had two educational systems based on language as well as state and religious schools, each with proportions in the range of 60:40. The country has become a loose federation since 1988. Yet programmes across the two autonomous communities retain much in common.

Rational encyclopaedism can be reconciled with cultural diversity and a weak central state in ways that are not admitted in France, Greece or Portugal. Teachers maintain similar values about the national curriculum and ways of teaching it in Belgium, Spain and Italy as in France. One major reason for abandoning the 1970 school-controlled curriculum in Spain in the 1980s was that teachers applied standards that led to a failure rate of around 30%. Methods may be more child centred in Belgium or in parts of Italy, but teachers generally assess on a weekly and yearly basis without external intervention and all systems have grade repetition.

Teachers' public positions also follow a French model. Except in Belgium, with its large Catholic sector, teachers are national public servants though, unlike France and except in Greece, they are generally chosen by a rigorous state examination after qualification. Their status is under threat by decline in state commitment to educational expenditure. Yet their view of themselves as state agents of rational modernization remains. Italian primary school teachers, uniquely in the industrial world, still only receive an upper secondary level training and secondary school teachers are university graduates with no teacher training. In contrast, in Greece, unlike the other countries, primary and secondary school teacher education has been partly unified in universities since 1982. Traditions of worthwhile knowledge and of the social function of the teacher seem to survive major differences in educational organization.

Rationalist–collectivist educational cultures are not as monolithic as the French example may suggest. While the power of an ancient centralist rationality and uniformity survives strongly, it is possible to reconcile this view with great respect for children, communities and multiculturalism. The issue is not of a choice between collectivist–rationalist or pluralist–naturalist approaches but of drawing effective and realistic boundaries between the public and private.

Eastern Europe

Soviet education, dedicated to creating a 'new socialist man' and 'education for the collective', derived as much if not more from the seventeenth-century European Enlightenment as from Communist dogma. It was in effect a highly authoritarian form of rationalist–collectivism with more ambitious aims than western Europe countries. Though the Soviet system was imposed on other countries of east and central Europe it was not entirely foreign to their own traditions. The contemporary issue is in what survived the political changes of the late 1980s as much as what changed.

The contrast between a small modern sector and a vast traditional hinterland in the Soviet Union was always greater than in any western country. The common school covered the ages 7–14 up to 1956. It was only in 1986 than a 9-year school for ages 6–15 became general. The morning-only school prevailed with collective social activities of Communist youth organizations in afternoons. However, there was always an élite even in the basic phase. Special selective schools concentrated on music, ballet, mathematics–science and foreign languages though they never took more than 3% of the whole age group (Muckle, 1988: 174). But those selected often were treated as representative of their village or collective and given popular local support.

The common school had one curriculum and standards that all should achieve. Pre-school education was thoroughly provided and systematic in aim in urban areas. The elementary curriculum for children up to the age of 10 or 11 devoted half the time to the Russian language, stressing grammar and vocabulary and gave mathematics a further quarter. Language teaching did stress oral use and drew upon traditional stories emphasizing the cultural function of Russian (Muckle, 1988: 64–67). Mathematics aimed to ensure that arithmetic could be completed as a subject by the age of 10 or 11. Programmes were standard for Russia and mainly so in other republics. They were complemented by common textbooks.

The curriculum for children aged 10–15 followed the subjects of western Europe with specialist teachers. Sciences were introduced in succeeding grades – biology, then physics and finally chemistry. Mathematics concentrated entirely on algebra and geometry – the former having the objective of 'raising the level of pupils' "calculative culture"' and the latter 'to teach the pupil to reason logically, argue his statements and prove his point' (Muckle, 1988: 51, 53). Sciences, language and history also emphasized understanding of abstract principles, concepts and deductive processes (Muckle, 1988: 48–73). Despite compulsory labour training, 'political education' and a patriotic tinge to humanities areas, rationalism was predominant in the Soviet school.

Whole-class teaching, teacher questions and pupil response predominated. The number of correct responses was totalled in each lesson for each row of children. Authoritarian classes were those where sanctions were applied to underachieving rows while in the permissive the exercise was a competitive game. Students were constantly assessed. Teachers provided grades for each child and the parents of underachievers could be harassed at work as well as by teachers. Students who failed to reach the standard were humiliated in ways reminiscent of political show trials.

The reform of Soviet education reflected both the collapse of the administrative system of sanctions and the decline of motivation. Soviet educators claimed that standards of achievement declined from the 1970s (Dunstan, 1985: 169). With the changes of the late 1980s, concern was raised in government about the effect of overdemanding education on the health of children as well as over a view of the '"normal-child", extinguishing his curiosity, agility and unconventionality' (Yagodin, 1989: 14). New aims of humanization, democratization and individualization permitted an emphasis on humanities, emotion and individual aspirations (Suddaby, 1989).

Yet the new educators retained a rationalist view of a curriculum that encouraged 'the ability to think, to understand, to analyze, to compare, to generalize or to draw conclusions' which followed a didactic sequence of 'first a law was formulated, then the stages by which it was mastered were determined and the facts were selected, examples from life were drawn which confirmed the accuracy of the law' (Karadovsky, 1993: 278–80). These features survived despite the emergence of selective and private schools, a degree of school autonomy outstripping that of England after 1988 and a new curriculum emphasis on ecological, moral, spiritual and aesthetic matters.

Soviet education drew from pre-revolutionary culture. Collectivism came as much from an ancient view of 'social life ... based on a willingness of each person to pawn part of himself to his fellow men ... (where) privacy was the worst form of mental exile' (Nettl, 1967: 64). Teachers were devoted despite poor conditions of work because they were members of the 'intelligentsia' which had an ethical vocation long before 1917 (Walicki, 1980: xv). And this culture may have created the unique achievement of Soviet education to accentuate the rational and standard in the school and the affective, social and practical in the out-of-school youth organizations. The question is whether this culture can be revived beyond Soviet totalitarianism.

Other Communist regimes in eastern Europe had similar systems. They also had older roots of a rational view derived from Comenius as much as Descartes as well as collectivist political systems. The direction of educational change has been similar to Russia after 1990. Yet there are also specific traditions for each country. Hungary, for instance, had equated the search for high standards of achievement with selective secondary schools even during Communist rule (Nagy and Szebenyi, 1990) and this Germanic approach seemed to produce student achievements on a German level (Foxman, 1992: 77). Poland, in contrast, has had also a powerful humanist–historical–religious tradition in the curriculum which has produced a somewhat nostalgic element in recent reforms (Pachocinski, 1994).

Rationalist–collectivist approaches survive in eastern Europe despite the weakening of the state. Standardized, scientific education has attraction to parents and students in a harsh economic climate where a universal rational education may be traded for work outside as well as inside the country. Yet there are a great variety of naturalist and humanist views of education which are in the early stages of revival but which may yet offer accommodation between the public and private.

Naturalist and community traditions in northern and insular Europe

Basic education in the northern countries in continental western Europe has a character which is clearly distinguished from the rationalist south but which differs from Britain and Ireland. There are still marginal rationalist–collectivist elements in education, not found in Britain, but also a pluralism, localism and naturalism in line with British traditions. Yet this bloc also divides, especially in the basic cycle. The Scandinavian community school is not paralleled in the central group of countries whose continued attachment to stratified secondary education is anathema to many of its neighbours.

Germany and the Netherlands

These two countries are distinguished by the variety of their school systems in contrast to the uniformity of France. German and Dutch basic education is never allowed to encroach on the family and social grouping. Pre-school education is marginal in Germany and has only began to develop in the Netherlands since 1985 when elementary education was defined to cover the ages of 3–12. Children in Germany spend only mornings in school. Rather than schools attempting to compensate for the family as in France, Britain or the USA, their effects are deliberately limited.

Selection for secondary school occurs at the age of 10 in Germany In the past, there was an examination. Since the 1970s in both countries internal teacher assessment together with parental choice have been decisive. Falling birth rates led to the decline in proportions entering non-selective schools, the *Hauptschule* in Germany and the MAVO, LAVO, and LBO in the Netherlands. Yet common lower secondary schooling has not developed, as in most of the industrial world. The comprehensive *Gesamtschulen* are attended by only 10% of children in Germany and none in the second largest state of Bavaria.

The array of selective secondary schools include academic institutions taking around 30% of students – the *Gymnasium* in Germany and VWO in the Netherlands – which take students to university entrance and the technical–academic schools (the *Realschule* and the HAVO) which prepare for higher vocational education. Yet all schools have a common curriculum in the first two grades. Only after the ages of 12–14 do the courses diverge. In both countries, many of those completing the unselective school courses successfully transfer into a selective institution.

In both countries, elementary education is more local and child centred than in France. In Germany, there are differences between the emphasis on standard achievement in conservative southern states and the social democrat *Lander* in the north where frequently schools may be encouraged to follow a school-based approach to teaching. The subjects and timetable of the curriculum are determined by each state. The Conference of Ministers of Education have sought harmonization since 1964 but roughly 30% of teaching time follows patterns unique to each statc. This diversity is greater in the Netherlands which has a national elementary curriculum, but where each school since 1985 can create its own programmes with the approval of the School Council and the confirmation of inspectors that the school plan is consistent with the broad national guidelines (England and Wales DES/HMI, 1987b).

Teaching methods and assessment are similarly diverse. The richness of student experience is emphasized in many German schools and also in the Netherlands there are frequent appeals to practical examples in teaching (Brink and Bruggen, 1990: 286–88). In both countries, the national constitutions forbid interference by government in teaching methods, though schools in the Netherlands have free choice of textbooks whereas the *Land* approval is needed in Germany. Despite selection to different kinds of secondary schooling, assessment is left to teachers who also share a concern to help students to succeed rather than, as often in southern Europe, in finding ways to fail them.

Though confined largely to private schools, the impact of Rudolf Steiner's ideas in Germany indicate a richer concept of child development than found in most other countries. Science in primary schools should start from exploring honey as a soft, sweet, malleable substance appropriate to the biological development of young children. At later stages (aged 15 or 16) it can move to iron as hard and resisting when children are biologically ready to absorb such an experience (Lauterbach and Frey, 1987: 41). The view of child development is sustained by a holistic view of knowledge in which all aspects – biological, social, practical, rational and spiritual – have a place and may, ideally, achieve a union at the end of the educational process.

The lower secondary school curriculum, in contrast, is much more rationalist and encyclopaedic. It is heavily prescribed and overloaded. In the Netherlands 14 compulsory subjects include two foreign languages while in the German *Gymnasium* two or three foreign languages (including sometimes Latin and Greek) are taken after the second grade. In both countries there is an emphasis on a standard achievement, reinforced in the Netherlands by a set of national attainment targets in 1987 which are similar to those of England and Wales (Brink and Bruggen, 1991: 280).

Languages and mathematics dominate the lower secondary curriculum. The emphasis in content and teaching is on rules and structures with little concern for pupil expression in language or practical application in mathematics. Factual learning is a strong feature in other subjects (Brink and Bruggen, 1991; England and Wales DES/HMI, 1987b). Teaching is mainly of the whole class type and is narrowly focused especially in mathematics where the blackboard is the centre. Grade repeating as well as stratified secondary schools produce a greater homogeneity of levels of student attainment which makes this possible.

The reconciliation of rational and earthy strains in German and Dutch cultures is achieved by isolating practical elements of the curriculum. In Germany, the subject 'Learning about Work' (*Arbeitslehre*) since the 1960s has combined career guidance, learning about the social–economic–legal contexts of work and work experience. Its core is a project where students design, manufacture and market a product in a co-operative, practical yet challenging way (Kledsvik, 1989). In contrast, in Dutch unselective schools practical studies relate more to specific vocational training but, as in Germany, focus on accuracy, reliability and 'making something and making it well' (Bieroof and Prais, 1993: 222). These practical courses are confined to the last two grades of non-selective schools in both countries.

Assessment has been very serious in the German system with students given grades at frequent intervals but also tested once or twice yearly. Assessment is controlled by teachers and the recipients of the results are students and parents (England and Wales DES/HMI, 1986). However, there is a final examination for the *Hauptschule* at the age of 16 and, a year later, for the *Realschule*. Teacher assessments and external examinations are combined. Performance across all subjects is taken into account.

Germany, particularly, has persuaded its below-average students to take study very seriously and reach standards where no more than 5% can be regarded as failures. Germany has not participated in recent international tests but the Dutch 14 year olds have been among the highest average performers (Robitaille and Garden, 1989: 105–24). The basis of this achievement clearly comes from the motivation of students. While some content and teaching are attractive, there is much that demands great effort without the instantaneous reward of satisfied interest. Yet the devotion and determination of teachers to ensure that students succeed is of great importance as is the insistence of employers and higher level educational institutions that recruitment depends on educational performance.

Teachers also provide the key to success. Teacher commitment comes from a professional pride with deep roots in historical culture. Teachers are civil servants in Germany. Yet teachers are stratified by grades related to levels of training in both countries in ways that are no longer acceptable in Britain and France. Training is based on schools and regional centres, especially in Germany and to a lesser extent in the Netherlands but this attracts criticism that theoretical and practical elements have little contact (Busch, 1982). Perhaps more important is that teachers have clear views of their function, even though this function differs between levels of schooling and perhaps the region or sector in which they work.

Indeed, compared with other European countries, it is remarkable how little basic education has changed in the Netherlands and Germany in the second part of the twentieth century. With reunification, the West German model was adopted by or imposed on the East. Rather than engage on reform, which is difficult in their pluralist cultures, they have succeeded in preserving archaic practices. Such conservatism may not work elsewhere.

Scandinavia

Nordic countries, while integrated into an overall continental European educational civilization, possess a distinctive culture of schooling. Yet the variations between the extremes of centralist Sweden and localist Denmark obscure this communality. One common, community school serves all children up to the age of 16. Only after then is there accession to the demands for occupational diversification.

The community school has its strongest expression in Denmark and Norway. It comes from views that schools should support local village economic, religious and historical cultures, notably of Grundtwig in nineteenth-century Denmark but also of Erling Kristvik in early twentieth-century Norway (Lauglo, 1994: 9). The school does not invade the private sphere too early so that 7 is the beginning of compulsory schooling (though reduced to 6 in Sweden). Less than half the population of 4 year olds was in pre-school education in 1990 in Sweden (OECD, 1992b: 92). And in Denmark and Norway state-supported private education since the 1970s has been provided for those parents who wish to give a traditional rural-religious character to the schooling of their children (Rust, 1989: 237–39; Winther-Jensen, 1994: 50). Even in Sweden the centralized introduction of common lower secondary schooling in the 1940s – ahead of any other western European country – was accommodated in all-through basic schools. Norway and Denmark followed on a more localized pattern in the 1970s.

The Scandinavian basic school has taken forms that differ from the rest of continental western Europe. Grade repeating is unknown. Even teacher testing has been resisted though national assessment was introduced in the late 1980s in Sweden partly in response to low levels of performance in international tests (in contrast to high achievements in Norway) (Robitaille and Garden, 1989: 124–29; Svingby, 1990). The ideal of maintaining social solidarity in traditional communities is preserved for as long as possible. However, the gulf between the approach of the community school and post-16 education has been a matter of concern, with government calls in 1992 in Denmark for more testing and greater rigour in the upper grades of the *folkeskole* especially in languages and mathematics (Winther-Jensen, 1994: 51–52).

A national curriculum exists through Scandinavia but its application differs. In Sweden, it is treated as a law to be obeyed by teachers but in Denmark as guidelines which may be adopted or ignored. The school council in Danish schools, dominated by parents, as well as the local authority may sanction deviation. At school level, teachers must secure the agreement of pupils before they teach a course. And in the overall curriculum the social studies subjects have had a strong place with a role of cementing local community identity.

Teaching methods reflect this communalism. One class teacher tends to cover all subjects in Denmark with reluctant concession to specialist teachers for some subjects in the upper grades. The teacher also moves up with the class from the beginning to the end of the nine grade *folkeskole*. Denmark was one of the first industrial countries to integrate children with special educational needs systematically into mainstream schools in the 1970s.

The role of curriculum actors differs from other systems. In Denmark, parents intervene in curriculum matters and, through the control that parent-dominated school councils have in the appointment of teachers, are able to influence teaching in other ways. Yet the private school movement suggests that parent control is not as great as desired by some groups. Furthermore, teachers themselves have been important community leaders in Norway (Lauglo, 1994). Tensions between national and community roles of teachers have been found as rural communities are turned into diverse urban areas with weaker social ties. Teachers – as in Germany, Belgium and the Netherlands – are graded by level of training and type of school which tends to maintain the unity of the basic school. But in Sweden, teachers submit to the national curriculum and national government, as in France, and the direction of change since the late 1980s has been to give local groups a greater leverage to produce higher standards

The Scandinavian community school has its origins in geographically dispersed rural communities of one race, language and religion. It is undermined by urbanization. But attachment to old values is powerful. Sweden, which introduced centralized planning early, differs from the others. In Norway with relatively even levels of student attainment and Denmark with very powerful local attachments the community ideal survives most strongly.

Britain

British traditions lie at the privatist and individualist end of the European pluralist spectrum, almost untouched by continental Jacobinism and perhaps closer to the USA than any other European state. Abrupt change in government policy from the mid-1970s may be linked to an older early-nineteenth-century approach which also has some North American resonances.

The direction of change in structure and access, in contrast, has been similar to that of southern Europe. Universal, free and compulsory public elementary education, as in France, was completed by the 1880s as part of a process began in the 1830s. A minority of the students from these institutions entered older academic secondary grammar schools from the late nineteenth century. Unselective secondary schools provided universal access after 1944 and the common secondary school became the norm after 1965. By 1980, over 80% of students were in comprehensive secondary schools.

There are unique features. Around 8% of pupils attended socially and academically élite private schools. The separate lower secondary common school did not emerge cleanly, with a number of variations in the ages at which students changed institutions. The predominant original scheme of 11–18 comprehensive schools only gave way to a clearer distinction at 16 in the 1980s. Scottish secondary education had a different pattern, historically higher participation rates and a curriculum with rational-encyclopaedic elements.

Basic schools were communities of children and teachers rather than organs of a wider community. Schools saved children from their homes as much in the élite independent secondary schools as in public primary education. Uniquely in the West, elementary education began at the age of 5 from the nineteenth century and children moved through the grades as family groups regardless of achievement. Selection to grammar schools by external examinations did create divisions within elementary schools (Jackson, 1964) but its end in the 1960s allowed schools to revert to community ideals.

Five-grade lower secondary schools were internally divided into streams by attainment. Many schools moved to 'mixed-ability' groupings in the first three grades from the 1960s but the external examinations, notably the General Certificate of Education 'Ordinary Level', designed for about 20% of the age group, forced separation in the last two grades. The General Certificate of Secondary Education was introduced in 1986 to reduce segregation. To date, less than half the age group achieve the examination grades in the range of subjects which are considered necessary for progress into higher level upper secondary courses. The failing group at 16 seems to be higher than in most other industrial countries.

A national curriculum had existed in the late nineteenth century but had been allowed to wither in the early twentieth (Aldrich, 1988; Gordon and Lawton, 1978). From the 1930s, teachers in elementary schools were encouraged to take the curiosity of children as the starting-point of the primary-school curriculum (England and Wales Board of Education, 1931). By 1967, officially supported recommendations were that subjects could disappear into co-operative projects and individual activities of children (England and Wales DES, 1967). The government policy statement of 1977 which produced the opening salvo in the move towards national curriculum described its strengths:

'Children engage in work designed to increase their control over themselves physically and mentally, to capture their imagination.... The child-centred approach takes advantage of the child's individual stage of development and of his or her interests: it complements the wider curriculum by harnessing the natural enthusiasm of young children to learning things by their own efforts instead of merely being fed with information.' (England and Wales DES, 1977: 8)

This approach was possible because there were few curriculum requirements except for religious education. There was no mandatory or even systematic informal testing of children. It has been difficult to determine what was the prevailing pattern of teaching. At the extreme, the teacher would negotiate with each child or small group their individually chosen activities. It was probably the predominant activity only in a minority of classes. More prevalent was individual and small group activity within the frames of a subject or topic and some common objectives. Whole-class teaching occupied a small part of the day. Children worked on their own and made sense of materials from books, worksheets and objects or visits rather than of a teacher presentation. Individualism, inductionism and a pastoral teacher prevailed in the primary school.

In the lower secondary school, separate subjects were taught by specialist teachers who defended their content boundaries as fiercely as those in any encyclopaedic system of education. In the absence of a national curriculum teachers varied widely in what they believed should be taught. Learning by discovery prevailed as much at this level as in elementary schools even though the source of learning may have been a laboratory experiment, worksheets or a range of textbooks. Traditional teaching produced total silence for three-quarters of the time interrupted only by hushed conversation between the teacher and one student. 'Progressive' teaching only differed in that children moved about in search of materials and consulted one another.

In the last two grades of lower secondary education pupils or teachers made their own decisions about their strengths. The General Certificate of Education examination rewarded attainment in each subject separately. The shrewd student narrowed his or her options to the minimum needed for future progress. A reasonable but not extravagant effort in two or three subjects to be dropped after 16 together with real concentration on the three areas of later specialization was most economic. Underachievers confused dislike for the teacher with an undiscriminating abandonment of effort in the wrong subjects.

But aims of subjects also contributed. Mathematics was seen to be important for its practical use rather than its training of thought (England and Wales DES, 1982). English could be an exploration of personal and moral issues through literature rather than systematic learning of linguistic structures. Naturalist and humanist justifications overlapped. Modern languages suffered when it was difficult to establish a base either in experiential learning or in natural student interest.

Teacher curriculum design and child-centred teaching were demanding especially when combined with expectations that the teacher was a substitute parent responsible for the social, moral and emotional development of each individual child. Distrust of parents meant that teachers did not enlist their help nor even expect that students would do very much school work at home. Unevenness between schools as well as neglect of attainment targets in mathematics and modern languages were cited to support a national curriculum and national assessment.

National curriculum and assessment introduced with the 1988 Education Reform Act appeared a complete revolution. Ten subjects were prescribed for children aged 5–16 with a modern language added at 11. Curriculum statements differed from continental European patterns. Attainment targets for each subject conflated objectives and content. Broader aims had to be gleaned from advisory committee reports. The curriculum was assessment driven. Nationally standard tests for students aged 7, 11, 14 and 16 provided the frame of content and teaching. These four key stages were placed alongside ten levels of attainment so that an average 7 year old would reach level two and an 11 year old level four (England and Wales DES, 1989).

The broader purpose of this curriculum was to provide information to parents about the achievement of their children by national standards and to allow them to judge the comparative performance of the school through its results which had to be made available. Standardization gave enormous power to central government bodies but the underlying political–administrative philosophy was utilitarian. Government provided means by which the efficiency of public institutions could be judged by parents who – through their choice of schools and as members of school governing bodies with enhanced powers – could take action to force schools to be more effective.

The national curriculum is not as draconian as it may appear. There were no specified times for each subject nor mandatory texts. Cross-curriculum themes such as careers education, gender and multicultural issues were to be covered. Complaints about overloading led to a reduction in compulsory studies to four subjects for the 14–16 age group in 1994. Ironically, in view of developments in other European countries and the government statements of the 1970s, modern languages were not taught in primary schools and were not mandatory throughout the lower secondary phase. Despite the invective of ministers (over, for instance, the teaching of reading) and the disapproval of the inspectorate of badly managed topic-based approaches (England and Wales DES/HMI, 1992a: 3) teaching methods remained free of central prescription.

The most dramatic change was in assessment. Teachers lost real power in this area which was enjoyed by their equivalents in other European countries (and Japan). Teacher demands for individualized records of achievement for each pupil were undermined by standard comparative measures. The politics of curriculum construction had swung decisively against teachers. Both major political parties, when in government, supported a national curriculum though based on different political–administrative philosophies. Teacher unions briefly resisted national assessment. The inspectors, who had some sympathy with teachers, were purged. The crucial issue was the position of teachers and, to a lesser extent, parents. Unlike most other countries, primary and secondary school teachers had had a unified grade for many years. Teachers, without a status based on civil service rank or community function, had sought an independent identity based on a pastoral commitment and pedagogical expertise. A national curriculum and assessment undermined the latter and parental power the former. They were forced into a narrower definition of competence based on skill in classroom management and on social responsibility in conjunction with parents.

Parents were to be the driving force of the cultural revolution of the 1988 Education Act. Their response has not been properly described. A traditional passivity combines with both the self-interest and public responsibility which the reforms of the 1980s encouraged. Parents have supported teachers and schools against higher authorities yet decisively have withdrawn support from school as they dislike. In primary schools they are caught between instincts to demand higher standard attainments and to support school communities concerned with the whole child. A clearer distinction between the cognitive and affective, the public and the private, the local and the national would make both teacher and parent functions easier to define.

Extra-European cases – the USA and Japan

The American school and its development suggests parallels with European pluralist traditions while Japan seems closer to collectivist systems of Europe. The unique traditions and the particular contemporary contexts of both may throw light on European options.

Basic schooling has been the subject of less public debate in the USA than upper secondary and higher education. Problems of attainment at the lower levels tend to be related to social–cultural characteristics of children, parents and community rather than the content and teaching of schools. Pre-school education has tended to lag behind other industrial countries, with only 51% of 4 year olds participating in 1990 (OECD,

1992b: 92). The Federal government, as part of the attack on poverty in the 1960s, launched the Headstart Programme to provide pre-school education for socially disadvantaged children. While the aim was to provide intellectual stimulation to allow poor children to compete in mainstream school, the programme as a whole focused on health care and education for parents (Spring, 1978: 153). Most families could educate their infants without public aid.

Elementary schools commonly cover six grades from ages 6 to 12 followed by 4 years of junior high school, though there are variations. One school without internal divisions or selection has predominated from the nineteenth century. The basic school turned immigrants of many cultures into Americans through a common language and common political socialization. The adage that the little red schoolhouse created the American nation still underlies American basic education despite local community control and the legacy of the Progressive movement associated with Dewey.

The standardization of American elementary education without external controls is one of the puzzles of comparative study. Learning English has been a more mandatory and standardized exercise than in Britain. American elementary school children are divided into graded reading groups ('Robins', 'Bluebirds' and others) following standardized texts, often containing test questions. Explanations have been offered which focus on the structure of the American textbook publication – states which prescribed textbooks were persuaded by national publishers to use a narrow range of books (Spring, 1978: 147–48). Yet the power and centrality of the written word in American culture is also important; apparent, for instance, to Europeans who find a strongly literary street furniture in comparison to their own graphics.

The social studies curriculum is also more central in American basic education than elsewhere. A Californian programme of the 1960s indicates a political socialization purpose in the eighth grade:

> 'How our country fosters the democratic way of life
> How our people meet their needs through participation in groups
> How our American heritage continues to grow
> How our ways of governing compare with other ways of governing.' (Raynor and Grant, 1972: 115)

Yet this apparent uniformity is also an attempt to achieve a national consensus overriding the differences of local communities, illustrated by the exclusion of religious education and inclusion of the saluting the flag in all public institutions. One of the few federal curriculum projects concerned with the basic phase 'Man: a course of study' aroused local opposition in the 1970s because its anthropological approach offered 'lurid examples of violence and sexual promiscuity' (Spring, 1978: 150). More recent problems have emerged over demands of cultural minorities to a social studies curriculum which will reflect specific histories and identities.

This debate has obscured that on whether basic schooling is about standard achievements or co-operative learning for social–economic goals. Dewey's conception of learning was to allow children to grow and to prepare for occupations. Utilitarian concerns for external standards were reflected in the textbook dominated teaching. The rationalist–intellectual justification which concerned continental Europeans had a relatively uninfluential expression in, for instance, the concept of the 'spiral curriculum' of Jerome Bruner where rational concepts could be introduced in early schooling for intuitive rather than systematic apprehension (Bruner, 1960: 52–53).

The undemanding yet informally standardizing character of American basic education may be related to processes of determination of content and teaching. American teachers have had fewer external restraints determined by public service functions in Europe or Japan. They are free professionals or workers employed by the school. A university-trained profession lacks status where university graduates are commonplace, and it is the state rather than federal government that controls certification. As autonomous professionals teachers may have complete freedom to teach as they wish and judge appropriate to children. Yet as workers without public status they are also subject to interference from school principals, parents and local superintendents. They are more likely to be identified as substitute parents or child minders.

In the 1980s, the emphasis on basic competence did affect elementary schools. States and Districts set tests. Grade repeating, after disappearing for a century, began to reappear (Shepard and Smith, 1989). Unlike Britain, there was no national prescription. Yet, in elementary schools, the revival of measurement of outcomes was not only consistent with a long American tradition but was also more congruent with long-established traditions of standardized aims for elementary schooling.

Japanese basic education offers a picture with some American parallels derived from the American occupation after 1945. Overall, Japanese schooling provides a distinctive refrain on the European collectivist approach. Unlike European collectivist systems, Japanese early childhood education is limited with less than 20% of 3 year olds and less than 60% of 4 year olds in school in 1990 (OECD, 1992b: 92). Growth has come from pressure of parental demands so that almost 80% of children in pre-school education are in private institutions (Japan, 1993: 22).

Basic education is provided in 6-year elementary schools which have provided universal education since the late nineteenth century followed by 3-year common lower secondary schools which are mainly unselective neighbourhood schools without any differentiation of curriculum or students. While automatic transfer to upper secondary schools, on the American pattern, is the overt norm, in practice the later grades of the junior secondary school are dominated by preparation for entrance tests of the most sought after public upper secondary schools.

The curriculum is national, standard, specified in detail and accompanied by a textbook for each course which is provided free to children. Japanese and arithmetic dominate in the elementary grades with somewhat less time for social studies, science, music and art/craft and physical education. A foreign language is added in the lower secondary school. Moral education has a place similar to religious education in European schools and 'extra-curricular' subjects are included in the curriculum. In response to criticisms of lack of active learning, a more discovery based Life and Environment course was introduced in the first two grades of the elementary school (Japan, 1993: 58–59).

Unlike some western systems, subjects other than Japanese and mathematics appear to have informal status. Traditional forms of social behaviour and personal responsibility are stressed in moral education while art and music encourage Japanese appreciation of beauty, even though music includes substantial attention to western composers. (Japan, 1983b: 61–75, 121–25). The search for a total and thorough learning puts great pressure on pupils in both elementary and lower secondary classes (England and Wales DFE, 1992b: 17).

Standardization is maintained but appeal is made to other forms of content and learning, notably the tangible, concrete and intimate. Reading and writing in Japanese and Chinese cultures have to face a separation of sound and sight. There is an obligation to learn 2000 idiographic characters by the end of elementary schooling in Japan (Japan, 1983a: 24–26). This may have an artistic orientation emphasized in the importance of calligraphy as a moral–aesthetic exercise from the third grade (England and Wales, 1992b: 8–9). The initial learning of phonetic characters in the first two grades therefore becomes a naturalist prior experience drawing on children's experience of sound in which greater attention is given to individual experience as well as leading to the public, moral–historic code of idiograms (White, 1987: 110–15).

Japanese elementary school teachers, it is claimed, achieve a warm relationship with children whom they know intimately yet emphasize the achievement of accuracy and skill. They teach not only to the specified curriculum but also follow the prescribed textbook. Yet they lay store on children finding answers for themselves, often through intuition, before the teacher reinforces the correct response. They stress harmony and collective effort while demanding that children early on acquire, sort and classify large amounts of information (White, 1987: 43–45, 116). Teaching is teacher centred, of a whole class type and uses few materials outside the textbook (England and Wales DES/HMI, 1991a). And teachers assess pupils at least every 2 weeks and communicate results to parents. But teachers have unchallenged rights to assess without outside intervention. The all-important entrance tests for prestigious upper secondary schools are not part of the official system.

The roles of the various actors in the achievement of high standards for large proportions of students in Japan has been a centre of much western analysis and speculation. Western frames have not provided very satisfactory answers. Popular demand and motivation are often cited yet parents have little part in the running of schools outside the fund-raising parent-teacher associations. Teachers do not have a particularly long or specialized training and enjoy little professional autonomy. While teachers draw upon traditions of an ancient priestly caste, their high popular prestige has little to do with either the public functionary or independent professional role models of the West and their union organizes them as if they were a section of an oppressed proletariat. Central government dominates curriculum content yet local authorities and school principals have greater impact on teachers' condition of work. Powerful traditions of respect for and commitment to education of teachers, parents and students seem to overcome obstacles. And standardization does not suppress individuality, personal relationships or delight in the natural beauty of the world.

While all Japanese groups criticize uniformity and pressure for undifferentiated pupil achievement, the temperature of the hothouse continues to rise until the 'examination hell' is reached at the end of lower secondary and through upper secondary education. Uniformity has been possible because of the particular social–cultural conditions of Japan and pressure is also a reflection on the expansion of occupational opportunities that economic growth has provided. But the Confucian imperative of harmony seems to have maintained some balance between individuality and collective aims and between affective, tactile experience and the public, intellectual and utilitarian. There may be questions about how long the reconciliation of opposites can be maintained yet western responses, based on the firmer separation of the public and private, may not be relevant.

Conclusion

Suggestions that basic education is converging across countries need to be treated with some scepticism. There are pressures for young children to acquire fundamental linguistic and mathematical skills in similar ways because of their importance for later learning which is affected by international economic competition. Other global imperatives encourage similar movements to achieve comparable cost effectiveness across countries which lead, for instance, to greater parental responsibility and a more standardized role for teachers. Yet basic education now collides, especially in pre-schooling, with traditional family education while its upper extensions takes in lower secondary phases of older élite schooling which has been distinctively different between countries. Quite apart from the obvious point that basic education is concerned primarily with linguistic skills in many different national languages, there may now be as much difference between countries as a century ago.

Children grow physically and psychologically between the ages of 2 and 16 in ways that are not paralleled in later ages. Parents have a more direct involvement in basic schooling than in other phases. These two elements, rather than producing convergence, lead to greater diversity. For there is no universal scheme of child development, and parents – despite economic pressures to act in similar ways across countries – look to older values in raising their children.

Concepts of child development influence basic education. Views that have been influential in the later twentieth century – Jean Piaget, Lev Vygotsky or Jerome Bruner – have simply been the internationally known tip of an iceberg which has many expressions in different countries. These views themselves reflect national traditions of knowledge. Piaget's cognitive scheme which assumes standardization yet warns against artificial acceleration of natural processes allies with a rationalist concept of mass education of Condorcet while Vygotsky's rationalist utopianism is not far removed from that of Comenius or of the revolutionary ideals of post-1917 Russia (Ivic, 1989). Bruner's role for intuition is consistent with a Platonic humanism which Anglo-Saxon cultures find more acceptable.

Child-development theories are often confined to certain cultures. Decroly, Freinet and Steiner proposed views that have had an impact in some countries but not others. The foundation of the 1967 Plowden Report in England on conventional child development theories was attacked both by those who argued that the social–cultural context of children was ignored (Bernstein and Davies, 1969) and by others who preferred a more 'English' view of personal autonomy (Wilson, 1976).

The problem for those who seek universally valid accounts of teaching and learning among young children is that the fundamental processes of basic education are mysterious. Despite a vast amount of research which nibbles away at the technical circumference, how children conceptualize language, number and space is still in the realms of magic. All those involved in education must stand back in wonderment rather than try to explain convincingly why 3-year-old children exhibit skills in language more advanced than those they develop in the following 20 years. The failure of the science of education to jump its first hurdle allows the basic processes to remain under the control of familial and folk cultures rather than any external agency. The rationale for the basic school is not that it can uniquely provide those skills which are fundamental to all future and higher level learning. It is that it provides an environment where children can learn together and be socialized early into that combination of co-operation and competition upon which future social relations are based.

Basic schooling has invaded parental spaces. So it must be reconciled with familial values. What parents expect of their children is likely to derive from ancient beliefs as much as from contemporary exigencies. These expectations may vary between social and cultural groups. On an international scale differences between nations and civilizations may be more important. So one American observer of education in the Soviet Union in the 1960s stressed that Russian parents treated their children with warmth which quickly turned to sustained coldness and withdrawal of privileges on even minor lapses from strict norms (Bronfenbrenner, 1970: 9); while another in the 1980s suggested that Japanese parental motivation comes from a cultural belief that the country has always lived on the edge of survival which is communicated by mothers to children at an early age because 'Japanese women have developed the production of guilt in others into a transcendant cultural art form' (White, 1987: 12). Such comparative cultural anthropology is still undeveloped. Without it, comparative study of basic education is still limited.

Whether the traditions of educational knowledge, access and participation are adequate in describing these differences in basic education also needs to be considered. If traditions have survived, then they are likely to have some authenticity. They are likely to have some consistency with traditions of family education and popular motivations. There are two caveats. First is that naturalist traditions of each society may be more useful for describing ideals of past social–cultural forms rather than the present. Secondly, traditions of higher levels of education are likely to be imposed artificially upon basic schooling. Whatever the forms of contemporary basic education, traditions may need to be reinterpreted to produce the most appropriate contemporary forms of education.

Future developments are affected by other conditions which are beginning to have an impact on all systems of basic education. Basic schooling in the nineteenth century corresponded to childhood. Children now reach puberty long before the end of basic schooling and face at least another 3 years – in many cases 7 or 8 years – of education before they can become workers and thus full adults or citizens. The private and public spheres of education need to be readjusted to meet this change.

The other universal change is the impact of telecommunications and information technology. If children could acquire some rudiments of literacy in cities a century ago simply by observing street signs, they can receive a total education at present through readily accessible information technology. Schooling is redundant simply as a source of content and its transmission. Information technology does it much better. Basic schools exist only for children to meet each other and the adult referees of this discourse. But the conditions of meeting need to be negotiated. Children need to learn to co-operate and to compete. Competition needs to be open and equal and its aim needs to be related to future education and life even though its form – as much in rationalist systems as in others – can be cathartic and based on games. Co-operation needs to be delicately combined with competition if preparation for adult life is to be real. Yet co-operation is also intimate and may have to be placed in the setting of particular cultures rather than indiscriminately linked to public access.

6
Upper secondary institutions: General and vocational

Two traditions collide in the years between the end of basic schooling and entry to higher education. General education reaches a rite of passage in the final secondary school examination. Vocational education is a separate stream, determined as much by national differences in employment as by educational cultures. The current reconciliation is parallel with that of the 1960s to create common secondary education. For the assumption is that comparable teaching, learning and assessment need to be provided for all students up the age of 18–19 even though, subsequently, they pursue different paths.

National traditions differ. The final certificate of general education is of great symbolic value in much of western Europe but has lost currency in the USA and Japan. Specialization has been intense in Britain. Elsewhere a broad curriculum has prevailed but most countries have tried to find a balance between generalism and specialism. Distinctive philosophies of education of each country reach their highest expression in academic upper secondary education. Vocational education diverges between those countries such as France and the USA where it has traditionally been the function of public educational institutions and those such as Germany and Britain where employers for long have determined training.

Categories of collectivism and pluralism and of rationalism, humanism and naturalism help to describe these variations in the context of common pressures for change. Issues of access and control focus on the relative power of government, employers and higher education institutions rather than on families and local communities. In content, teaching and learning the humanist tradition, which was suppressed in early education, resurfaces while the naturalism of the family and growing child is replaced by that of adults at work and play. Specific questions focus less on methods of teaching and more on the assessment of skills and aptitudes.

Traditions and change in nations and regions

France and the European collectivist tradition

The collectivist tradition subordinated upper secondary education to state economic and social planning. The general and vocational branches are linked in content and control. The questions are how far 'inserting' individuals into occupational slots can survive when national economic planning is under threat and individuals no longer accept a state definition of their future lives. France represents a 'pure' wing of this tendency which, however, was exceeded in rigidity in the old Soviet Union while other European 'collectivist' systems exhibit significant variations.

France

Rational–encyclopaedic concepts of educational attainment and state prescription of national occupational needs have given a unity to French upper secondary education. The coherence was established by the creation of the *baccalauréat* by Napoleon in 1808 as a state certificate. Its contemporary expression is the 1989 government policy that 80% of the age group should reach *baccalauréat* standard by the year 2000.

This plan not only establishes universal upper secondary schooling. It also assumes an equivalence of general and vocational education. For most of the twentieth century, the two were kept separate. General education occurred in *lycées* which, although state schools, selected students at 11 or younger, and until the mid-century charged fees. Only 4% of the age group obtained the *baccalauréat* in 1946 and 12 % in 1965 (Halls, 1976: 129). The expansion of upper secondary education came after the creation of the common lower secondary school (*collège*) after 1963 and the transformation of the *lycée* into an upper secondary institution. The proportions of the age group gaining the *baccalauréat* rose to 26% in 1981 and 51% in 1992 (Robert, 1993: 168). Furthermore, almost 40% of those succeeding in 1992 gained the certificate in technical–vocational areas (France, 1993c: 68).

The integration of general and professional studies was made possible because vocational education has been a state responsibility since the late nineteenth century. The precedent was set in the Napoleonic period with the creation of *grandes écoles* in the higher education to train engineers for government service. Industrial competition from Britain and Germany in the late nineteenth century led government to take over lower-level vocational training culminating in the 1919 Astier Law through which employers paid a levy in return for the training of their young craft workers, part time, in state institutions (Charmasson, 1987: 470). The ensuing qualification, the *Certificat d'Aptitude Professionelle* (CAP), was awarded by the state and became a legal sine qua non of occupational practice.

With the introduction of common lower secondary education, the CAP courses transferred out of apprenticeship centres into technical upper secondary schools (*lycées professionels*) which provided courses also for technician level qualifications. In 1968, attempts were made to create equivalent general and vocational tracks through the *baccalauréat de technicien* (later *baccalauréat technologique*). The 1985 *baccalauréat professionel* in effect drew students from lower level vocational courses and was seen as the vehicle for the achievement of the target of 80% reaching *baccalauréat* standard. The CAP, which had been taken by over 40% of the age group in 1983, was expected to decline to cover the intractable 20% of 'failures' of French schooling.

This pattern of development was the product not only of state control of vocational education but also of state planning. The phase of *détermination* of future occupations after the age of 15 was controlled by French state economic planning which, since 1945, had related the provision of post-compulsory education to economic and occupational targets (Hatcham, 1992; Paul, 1985). However, national plans do not always accord with individual aspirations. There was resistance from those who were allocated to craft level preparation and a low rating by mature craft workers, compared with technicians, of the training they had received in the past (Tanguy, 1991: 138–42).

Unification of the broad principles of content across general and vocational courses had existed long before attempts at the creation of equivalences from the 1960s. All post-15 education was based on a core of rational–encyclopaedic study. Vocational elements were simply the equivalent of specialisms in the general education area. The programme of the three grade course leading to the *baccalauréat* covers the subjects of the lower secondary school with the exception that French is replaced by philosophy in the final grade. All students, whatever their specialism, must cover French, mathematics, science, a modern language, social studies, philosophy and physical education. All but the last must be passed in the final examination. With the exception of philosophy, the same applied to the *baccalauréat professionel*, the CAP and other courses (France, 1993c: 40–63). It is expected that all who have been awarded a certificate of the state will have demonstrated breadth of general education necessary for a citizen.

The rational ethos of this study is evident particularly in the specialisms and the kinds of aptitudes which the *baccalauréat* examinations test. The *baccalauréat* had divided into philosophy/letters (languages, literature, history) and mathematics/science branches in the 1850s. It was not until the 1960s that social sciences and technology were added and the sciences were split into separate physical and biological sections and a further three (industrial studies, business studies and information sciences) emerged in the *baccalauréat technologique*. Each main branch was divided into sub-sections. Students, in effect, spent a little more time in their specialist subjects (typically 6 hours when a subject was a specialism compared with 3 hours a week when it was basic) and were expected to reach higher standards. It was out of these divisions that informal status rankings emerged.

The classics section of letters retained predominant place at least until the 1950s and philosophy was the pre-eminent subject. Then mathematics and physical sciences replaced it and by the 1990s had such status that even those wishing to study, for instance literature, in higher education would choose the mathematics–physical science branch. Indeed its status had risen to such an extent that fears were expressed in government that it would produce a future élite of technological barbarians. Reforms of the 1990s counter this tendency by amalgamating the two science sections but their impact has yet to be seen. In contrast, the business studies section was the soft option despite the generally high standing of other parts of the *baccalauréat technologique*.

While status rankings may emerge because of job and higher education opportunities, the physical science section was seen as the best preparation for entry to *grandes écoles* most of which specialized in engineering; the technological version of the *baccalauréat* was needed to enter the popular university technological institutes, which also reflected the continued power of rational knowledge. Mathematics became the supreme test and indicator of capacity for rational thought.

Philosophy, in contrast, lost some of its lustre and its boundaries with French were weakened. Thought and written expression merged. 1993 papers on philosophy contained questions such as 'To what extent does imagination contribute to the happiness of man?' or 'Is it possible always to distinguish between work and leisure?' which in form, if not content, had changed little over 100 years. French offered passages from contemporary journalism or popular books of social comment for résumé and writing extended responses to quotations like 'Sport is the new religion of a world that believes in nothing'. Even essay titles which required reference to set texts were of the type 'What in your view is a good book?' (*Le Monde de L'Education*, September 1993: 103, 121, 127, 129). In effect thought and literary expression became characteristics of second-order rationality after the logic of mathematics.

Specialization is not allowed to undermine the demonstration of competence in a broad and standard examination. All subjects are tested by a combination of written examinations, oral tests and occasional practicals. A student in the science branch in 1995 is required to take nine written examinations of 3–4 hours each, one 4-hour practical and four orals of 15–30 minutes. A complex system of weighting gives much more importance to the specialist subjects of the branch studied by the student.

Standard and objective examinations have been sacrosanct in the French tradition. Any other form of assessment 'smells [of] privilege, political intervention, occult influences or even bribery' (Legrand, 1969: 128). While papers and examining are controlled regionally, results for each region have been published. Since 1992, the results of every upper secondary school in the country have also been made public in ways that allow national league tables to be constructed (*Le Monde de l'Education*, January 1995: 94). Yet achieving a pass is what matters rather than grades which have only a marginal impact on the value of the *baccalauréat* in gaining places in a few institutions of higher education. Entrance examinations for the élite *grandes écoles* are taken 2 years after the *baccalauréat*.

France has a different form of selection than northern European countries. It is the branch of study that distinguishes between élite and mass and that selection occurs at the beginning of the upper secondary course. Final results above a bare pass matter little. But the status ranking of the different branches is informal and to a degree reflects long established valuations of rational knowledge. Even with the expansion of the proportion taking *baccalauréat* courses, the core of rational skills is carefully maintained even through extreme simplification of the required tests. Furthermore, the intensity of the requirement of demonstrated capacity for rational thought at *baccalauréat* level inevitably trickles down to reinforce rational demands at lower levels of the system.

The control of vocational courses by the state allows the same principles to apply outside the traditional general academic area. All practical affairs could be based on rational first principles. Competence in science and mathematics especially was the basis of any vocational preparation. The industrial branch of the *baccalauréat technologique* had sub-sections in mechanical, electrical, electronic, civil and energy engineering; the *baccalauréat professionel* had 35 occupational sections and the CAP 235. Yet all courses were founded on firstly the core upper secondary course and secondly on the theoretical studies (usually mathematical and scientific) needed for the specialism while the required work experience elements for full-time courses (and many CAP students were part-time) ranged from 8 weeks over 2 or 3 years up to a maximum of a quarter of total study time (France, 1993c: 48, 58–63).

Despite the rapid growth of upper secondary education in France, certain traditions survive. The *baccalauréat* has almost mystical significance as a core national institution. It is also the perfect vehicle for the maintenance of a rational–encyclopaedic view of knowledge. As a result other agencies fail to exert an impact on upper secondary courses. Employers are relatively weak, though they complain about the flaws of the system. Higher education has less of an impact than in other systems since *baccalauréat* holders still largely choose their universities rather than the universities choosing their students.

Teachers in the *lycées* traditionally were a powerful intellectual caste, especially in the mid-twentieth century when they included so many of France's leading intellectuals, but the scholar apprentices who taught in *lycées* while spending 10 years to complete their *doctorat d'état* which assured academic careers have declined with the phasing out of this degree. The *agrégés* are still a powerful state–intellectual caste but are as likely now to teach in first cycle higher education as in the upper secondary course.

Changes in control have focused on institutional management. While 'market' approaches are limited in a system where young people can only attend the *lycées* in their own catchment area (*district scolaire*), the organizational complexities of running institutions with many branches have led to devolution of more power to school principals and their deputies who are responsible for the general climate and dynamism of the institution, the provision of a proper range of courses and relationships with students, parents, employers and the local community (France, 1993c: 39). Specialism in student courses creates organizational problems which can be resolved best at institutional level.

French upper secondary education is linked increasingly to higher education or work. Courses, teaching and assessment differ little between upper secondary education and first cycle higher education. As in other countries, employers now provide in-house training for recruits so that upper secondary qualifications, even of the vocational type, only signify capacity to undertake training. Courses provide the means to ensure that a majority of the age group continue education up to the age of 18. Inevitably standards of achievement may not be what they were when courses were confined to élites but the combination of the expectations of a minimum of rationally based intellectual competence and the survival of state qualifications reduce the size of the dramatically underachieving group found in some other countries.

Other countries in south and east Europe

Other European collectivist regimes share the French standardization of the upper secondary course, the pivotal position of state certificates of upper secondary education and state control of vocational education. However, the certificates of secondary education have not enjoyed in the other countries the currency they have in France. There are variations in the extent of economic planning and, crucially, in the status of vocational studies.

Access to upper secondary education has been open in most states though participation rates, while incorporating over 60% of 17 year olds in Spain and Greece, are still low in Portugal. All have distinctions between general and vocational courses and, among the latter, between those aiming at craft and technician levels. Proportions vary. More enter vocational than general courses in Italy but the reverse is the case in Spain and Greece. In all countries, craft level courses – often in separate institutions and provided in Italy by local authorities – tend to cater for those who underperformed at lower secondary level.

Italy, Belgium, Greece and Portugal have similar forms of progress through general academic education. In Italy, there is a drop-out rate of almost half in the 5-year course leading to the *maturità* but a 94% pass rate in the examination (Monasta, 1994: 168–69). This state certificate and its equivalent in the vocational section give automatic right to enrol in any university faculty. The Belgian five-grade academic course leads either to universities or non-university higher education. Greece has a 3-year course leading to a state certificate which allows entry to higher education but is delayed for those with lower grades. Spain differs. The *bachillerato* is awarded by internal school assessment, after three grades to the age of 17. Students are then required to follow a further year's course and take entrance tests set by universities – a procedure with parallels in Portugal.

In contrast, in eastern Europe, completion of upper secondary education over three grades usually was signified by internal assessment and higher education institutions invariably held their own entrance tests.

A common curriculum prevails in southern and eastern Europe which all should follow based on the same kinds of subjects as were taken in lower secondary education. This usually came from survival of the undifferentiated course which prevailed up to the 1960s and survived even longer in eastern Europe. Except in Spain and eastern Europe, the final certificate is awarded after external controlled traditional written examinations. Some specialization has entered most systems. Distinctions are made between humanities and sciences in Italy, Greece,

Spain and Portugal. Both sections focus largely on the same general list of subjects and specialization is usually delayed until the later part of the course.

While a humanist orientation is found to some extent in Greece and Italy, especially in the amount of time given to the classics and literature, broadly a rational–encyclopaedic ethos prevails even in the panoramic view of literature and history within a humanist perspective in Greece (Hodolidou, 1994). As in France, mathematics has become the prestige subject in most countries (Olmedilla, 1992: 138). Spain and Portugal also have philosophy as a core subject. The general trend towards a high status ranking of scientific–rational study of France is experienced elsewhere in southern Europe.

The vocational sector has not developed as effectively as in France. Italian vocational schools have drawn on a tradition of Catholic technical education but they attract students in part because the academic element is identical with that of the general education stream. Students lose little in future chances by opting for vocational education. In contrast, in Spain, despite recent industrial growth, as with Greece and Portugal vocational education cannot draw upon a traditional prestige nor a developed industrial system to support it and vocational courses do not give equal access to higher education (Meijer, 1991).

Vocational education in East Europe, though not enjoying the status of general education, was linked closely to employment during Communist rule. With the collapse of old economic institutions from the late 1980s this link was broken and the vocational institutions faced a loss of role. Where new economic activities emerged so did private vocational institutions charging high fees to train students in the relevant skills (Tomiak, 1995 56–57).

Pluralist traditions in Europe

There is less concordance among the pluralist societies of northern and insular Europe about upper secondary education than among the collectivist nations. General academic education moves towards humanist and individualist approaches. Yet rational encyclopaedism still infiltrates the content of upper secondary schooling in Germany and the Netherlands. Britain and Germany share a sharp separation of general education and vocational training which is more extreme than elsewhere in northern Europe. Despite these cross currents, Germany and the Netherlands can be viewed together while Scandinavia and Britain can be taken as contrastive cases.

Germany and the Netherlands

These countries are united in having selective academic all-through secondary schools, upper secondary general courses which have attempted to move from an older encyclopaedic to more individualist and specialist approaches and a more distinct separation of general and vocational education.

German upper secondary education has had a reputation for greater rigour and higher standards than other advanced countries since the nineteenth century. Not only the reports of Matthew Arnold and Michael Sadler reinforced this view. It is claimed that French *baccalauréat* pass rates are lower in regions close the German border because of the informal impact of these German standards. Students do not complete the course at least until the age of 19. The final state examination – the *Abitur* – was established in 1788. Yet its high standards have been associated with a conscious break in the whole ethos of study on entry to higher education and this shift makes the course leading to the *Abitur* more subject to political debate than the studies which precede it.

Until 1960, the three-grade upper secondary course was thoroughly encyclopaedic culminating in examinations in 10 subjects. The mid-nineteenth century orientation had been classical and humanist based on Latin and Greek (Teichler, 1965: 48). A division between language–humanities and mathematics–science specialisms had occurred at the end of the nineteenth century in *Gymnasien* of different orientations but this had not affected the common requirement to cover all subjects. The fundamental purpose was to complete general, standardized education so that the university student could be intellectually independent, mature and self-reliant. The course and examination were controlled by individual states rather than national regulators. But until 1970 only a minority participated. The proportion of the age group gaining the *Abitur* was 6% in 1960 and 11% in 1970 (Teichler, 1985: 51).

Despite protests from university academics and professional associations, the West German Conference of Ministers of Education agreed to a reduction in the number of compulsory subjects in 1960 and a range of branches not unlike that of France. Reform culminated in a much more specialized course in 1972. The compulsory course was to cover two-thirds of the time and would include, among others, German, mathematics and a foreign language. However, compulsory subjects could be confined to the earlier grades and examined by the school. The specialisms could include subjects such as law, geology and sociology (Fuhr, 1989: 105–6).

The weight of opposition to these proposals, especially in universities, led to revision in 1988. Basic courses in two of German, mathematics, or a foreign language must be taken in the external *Abitur* examination and the weighting of examination marks was tilted away from specialized advanced courses towards basic achievements in core subjects. In practice, as in other areas of German policy-making, federal compromises allow for individual states to move at different speeds. Southern states adopted the return to basics with enthusiasm whereas some in the north tried to delay implementation and maintain diversity of student choice (Fuhr, 1989: 109–10).

The crucial undercurrent of the debate was the numbers taking the *Abitur* and its articulation with entrance to higher education. By 1986 over 20% of the age group received the *Abitur* (Fuhr, 1989: 208–9). It had been a universal passport to any university and any faculty. But in the 1970s it had become possible to enter non-university higher education by other means and certain university courses required higher grades or further tests for entry.

Lengthy written examinations, often as long as 6 hours, prevailed in the *Abitur*. The debate over reform centred upon school level assessment of part of the course. In the diverse pluralist culture there was also confusion between specialization as an inevitable process to prepare for higher education and as a reflection of the range of personal interests of students. Commitment to standards in intellectually demanding areas remained powerful.

The Netherlands, like Austria and parts of Switzerland, had much in common with Germany. The general upper secondary education was provided in selective academic schools. Separation between humanities and sciences was stronger in the Netherlands than in Germany and the curriculum was more open to school determination. But the final examination is centrally controlled and includes six or seven compulsory subjects. Debates in the late 1980s focused on whether mathematics and a second foreign language should be added to Dutch and a first foreign language as compulsory subjects (Brink and Bruggen, 1990: 285). As in Germany, there was a continued commitment to a broad, standard, encyclopaedic curriculum and also pressures for student choice of specialisms which, in the minds of some, prepared for higher education and, for others, responded to personal student choice. The desirable balance between school-based courses and assessment and central control provided another dimension to this debate.

The Dutch debate, like that of Germany, emerged in a stratified secondary school system and in a tradition of university education that has been humanist in orientation and emphasizes student intellectual independence. While proportions taking the general academic course have risen substantially, the Netherlands has a majority of higher education students in specialized non-university institutions while universities have demanded additional qualifications for subjects in high demand. The old standard academic upper secondary course is still peripheral in the whole system.

German upper secondary level vocational education has excited world-wide interest and admiration, often based on misapprehension, in recent years. In the late 1980s close to 70% of the age group gained a vocational qualification and, remarkably, less than 10% gained no recognized certificate.

Despite the growth of full-time vocational schools (*Berufsfachschulen*) in Germany which combine rigorous general education with vocational training (England and Wales DFE/HMI, 1993) the foundation is the dual-system. The majority of young people leaving school at 16 are taken on as apprentices and combine systematic training in work with part-time general education in *Berufsschulen*. Apprenticeship and training have been rigorously protected by government. A vocational training act of 1969 required planned in-company training in 374 recognized skilled occupations. The norm was for particular workers – *Meisters* – with special qualifications to take responsibility for training apprentices. Certificates of qualification had a legal force and monopoly and were based on examinations which were controlled mainly by employer organizations.

This survival of apprenticeship – covering more occupations than in other countries – had its origins in nineteenth-century legislation. The medieval guilds of skilled workers had been maintained by law in 1731 in Prussia. Bismarck's federal industrial legislation of the 1880s – notably a law of 1897, which was designed to maintain traditional institutions against the socially disruptive forces of industrialism – required that the guild structure and especially apprenticeship should be maintained in the new industrial cartels. The German craft system was based on protectionism (Dessinger, 1994).

The *Berufsschulen* have provided general education in German, community studies and religion as well as vocationally related studies in science and mathematics. The outcome has been a vocational system which is dislocated from general education and whose origins and survival are better explained by the structure of German industry than by education (Marsden and Ryan, 1991).

Education and training are separated in ways that would not be acceptable in France. Training has status not only because of the strong practical tradition in Germany but also because of the peripherality of higher academic education. Yet individual students ·negotiate this difference with some skill. Up to 20% of apprentices since the late 1980s have gained the *Abitur* before beginning work. Substantial numbers of university students have a legally recognized vocational certificate. German students are brought up in a tradition which would be unacceptable elsewhere – that education is completed nearer the thirtieth birthday than the twentieth – and can gain the best of both educational and training worlds. The archaic tradition of the nineteenth century perpetual student may now be appropriate for the contemporary world.

The Netherlands had the dual-system but never quite in the central position of that of Germany. Vocational training, also with a high residual status closer to Germany than to Britain and France, was conducted more completely in full-time upper secondary and higher education institutions. Government has intervened because of the tendency of such courses to fail to keep up with changes in work (Liebrand, 1991). However, as in France and Britain, full-time vocational courses take on the function of absorbing those who cannot find work and educational underachievers and have a second obligation to offer open opportunities for higher study (Vonken and Onstenk, 1995).

Scandinavia

Scandinavian countries have had an upper secondary school very similar to that of Germany together with separate vocational education. They have attempted since the 1960s to democratize this sector from different conceptions of democratization. Denmark, at one extreme, followed the individualization associated with the liberal wing of the German reform movement while Sweden, at the other, sought a more radical version of the integration of general and vocational education of France. Both views were proposed within a general conception of local, institutional choices but the Swedish version retained some residual collectivist elements.

Nordic countries until the 1960s had a *gymnasium* which was Germanic in character as well as in name. A standard, many-subject course was divided into broad humanities–languages and science branches. Vocational education was linked to apprenticeship and separate training institutions. The general aims of academic education were encyclopaedic preparing for a humanist university.

The Danish reform strategy in the early 1980s, with some echoes in Norway, was to import the socially co-operative, democratic ethos of the *folkeskole* into the *gymnasium*. The U90 reform of 1978 proposed individual student choice of subjects, together with a topic-orientation and interdisciplinary teaching. Foreign languages were to be less important. By the time reform began to be implemented after 1987, there was a return to branches of study and a common core. The core included Danish, history, art and religion but not a foreign language or mathematics. Branches such as languages or mathematics had compulsory subjects attached to them. But optional subjects, including those studied at an advanced level, occupied almost half the teaching in the final year of the three grade course and were assessed through a large individual student written assignment in contrast to the central, state examinations for core and compulsory subjects.

Yet the broad structure of upper secondary education was not changed. Only about one third of students entered the *gymnasium*. The others entered vocational courses which distinguished between those at a higher level with substantial general education elements and the craft courses usually taken part-time by apprentices in work. A law of 1989 attempted to integrate the two while maintaining work experience elements. Yet, less than 10% failed to get any post-compulsory education and Danish vocational education has been well regarded by students and employers (Winther-Jensen, 1994: 46–58).

The Swedish reform was unique in Europe but, as in Denmark, came from the imperative to extend the common school beyond compulsory education. From 1968, general and vocational education was integrated in multipurpose three-grade institutions. The aim was to remove distinctions on social grounds and to permit students to combine general and vocational courses. But, in practice, long academic courses were distinguished from shorter (1- or 2-year) practical–vocational lines. And the 25 subject list from which choices were made did not provide sufficient specialization in vocational areas which increasingly began to be grouped (Ekholm, 1985: 104–7).

The integration was taken further by abolishing the final examination in 1977. Assessment was entirely school-based though carried out with reference to state-determined scales of achievement (reinforced by national evaluation of the assessments of each institutions). So universities select students through their own entrance examinations (Fagerlind, 1992).

The puzzle, from the perspective of other countries, is that the Swedish government tests and evaluates students more systematically than other countries but has no final certificate of upper secondary education. Individual choice and social equality have been sought within a framework of close central evaluation. Yet Sweden in this respect has moved towards a British, American and Japanese approach of selecting students at the end of upper secondary course rather than at or near the beginning when allocation to branches of study occur as in most of the rest of western Europe. In both Denmark and Sweden a collectivist commitment to standard programmes and/or examinations and, indeed, to rationalist–encyclopaedic knowledge was weaker than even in Germany or the Netherlands.

Britain

The impact of Britain's privatist political culture becomes clear in upper secondary level education. General academic education, in England but less so in Scotland, is dominated by a certificate awarded by universities and not by the state. Vocational education traditionally has been controlled by employers and professional bodies in co-operation with minor partners in peripheral sectors of public education. Yet Britain has for long had the specialism, student choice and the university-controlled entry to higher education to which other countries are moving.

There is strong defence in England for a supposedly traditional form of upper secondary education which in fact is younger than many of its supporters. The older final qualification of secondary education, the School Certificate, itself was born in the late nineteenth century. It was transformed into the intermediate qualification, the General Certificate of Education Ordinary Level in 1951 and then the General Certificate of Secondary Education in the 1980s, taken at the end of lower secondary school. There has never been an equivalent of the *baccalauréat* or *Abitur* in England.

The upper secondary course, which usually only lasts 2 years, only grew in the mid-twentieth century to select students for scholarships rather than to provide for general university entrance. While Oxford and Cambridge maintained their own entrance tests, universities established from the nineteenth century used the School Certificate. In 1939, it was still possible to enter universities on the basis of this lower level qualification. Only after 1945 did universities in general demand the Higher School Certificate renamed the General Certificate of Education Advanced ('A') level, in 1951. Yet the 'A' levels had never applied in Scotland where four or five subjects were studied and examinations taken a year earlier.

The privatist and especially selective nature of the 'A' level came from its origins. Examinations were run by universities or groups of universities, initially as entrance tests. Government exercised only light regulation over these semi-autonomous bodies while the content of courses reflected the specialist studies that universities wanted from their entrants (Petch, 1953). Proportions studying 'A' levels remained small and even to date have reached only about 25% of the age group. Furthermore they are stringently graded with a pass rate of around 70%

and grades of pass ranging from A to E.

University control meant that the 'A' levels mirrored university study rather than that of the school. Typical questions in an externally set written paper called for considerable analytical and/or literary abilities for success. The depth of study frequently exceeded that required in universities. And higher education institutions were concerned about the grade in the subject which the candidate proposed to study in higher education. Sometimes two, usually three and occasionally four subjects were followed most frequently in cognate areas. Very few candidates would have studied all of English, a foreign language and mathematics. Some would have studied none of these.

Criticisms of lack of breadth of study and of the élitist character of the 'A' levels have been common since the 1960s. These are not entirely justified since entrance to higher education required also passes in additional subjects at the 16+ examination but specialism lowered the status of all but the 'A' level subjects. The depth of study permitted short degrees in higher education. But élitism became a barrier to expansion of higher education in the 1990s. Though of much later and less legitimate birth than the French *baccalauréat* or German *Abitur*, the 'A' level acquired a similar cachet of a distinctive national institution. The Prime Minister's forward to a government reform document of 1991 described the 'A' level as 'the benchmark of academic excellence' (England and Wales DES, 1991: 1). The 'A' level course is not regulated by the National Curriculum or national assessment.

'A' level was the conduit for the inclusion of humanism as well as specialization and individualism in the upper secondary course. Humanism assumed intuitive, revelatory responses of learners to texts. The possibility of moral enlightenment, of sensitive appreciation of moral choices in human action could come as much from a narrow choice of sources as a wide one. The typical humanities courses in 'A' level permitted such approaches, notably in English literature (since English language courses in 'A' level were rare), history and modern languages concentrated on humanist study of foreign literature rather than the linguistic structures. 'A'-level history courses focused on narrow areas such as English history from 1066 to 1307 and its European background from 800 to 1485 even though a university history course would expect a wide sweep of the whole of English history. Literature for the 2-year course could be confined to six books – two Shakespeare plays, the works of two poets and two novels each of which could be taken indiscriminately from five centuries (more if Chaucer was one) – of English literature where university courses would expect a synoptic coverage.

Sciences and mathematics did not fit easily into this scheme. Mathematics was concerned with the solution of problems exclusively using mathematical notation. Physics, chemistry and biology focused upon the systematic reporting of scientific processes and the exhibition of capacity to exemplify these schemes in practical demonstrations. At the highest levels, mathematics and science were seen to be deficient because they did not have a literary and moral content – so that students competing for élite universities were required to take literary/moral/philosophical examinations while the literary skills of others were neglected which could reinforce the sense of inadequacy of these specialists.

With the expansion of numbers taking 'A' levels so the tables were reversed. Low attaining humanities students were required essentially to have a basic capacity for literary presentation through which to organize factual information and to provide not particularly insightful personal responses. Mathematics and science students were still expected to solve specific mathematical problems or describe scientific processes in ways that expected accuracy and convergent understanding. So mathematics and science were perceived to be more difficult for average students.

Vocational preparation in England traditionally has been totally divorced from education. This institutional separation has been greatest at higher professional levels where qualifications to practise law, engineering or accountancy were controlled entirely by professional associations unconnected with education, and even now are taken part-time, often by independent study by those in work. Craft and technician qualifications have also been controlled by employers as in Germany but state institutions emerged in the late nineteenth century to provide courses to prepare for them. Courses and examinations were determined and regulated as much by employer associations as educational institutions. Study was by day release or in evenings. And craft workers, in contrast with France, had no requirement to gain such qualifications to be regarded as skilled and fit to practise.

Vocational qualifications for both technician and craft levels emerged which were unconnected in level to GCE. Separate courses and diplomas emerged at broadly three levels, the highest of which was generally regarded as above 'A' level. But there was no rate of exchange between a general education and a vocational qualification. They had different purposes. Formal vocational courses were often about learning the manuals of standard, agreed professional practice. Intellectual, cognitive, rational and literary skills were simply means to being able to show this familiarity. Certain courses would have the educational prerequisites to be able to systematize professional practice.

After a number of initiatives in the 1980s, including attempts to identify core skills with a generic vocational application (Lawson, 1992), a new system of equivalences emerged in 1991. National Vocational Qualifications (NVQ) were made equivalent to general education certificates (England and Wales DES/HMI, 1991c: 18). And expansion of provision occurred in further education colleges, hitherto institutional anomalies that became part of a separate upper secondary education sector from 1992. The major difficulty was that NVQs had both general and specific branches. The general (GNVQ) became a vocationally coloured version of GCSE and 'A' level which were treated with suspicion by universities while the specific vocational courses (NVQs) were not always viewed as providing an adequate practical training by employers.

The British system, despite its many critics, has great strengths which were vitiated by inadequate or over-zealous application. 'O' level GCE and GCSE in their previous incarnation as the School Certificate were the equivalent of the intermediate 'basic' course element of upper secondary education which developed elsewhere in the 1970s. Instead of being lengthened by a year to justify this equivalence it disintegrated into separate subjects to allow more students to achieve passes in a few subjects in which they were talented. The 'A' level is a specialist course of the type which began to be introduced in other countries as the advanced element of upper secondary education. It would have made more sense for it to be a 1-year course especially designed for higher education entrance as developed in Scotland. A similar but so far failed experiment of the Advanced Supplementary level has been introduced in England but cannot supplant the well-rooted 'A' level.

The problems of reform partly spring from politics and political ideology. When examinations are used by higher education institutions and employers to select entrants, it is difficult to change what has become the equivalent of a monetary currency. The major source of change is likely to be the introduction of tests by higher education institutions and employers.

Similarly the major problems of vocational education came largely from the unwillingness of companies to train young workers or to insist that they succeeded in vocational examinations. As vocational education becomes a form of general education so it loses its vocational status. While similar problems may exist in France, there is the residue of a French state responsibility for vocational qualification to support an otherwise flawed approach. In Britain, the expansion of vocational courses was a reaction to the sharp decline in employer training for those completing lower secondary education as well as the growth of youth unemployment since mid-1970s (Marsden and Ryan, 1991). In view of the tradition of on-the-job training, the real revival of vocational education is likely to be sparked by employers.

The USA and Japan

Solutions have been found to European problems in the USA and Japan. Both have serious weaknesses but the skeleton of an upper secondary education for all has existed in the USA for a century while Japan has more fully, though not completely, made vocational education a matter for employers and workers following a universally provided full general secondary education.

The USA

The identified, public 'crisis' of American schooling, even though it had separate phases in the late 1950s and early 1980s, has concentrated on the 4-year High School which has been completed by about 80% of 14–18 year olds since the 1970s. Ironically, this neighbourhood High School, which has been accused of failing to maintain basic educational standards, has the breadth and variety of courses and in other countries is still seen as the model for future development.

The American High School provided a comprehensive curriculum of academic, vocational, social adjustment and recreational subjects. It catered for those who would enter higher education and those who would enter work. It also prepared students to be well-rounded participants in local communities. In the late nineteenth and early twentieth centuries, the High School prepared students for local futures so the employers and higher education institutions of the vicinity would have knowledge of the standards and achievements of the High Schools. There was no official system of external examining or curriculum control. High Schools assessed their own students and awarded their own certificates. Upper secondary education was unified and local in control and content with over half the funding coming from School Districts in 1960 (Stocking, 1985: 240).

By the 1960s, a majority of high-school leavers were entering higher education. Vocational courses to prepare for jobs were provided in the post-High School Community Colleges. The High School curriculum was associated with undemanding standards in general education and the neglect of mathematics and foreign languages, especially in the period following the launch of the Soviet Sputnik in 1957 which created a climate of recrimination about American education. An influential book by James Conant proposed fast-track academic courses and attention to mathematics, science and foreign languages (Conant, 1959).

The strictures emerging from the debate in the late 1950s had an impact. Fast-tracks emerged including those which allowed students to take higher education level courses in High Schools. 'Magnet Schools' in deprived urban areas offered high-standard education from the 1970s. By 1982, 38% of students were in High School programmes that were designated as 'academic' (Stocking, 1985: 241). Private testing agencies, which had been used since 1900 to select students for élite higher education institutions and especially the Standard Aptitude/ Attainment Test (SAT) which had existed since 1927 flourished so that about a third of all students were taking them by the 1980s. State governments introduced their own tests of basic competence. Again, as in the 1920s, within the American localist–privatist culture, a hard 'utilitarian' solution was found to problems of unevenness.

The remaining problem was that the new utilitarianism left behind a very substantial minority of underachievers whose lack of preparation came from both failure to achieve literary and mathematical standards in earlier education and from the unfocused nature of the High School curriculum. A study of 1981 identified three typical High School student transcripts which indicated that no students had followed any single subject over more than two grades of the 4-year course, that each followed between 25 and 30 distinct courses while at High School, none included a foreign language and that each student had between five and 15 courses of a social–recreational type (myths and folklore, science fiction, driver education, mixed glee club, ceramics, choir, family relations, photography, horticulture, team sports) compared with between three and 12 academic courses (Boyer, 1983: 81–83).

The great range of subjects taken by students in the American High School may encourage a flexibility of responses of students to different subjects which is missing in the narrower European content. This call for adaptability has been particular to American optimistic, future-orientated values and is relevant to expectations of whole-life learning which are stronger in American than European cultures. Teaching styles, despite large and diverse classes, emphasize group discussion and student response. Non-American observers find students are articulate and confident (England and Wales DES/HMI, 1990).

The deficiencies of the American High School have both culture-specific origins and general characteristics of universal upper secondary education which other countries are beginning to face. The local tradition of control does make it difficult to orientate students and teachers to national or international standards as has been possible in other countries. The pragmatic view of knowledge makes hierarchies of core, cumulative and peripheral studies difficult to construct and operate. Examinations without a powerful symbolic national cachet cannot easily be introduced. Testing by both national agencies, including the SATs, and within schools tends to be of a multiple-choice, single response type because of lack of a national standard. Reductionism, as in Henry Ford automobile factories in the 1920s, prevails in testing with the result that teaching and testing are one dimensional and there is little scope, for instance, for the sustained student writing which is the mark of almost all European systems (Boyer, 1983: 88–91, 142–49).

Yet American High Schools are for all so that 'drop-outs' are viewed as deviants. And the range of relevant knowledge and skill for 14–18 year olds is vast. Institutions have difficulty in organizing teaching in the face of this diversity. An American teacher suggested: 'Time is the currency of teaching. We barter with time. Every day we make small concessions, small trade-offs but in the end we know it's going to defeat us' (Boyer, 1983: 142). The most successful students are those who develop their own effective strategies for handling diversity and the overcrowding of experience – a view of student progress consistent with contest values. The majority are far less effective, indicating the limitations of the contest norm. And High Schools as organizations are not able, especially with classes of 30 students, to provide sufficient real teaching and to encourage real learning. Other systems may face these problems increasingly as participation becomes universal yet individual futures become more diverse.

Japan

Japan provides an internationally relevant alternative because it has had higher levels of participation in upper secondary education than any other country, including the USA, since the 1970s. There is a peculiar vocational stream, catering only for about 25%, controlled by the education system yet providing for one particular sector of the economy.

Japan provides a benchmark for the rest of the world in having had close to universal three-grade upper secondary schooling since 1975. In 1920, 25% of the age group were students at this level, far above the European norm and not greatly different from the USA. By 1940 the proportion was close to 50% (Cummings, 1985: 145). In 1991 it was 96% (Japan, 1993: 21). But universality is combined with a selection process unlike western countries and, apart from the 25% in vocational schools, a uniform and unspecialized curriculum.

Parent and student demand has driven the expansion of upper

secondary education. Even public schools charge tuition fees which amounted to almost 30% of their total income in 1990 (Japan, 1993: 100). While a diverse, stratified system was replaced after 1945, under the influence of the American Occupation administration, by common neighbourhood schools, the pressure of parent demand has created schools of differing prestige, measured by their success in gaining places for their students in the best universities, and the more popular have highly competitive entrance examinations. There is a common school with a uniformity of basic achievement which is unmatched in the West but above it are those institutions which rise and fall in popular estimation. This peculiar combination of high uniform standards and intense competition is rarely seen in Europe or North America.

This characteristic, however, may be associated with curriculum conservatism. The upper secondary curriculum, even including the vocational schools, is standard and encyclopaedic. All students must complete at least 35 out of the required 80 credits in Japanese, history or geography, civics, mathematics, science, health, physical education, art and home economics. The elective courses are taken from a relatively small number of options in the same subject groups with the addition of foreign languages though vocational schools together with specialized schools and new 'comprehensive' schools from 1994 provide a wider range elective areas including, for instance, information science and international studies (Japan, 1993: 60–61, 64–65). In practice, students choose options in such a way that they specialize in humanities or sciences. These variations do not change a condition where there is perhaps a greater uniformity of upper secondary teaching than in any other large industrial country.

In contrast to basic schooling, uniformity is not entirely an outcome of central government prescription. Official syllabuses are less prescriptive for the upper secondary stage though the textbook remains influential. Teachers, in some subjects, introduce a variety of interpretations of subject matter as well as teaching with style, elegance and wit. Assessment is in hands of teachers at school level with no state external examinations.

Instead the major pressure comes from university entrance examinations. Each university (including the private) sets its own entrance tests in the range of subjects of the state curriculum. The emphasis is on knowledge tested by single response or multiple choice examinations (Rohlen, 1983: 90–99). Even when a common examination was introduced in 1979, the most prestigious institutions such as the University of Tokyo continued to set their own additional tests which have become more specialized (Frost, 1992: 28).

Competition matters because the great companies recruit from the most prestigious universities. The prestige associated with being a 'salaryman' in one of these industrial enterprises thus distorts upper secondary school teaching and learning. Yet in some ways the combination of employer policy and popular motivation have created an upper secondary school curriculum which has solved or evaded many of the problems of western countries. Training is so fully provided within the company that vocational concerns can be ignored by most students until they start work. In these conditions, students can concentrate single-mindedly on achieving basic standards or better of general education. Social, recreational, individual aims can be postponed to the more relaxed higher education course. The only clouds in this efficient system are the maintenance of self-sacrificing individual motivation and the encouragement of both more individual creativity and knowledge of the outside world, at least among some students, in the Japanese economic interest. Recent introduction of alternative high school courses is a recognition of these potential problems.

The discordant, anomalous element of Japanese provision is the vocational school. While the general educational achievements and the quality of vocational training of these institutions have been viewed favourably by western commentators (Prais, 1986), they have also been identified as the centres for congregation of school refusers who have dropped out of competition and exhibit a variety of delinquent characteristics (Inui and Hosogane, 1995). Their economic justification was the need of small enterprises for workers with vocational skills which the business could not provide. On a more general level, they suggest a less optimistic scenario of future economic–educational development in Japan.

Conclusion

The differences between major countries in educational provision for the 15–19 age group remain considerable. Each country has particular strengths and weaknesses which reflect political and economic as well as educational traditions. The attainment of a common international standard is unlikely as long as each country retains deep attachment to the achievements of the past. Yet there are some common international pressures which need to be taken into account by all.

Near universal upper secondary education cannot be avoided. Japan has had it for 20 years. All major industrial countries have over half the age group up to 18 in education. Young people below the age of 18 are unemployable, except in the most marginal areas, both because of their lack of currently relevant occupational skills and their incapacity to take on the great personal responsibilities for any kind of work in economies stressing the accountability of every employee. The contemporary issues are whether near universality means 80, 90 or 95% age group participation and how quickly first-phase higher education also becomes universal.

Education up to the age of 18 must necessarily be general. Narrowly vocational courses for this cohort are redundant. Future workers need general intellectual capacities which cannot be achieved for the majority at the end of basic schooling. Occupational training is no longer possible in state educational institutions. As early as 1981 American employers were recognizing that 'instruction must now be so specialized and the necessary equipment must be so sophisticated that it is difficult to create complete vocational programs' (Boyer, 1983: 122). Even the vaunted German dual system is taking increasing numbers of apprentices at the age of 19 after full secondary education. Employers inevitably will provide training for their recruits because of specialization. But they will require higher initial standards of education.

The content of general education is not internationally agreed. There is a clear need for higher standards of achievement in the national language, foreign languages, mathematics, science, social studies and technology. But national, standard curricula are no longer attainable as in basic schooling. After 10–14 years of education, the range of attainment of 16 year olds is too great for them to be taught to one standard. Particular gifts of all young people, of specialized as well as of a general kind, need to be developed after 16. Artistic, physical, manual as well as particular intellectual talents need space to flower. Yet general education to basic levels need to be maintained by all.

This diversity allows for often dysfunctional, archaic traditions to survive in different countries or, in many cases, temporary and inadequate solutions to take root. The common standard curriculum of Japan has universal relevance but the pressure for narrowly convergent achievement puts demands on student and parent motivation that cannot be sustained in most other countries, nor over a longer time span in Japan. The measurement of student attainment through narrow testing is a product of competition rather than of appropriate ways of judging what has been achieved. This danger of allowing means to determine ends, especially in competitive examinations, is found in several countries.

At the other extreme, practical and vocational studies in European countries give expression to the naturalism of being an adult with capacities well beyond the narrowly intellectual. Yet these courses should be part of general development rather than occupational preparation. Official disingenuousness prevails about 'vocational' courses which may have value in helping young people to develop and possibly to overcome an earlier distaste for academic study but are no longer properly vocational. 'Vocational' courses must be properly and primarily aimed at developing general intellectual capacities to higher levels. A naturalism which takes into account social and recreational interests of adult life is also important but can disintegrate into the ephemeral self-indulgence of the American High School.

Of course, these diverse aims need to be achieved within more limited public and indeed private budgets. To meet all the legitimate aims of teaching and learning in upper secondary education would be prohibitively expensive. Concentration on the basic general curriculum is more realistic and cost-efficient. Some kinds of non-standard education may have to be privately provided or offered to some on the basis of selection as with sports, dance and art. Furthermore, comprehensive upper secondary education institutions become so complex in their offerings that they run up against the limits of organizational capacity. American High Schools, often institutions with enrolments of thousands, face organizational overload. Two-tier provision with different institutions offering basic and public or specialized and private courses may be the solution.

The variety of provision across countries suggests a tenacious commitment to the past in face of the complexities of the present. State certificates of secondary education, nationally standard courses and separate vocational sectors in many European countries are indicators of ancient traditions which survive because a contemporary usefulness can still be squeezed out of them and their abolition may worsen matters if clearly better alternatives have not been developed. But their archaic nature and their short life span need to be recognized. They are certainly not transferable to other countries, especially when their current temporary usefulness is based on specific national cultures of control and content.

The viability of maintaining various established practices and of introducing innovations depends on the changing nature of employment and of higher education. The former requires a different kind of approach than this book can offer. Higher education needs to be examined more fully because its impact on earlier levels of education is crucial.

7

Higher education

Higher education is more complex than any of levels that precede it. While its students are no more heterogenous since they are only a selected segment of the same people who were in schools a few years earlier, the variety of functions of higher education creates complexity. Higher education institutions do more than teach for 'knowledge is the common substance ... research creates it; scholarship preserves, refines, and modifies it; teaching and service disseminates it' (Clark, 1984: 107). All these activities can be carried on not only in the same institution but also by the same teacher/academic. Knowledge creation has constituencies in the wider society beyond students. Even within teaching and learning, the expansion of higher education in most industrial countries in recent years generates more diversity since heterogeneous adult occupational futures and personal, social and cultural aspirations cannot be homogenized even to the limited degrees that applied to children and youth.

The idea of national higher education traditions raises objections. Higher education is global in ways that no other sector approaches. The term university emerged to describe an institution which served more than one country. Its teacher – researchers have contacts throughout the world which play important roles in the definition of their research and teaching. Students migrate, as much now between industrial countries as between rich and poor areas. Above all, knowledge circulates globally and this transmission is accelerated by specialization which can mean that a specific research topic may be investigated only by six people in six different countries.

Yet international convergence in what is taught and learned may be as elusive as it was in the early nineteenth century when universities were reformed and reinvigorated by nationalism as well as by industrialism and urbanism. Higher education provides the reservoirs of distinct national, sometimes also local cultures which differ markedly from each other and which replenish the pools of distinctive national characters of knowledge which mark out not only schools but the activity of public life more widely.

The variety of national traditions has been noted over a long period. Abraham Flexner in 1930 described differences between German, English and American universities but curiously omitted the equally distinctive French (Flexner, 1968). The recent expansion of numbers of students – to include those who will be future nurses as well as medical doctors; teachers in nursery schools as well as in higher education; and public officials in clerical as well as in administrative grades – has accentuated rather than reduced the differences between national systems. Higher education institutions are stratified vertically in some countries and horizontally in others. There is no standard in length or status of courses. Above all, what is taught, learned and assessed can still diverge sharply between nations.

As with other levels of education, these differences can be described and explained most effectively by relating them both to prevailing views of knowledge and to political cultures. The purposes of higher education differ between countries in terms of rationalist, humanist and, with different emphases, naturalist traditions of education as much as schools. The place of higher education in wider society still differs in collectivist and pluralist political cultures of varying hues.

Collectivist traditions in Europe

While higher education institutions in many countries are fully or partly autonomous, in the southern and eastern European tradition they are as much organs of the central state as schools. Their teachers are state officials and their courses need to be approved by government. Research and teaching are carried on in separate institutions. Above all rationalist views of knowledge prevail and inform the training of professionals in a wide range of occupations. Yet this type has taken on a number of different configurations with the expansion of enrolments in various countries even though there is a similarity in these responses when compared with countries with pluralist traditions.

France

Radical reform of French universities after the 1968 student revolt was unparalleled in modern Europe. Yet the university, while overwhelmingly the largest in student numbers, may not be the pivotal higher education institution in France. The University of Paris, formally established in the twelfth century, had been, with Bologna, one of the two great international and independent universities of Europe in the Middle Ages. Its decline was sharp. The pinnacle of contemporary higher education – the *grande école* – emerged after the 1789 Revolution as an organ of state planning and transformation. When the universities revived at the end of the nineteenth century it was as the second-class institutions which they have been ever since.

The *grande école* has remained an élite institution taking about 10% of all higher education students (Neave, 1985: 15, 23). Selection is through a competitive examination taken 2 years after the *baccalauréat*, in the past exclusively following a course in designated upper secondary schools but more recently also by students completing 2 years in universities. Two-year courses lead to diplomas which have no equivalent in the universities but which have great value in securing the best jobs. Of the 226 institutions some have a higher status, notably the *École Polytechnique* and the *École Normale Supérieure*, both founded by Napoleon, the first to train engineers and the second for secondary school teachers. After 1945, the prestigious *École National d'Administration* was created as a post-graduate institution mainly for working civil servants. Most institutions provide courses in science and engineering. They are run by various government ministries and their students, who are paid salaries and often wear military uniforms, do not experience the savage drop-out rates of universities. The state function and the predominant science-based teaching of these institutions in turn affects the values of French higher education as a whole.

Universities were more slowly conquered by the state. Despite the 're-creation' in 1896 of 15 universities, they remained loose federations of separate faculties – medicine, pharmacy, law, letters and science – each preparing for specific occupations. Possession of the *baccalauréat* gave students the right to enrol in any faculty of any university. The degree of *licence*, taken after 3 years, was a state qualification with state syllabuses but the majority of those who had enrolled failed to achieve this qualification. The student revolt of 1968, which almost unseated the President of France, was a product of overcrowding and failure. It created the conditions for a reform which more fully brought higher education under the direction of the state.

The outcome of 1968 Faure law was a sub-division of the old universities (with the University of Paris turned into 13 separate universities) and the creation of teaching and research schools each with designated areas and levels of work. More significant was the horizontally layered system of access and study. A 2-year first cycle led to the *diplôme universitaire d'études générales* (DUEG), its science and technology equivalent (DUEST) and similar diplomas. The intention was to reduce the drop-out rate by releasing many students into the labour market at an earlier stage. This had economic planning and statist–egalitarian functions. The first cycle was common to all students. It was even equivalent to the *grandes écoles* entry preparation courses and to sub-higher education institutions such as the primary teacher training colleges (which then began to prepare for the DUEG) and higher technician courses which remained in selected technical upper secondary schools. Two year *instituts universitaires de technologie*, created in 1966, in contrast became highly regarded institutions.

The 1968 reform has been relatively effective in absorbing the expansion of student numbers which reached 40% of 20 year olds in 1990. The imposition of this kind of uniformity depended on powerful government direction which has been less possible in pluralist systems. Students did not, however, obey these dictats. Most who completed the first diploma spent another year preparing for the *licence* or two for the *maîtrise*. Those entering schools of medicine or pharmacy followed longer courses also leading to state controlled degrees, which like lower level vocational qualifications, bestowed state certification of the right to practise a profession. Even post-graduate qualifications for those completing general degrees were predominantly diplomas with a combined intellectual–professional character, notably the *diplôme d'études approfondies*. The most prestigious post-graduate qualification for those in general areas remained the state-controlled and highly competitive *agrégation*.

A common first cycle assumed a certain communality of study. Rationalism pervaded French higher education as much as in the schools. Its most influential twentieth century expression as the basis for higher education came from the Spanish writer Jose Ortega y Gasset (1946). His concept of a general culture was Cartesian and was pointedly opposed to German and English humanism. He lauded the medieval conception where:

> '"General culture" was not an ornament for the mind or a training of character. It was, on the contrary, the system of ideas, concerning the world and humanity. It was consequently the repertoire of convictions which became the effective guide of existence.'

This scholastic view was still relevant because:

> 'Life is a chaos, a tangled and confused jungle in which man is lost. But his mind reacts against the sensation of bewilderment: he labours to find "roads", "ways" through the woods in the form of clear, firm ideas concerning the universe, positive convictions about the nature of things. The ensemble or system of these ideas, is culture in the true sense of the term; it is precisely the opposite of external ornament ....

We cannot live on the human level without ideas. We are our ideas.'
(Ortega y Gasset, 1946: 43–44)

This rationalism provided the cement of teaching and learning at every
level of higher education. This consistency may be indicated by placing a
1994 question for students at the *École National d'Administration* '"If
the state is strong it will crush us; if it is weak we will perish" Discuss'
alongside one of 1993 in the philosophy paper of the *baccalauréat* 'Is the
state the enemy of liberty?' (*Le Monde de l'Education*, 1993: 126;
Sunday Times, 1995: 23).

Yet rationalism was aligned to state-determined futures of students, to
an ultimate professional–vocational purpose of every course of study and
the divorce of teaching from research. French higher education was
about teaching. Research, though finding its way into some university
schools, had from the sixteenth-century foundation of the *Collègè de
France* been assigned to a separate sector (Neave, 1993). Research-
oriented aims never infected teaching as they did in Germany.

Forms of teaching could be distinctly different from those of Britain or
Germany. The rationalist university was based on the mass lecture and
relative lack of community or close contact between students and
teachers. A standardized course based on system and logic could be
taught by standardized ways. Students, at worst, crowded into lecture
halls in hundreds, often failing to find places and prepared themselves for
examinations with little help from tutors who had a commitment to teach
around 3 hours a week. Maturity did not mean a generic change in kind of
intellectual objectives but in self-responsibility of learning. University
teachers do not have offices – if they meet students it is in corridors or
cafés – and, with the late twentieth century development of roads and
railways, frequently commute across the whole country to work. The
distinction between full-time and part-time students was always unclear,
especially in massive universities like that of Paris before 1968.

Student responsibility was to learn with little special help and to
survive usually without maintenance grants, though with the benefit of
subsidized accommodation, restaurants and public transport. This
subsidized existence only marginally aided students in meeting the harsh
demands of survival. Maturity for the student meant being economically
self-sufficient. The penalties were usually exacted through failure to
complete courses. This Darwinist existence could be associated with
student radicalism.

There are ways in which France has departed from the purer
rational–collectivist traditions which are better exemplified in Italy or
Spain. *Grandes écoles* have no equivalents elsewhere in southern

Europe. They represent a Napoleonic strategy, adopted by governments in other countries in later times, of bypassing the traditional university rather than reforming it. Despite French complaints about Americanization of higher education, it has been French governments which adopted American patterns which were not found elsewhere in southern Europe. Reductionism characterized the 1968 reform. Teaching and learning units have been reduced to smaller parcels and assessment, which can be as much as 80% internal. Modularization has produced ten units per year up to *licence* or *maîtrise* level each separately assessed even though the have been described as 'a collection of unrelated scraps of knowledge' (Girod de l'Ain, 1994: 407).

France could contain much undistinguished higher education, especially in humanities and social sciences which grew in student numbers from the 1970s (Neave, 1993: 164–65) because of the élite sector, the university institutes of technology as well as the *grandes écoles* which protected science thus rationality. A double layer of rationality emerged in higher education as it had in upper secondary education where logic and system had different standards in humanities/social sciences and mathematics/pure science.

Southern and Eastern Europe

Italy, Spain and Portugal clearly have a French type of university, sometimes more authentically French than those of France where Belgium and Greece have combinations of the German and the French. Eastern Europe, under Communist rule, followed elements of the French approach.

Italy has the most traditional system. The conventional university predominates and is still organized on faculty lines. Students, with little help except state subsidized services which almost constitute a social welfare system, struggle to complete a 4-year degree (*laurea*). Terminal first-cycle courses are for a minority preparing for a limited range of occupations. Numbers grew, above the European norm, five times between 1960 and 1990 and put pressure on an unreformed system of teaching and courses. While the state controlled degrees, appointments and programmes, the feebleness of the Italian state was indicated by the immense power of a professorate which resisted change.

Spain, in contrast, reacted to growth by selection. First and second cycles were created to reduce the pressure of numbers, especially in massive institutions such as Complutense University in Madrid. The first cycle has been prepared in separate university schools. Full universities introduced selective tests for those who had studied for 1 year beyond the *bachillerato.*

The traditional university course, within a rationalist–utilitarian view, was of 2 or 3 years of general rationalist study in basic areas such as mathematics and pure sciences for engineering or political science and economics for law. The final 2 or 3 years leading to the *licenciatura* then concentrated on professional–vocational areas. This scheme was consistent with the rationalist ethos of theoretical, rational study as the foundation of professional competence. Yet the creation of two cycles, in Spain as in France, produced difficulties of maintaining intellectual coherence. Furthermore, the structure of theory then practice that had underwritten the most prestigious courses in southern Europe were in areas such as medicine, engineering and law. The rationalist tradition less easily accommodated a vocational course without a substantial basis in theory. So southern European countries suffered from not having an élite sector of higher education to protect traditional rational values while not being able to offer a coherent basis for study for others.

Eastern Europe had had a version of higher education which had much in common with France. Universities were selective with stringent entrance tests. A large sector of professional non-university institutions was developed from the 1930s to prepare people for particular occupations, sometimes of high status and in other cases of lower standing. The key to the status of higher education institutions was the standing of the profession for which they prepared. This link was reinforced by planning procedures which allocated individuals to jobs, within a range of occupations related to a particular course. Even more than in France, research was separated from higher education and located, in the Soviet Union, in the Academy of Science and its branches in various parts of the country.

So science, based on rationality, gave entry to certain highly regarded jobs and was also associated with prized intellectual status. Science had a high prestige in universities and other institutions. But the highest levels of education were contained within the research training courses of the Academy of Science which lay beyond the universities.

This arrangement could not survive the collapse of Soviet power. The Academy of Science and universities could no longer be funded relatively lavishly by state authorities. Monetary and market considerations surfaced. Institutions which could offer marketable skills, notably in business management, could charge high fees. Universities in general admitted students according to their capacity to pay. Rational–intellectual values might survive, supported by a revived humanism, but in very constrained conditions countries could no longer afford a class of intelligentsia of the Communist period.

Northern European pluralism

Where one model of a collectivist southern European higher education can be suggested, in northern Europe there have been two competing philosophies identified with Germany and Britain. The German tradition has been the dominant and most influential especially within Europe. Yet the two offer different approaches to a higher education guided by traditional humanist, moral and individualist principles.

Germany

The distinctive German tradition is identified with Wilhelm von Humboldt, the Prussian Minister of Education and the university he founded in Berlin in 1809. While universities would be funded by the state which also had some influence over appointment of their academic staff, they would also be independent. Universities trained state officials who were perceived to need that wisdom and morality that a knowledge of classical civilizations would bring. Above all German universities should be research institutions concerned with the disinterested production of learning. Students became apprentice researchers attached to professors rather than apprentice state officials as in the French tradition.

The German university – which developed with early nineteenth century nationalism and the flowering of its philosophy, literature and scholarship – changed little in the twentieth century despite student numbers more than doubling between 1960 and 1980. All universities were deemed of equal status though financed by and responsible to *Land* governments – an equality made necessary by the survival of the tradition of student movement between institutions in the course of their study. The *Abitur* remained the passport to entrance to any university, upheld by law in 1972 (Teichler, 1985: 57). Germany stood apart from other large industrial countries in the survival of the traditional equality of state universities and their general education function in preparing professional élites.

Government responded to expansion of numbers, not by reforming universities, but by creating a non-university sector. The *Fachhochschulen* after 1971 offered courses in vocational areas with entry via vocational qualifications as well as the *Abitur*. Students were expected – almost required – to graduate in less than 4 years compared with the average of 7 taken in the universities for nominally 4-year courses. Student freedom of study and the scholarly–research ethos of the university did not apply. As in upper secondary education, highly practical vocational courses emerged because of the archaic academism of the traditional institutions. Yet the non-university sector remains peripheral.

The universities could not resist all change. Limitations of the right of entry via the *Abitur* to any course appeared with *numerus clausus*, starting with medicine in the mid-1960s and then extended to other areas such as economics, as a means to regulate imbalance between supply and demand. *Abitur* grades, a centrally administered additional test and a lottery determined access to popular fields. Furthermore, German authorities in the 1980s attempted to distinguish between universities on their research achievements, in common with other countries, which affected informal student rankings of institutions (Frackmann, 1990: 195–98).

Teaching and learning in the traditional university are different in essence from institutions in France, Britain and the USA. The recognition of distinctiveness, indeed, created a conscious break between upper secondary and higher education in the nature of study. The essential difference lay in the concept of *Freiheit des Studiums*. Each student could construct his or her own programme, moving from professor to professor and from university to university and deciding the pace and timing of study. While courses had compulsory intermediate examinations, the ultimate piece of work was a thesis which would indicate, if not originality, then sustained and individual synthesis.

The German humanist ideal therefore aimed at a holistic and transcendental unity of knowledge and understanding but which was peculiar to each individual. Student freedom could mean they wasted their time and also that they had space for ultimate self-fulfilment. Flexner's observations in the 1920s have held throughout the twentieth century:

'the student is ... free ... he can go where he pleases .... He selects his own teachers; he wanders from one university to another; he may waste his time in fencing or drinking ... where a logical order of studies prevails, he may take advice or neglect it at his peril. He is treated like a man from the day he matriculates .... The student may be industrious or idle; may accomplish his purpose in the minimum number of semesters or may consume more; may stay in one place or go elsewhere .... He is regarded as competent to care for himself and he takes the full consequences. Finally, he has, when he thinks the moment has come, to submit to an examination. No calender tells him when or precisely on what.' (Flexner, 1968: 320–21)

Vocational imperatives have not been absent from this scheme.

Humboldt saw the two purposes of higher education to be interrelated. 'General education is meant to strengthen, ennoble and direct man himself, the specialist education will only provide him with skills for practical education.' This was developed into an idealism, derived from Kant, Hegel and Fichte where *Wissenschaft* (academic learning and research) was conceptualized 'as the moral and practical duty to organize reality according to absolute knowledge; the place where this knowledge would be discovered was the university' (Gellert, 1993: 7). The actual insertion of vocation came through state examinations, in general education subjects, which were controlled by the state but taken in universities for qualification in law, teaching and medicine. The university first degree, in contrast, was the doctorate examined by thesis (though the higher level qualification needed to enter university teaching was the advanced thesis of the *Habilitation*).

Great responsibility was placed upon the student to make choices and to decide and follow his or her own timetable. At best this allowed students to complete projects when they were ready intellectually and to exercise great self-control and autonomy. Individual responsibility and individual projects were accompanied by greater individual contact between teachers and students. But, as Flexner noted, the pinnacle of teaching was the research seminar organized by the professor, to which invitation was restricted to favoured and promising students. Intellectual élites were marked out for special treatment.

The non-university sector in contrast was marked by formal classes and timetables similar to schools with compulsory attendance and tightly organized assignments. The assumption was that students had not reached the maturity of autonomous independent study of the traditional university student. Maturity and academic freedom and intellectual attainment were seen to be interrelated. In effect maturity was marked by intellectual attainment and academic freedom required maturity.

Institutions are changed by students reacting to socio-economic pressures. Students in the 1990s, faced with interminable university courses and graduate unemployment at the end of them, responded by getting vocational qualifications first, an option exercised by almost a quarter of new students in German universities in 1990 just as increasing numbers entering vocational education had completed the *Abitur*. Sixty per cent of students delayed entry to university until the age of 21–23 rather than enrolling in non-university institutions which took less than a third of all higher education students (Rau, 1993: 42–43). And large numbers of students in practice followed lives of part-time study with part-time work. The irony was that student life-choice patterns allowed very traditional conceptions of university study to survive.

An archaic German university actually may accommodate contemporary diversity better than some of its reformed counterparts elsewhere. But the system depends upon a distinction between a high-standard upper secondary education and high-quality vocational education; and a permissive individualist and humanist higher education. These conditions do not exist elsewhere.

Other continental north European cases

The Humboldtian university has remained a powerful ideal in most other north European countries, and has an impact elsewhere including Greece. The Netherlands most closely followed the German pattern whereas Scandinavian countries differed from it in particular ways, especially in application of concepts of community and social equality.

The Netherlands has a humanist university, perhaps inspired by Erasmus rather than foreign sources. Student freedom and individual responsibility have also led to interminable study. Ancient universities are preserved through a binary system which has very different non-university institutions. The Netherlands also has introduced *numerus clausus* for popular areas of study by similar processes of additional student selection as in Germany (also including a lottery). Universities in the 1980s were ranked by research achievements.

Two-thirds of students enter vocational institutions. These were seen to provide the economic and occupational relevance which universities could no longer offer for students aiming at intermediate jobs. Yet, while Dutch governments were more forceful than those of Germany in seeking financial efficiency – including higher education institutions generating their own incomes – the view of equality between and distinctiveness of universities was maintained (Ruiter and Van Vught, 1990).

Scandinavian countries, in contrast, have moved from a version of the Humboldtian university to a view of higher education as a community of adults. In Sweden, the binary system was attacked by a law in 1977 which combined different lengths and orientations of courses in the same institutions (Lane, 1991: 160–62). The response of students was similar as in Germany – they postponed entry to higher education. In Sweden, the 1977 reform gave preferential access to students over 25 with work experience (and without formal academic qualifications), while the proportions of mature students rose in other Scandinavian countries, notably Norway where by 1987 45% of students were over 24 and 23% over 30 (Aamodt *et al.*, 1991: 132). Increasingly a view of higher education serving and representing a whole adult community emerged though its reconciliation with imperatives to provide for the coherent intellectual development of students and a preparation for a range of occupations was uncomfortable.

Britain: Reform within an alternative pluralist culture

Britain stood apart from other parts of western Europe, particularly after 1990, and, as in other matters, looked more towards a north American model. This was the system of minutely-graded and shifting hierarchies of institutions of higher education. Such a system had always existed in a country where universities were autonomous institutions with far less government control over students entry, courses, degrees, staffing and internal organization than in the rest of Europe (McLean, 1990b). Informal hierarchies were reflected in the differential entry requirements of departments within institutions relating not to possession of basic qualifications (which, unlike most other west European countries, never gave automatic rights of entry) but to grades obtained and, with Oxford and Cambridge, to special entrance examinations.

While there was a certain stability in these hierarchies – such as the long-standing predominance of Oxford and Cambridge in general education subjects and of some colleges of London University in vocational areas such as engineering and medicine – there was also change so that Sussex, which had been popular and competitive in the 1960s, was unloved by students in the 1990s while Nottingham experienced the reverse movement over the same time period.

Government, which in 1966 had adopted a binary system of vocational polytechnics alongside traditional universities, abandoned it in 1992 when most institutions became universities. Student demand established the pecking order of institutions in a market relationship though governmental bias in funding according to research achievements also would have an effect. This change coincided with the rapid expansion of numbers of entrants from less than 15% of the age group in 1985 to over 30% in the 1990s. As in Scandinavia, expansion was accompanied by the absorption of older students with less conventional entry qualifications (Halsey, 1993). Growth in effect allowed distinctions between institutions in their informal prestige while government abandoned aims to regulate course offerings.

The English university tradition was one of teaching rather than research and of humanist rather than rationalist or professional aims. Universities were separate from the state in every aspect until government funding was provided in the early twentieth century. As in France and Germany, the essence of the higher education tradition dated from the nineteenth century when decadent institutions were reformed. The new mission did not have governmental sources but was expressed most fully by J.H. Newman in his emphasis on a liberal education which had nothing to do with profession but with knowledge for its own end (Newman, 1931: 24–47). Newman's apparent other-worldliness was attacked by Thomas Huxley with his idea of the liberation that science brought. But Newman's starting-point was that through their community a group of scholars achieved a unity in their different branches and the student, though necessarily specializing in one area, came through social–educational interaction to see that part in relation to the whole with the result that 'A habit of mind is formed which lasts through life, of which the attributes are freedom, equitableness, calmness, moderation and wisdom' (Newman, 1931: 26).

This mission developed into a belief in teaching and the cultivation of morality rather than science. By the early twentieth century, the desired outcomes were listed by an American observer as 'knowledge, culture, the power of expression, character, manners, a rare balancing and maturing of qualities calculated to equip men to meet with dignity and competency the responsibilities of life' (Flexner, 1968: 274). The function of the university extended that of the reformed public school of Thomas Arnold in developing Christian gentlemen to participate in public life in political–administrative roles.

The most representative course of nineteenth and early twentieth century English higher education was that of 'Greats' at Oxford – Greek and Latin language, literature, philosophy and history – though which the finest achievements of man (in the humanist view) could be developed. Yet the order and content of this was important. Language and literature occupied the first 2 years, history and philosophy the last 2. Language built upon rational systematic preparation of the upper secondary school but was related to literature which gave both training in rhetoric (Cicero) and heroic examples (Homer, Greek dramatists). But the pinnacle was classical history and philosophy. Students specialized in one or the other and were encouraged to identify the contemporary relevance of each – a distinction being created already perhaps between public men of thought and of action.

Classics declined over time. By the mid-twentieth century, modern history and literature had surpassed them and again had a moral function of creating insights into heroic but personal achievements of individuals. History emerged at Oxford – though founded on constitutional law – while literature was pre-eminent at Cambridge, especially in the period up to the 1960s. The partial generalism of the classics course was replaced by increasing specialization through single honours courses from the mid-nineteenth century which permitted only the study of one subject in depth. This moralism and specialism infiltrated the higher education system as a whole by the twentieth century. Despite considerable variations in nineteenth century higher education, there was a convergence towards a version of the Oxford model in the later twentieth century.

The variations are interesting. The four Scottish universities had been pre-eminent in the eighteenth century when they were associated with both a rationalist scholarship and vocational courses which were absent from the two English equivalents (Davie, 1950). Scottish universities not only provided Britain with university trained doctors and engineers when the former were trained outside the university system in England but also had a broad course which avoided early specialization.

The second variation was the development of mathematics and science at Cambridge, since the seventeenth century, associated with a rigorous examination system in mathematics and a tradition of research which could endow Isaac Newton and James Clerk Maxwell with professorships. Despite the brilliance of mathematics and physics at Cambridge from a period which predated the reform of Oxford and Cambridge as a whole, this tradition never had a central place in English higher education except in a research ethos which never predominated as in Germany and only gained a central place in the 1960s.

The third variation was the development of the new universities in the nineteenth century. London and its colleges provided a part-time and vocational education (derived in part from bringing together old institutions) while Manchester, Birmingham and other industrial city universities offered courses related to local industry such as textiles and metallurgy.

Alongside university education, a strand of ancient vocational education existed provided by professional associations – notably in law and medicine – which were never totally supplanted by universities. Legal training in a narrow sense remained stronger in the professional associations than in the old universities. This tradition of professional training in the apprenticeship model continued in engineering and accountancy. It made possible the maintenance of a general education in relatively short courses of 3 or 4 years on the Oxford–Cambridge model since graduates would become professionally trained entirely outside the university sector.

The university tradition was an extension of the secondary school. It gave little specific professional training in contrast to French practice. It was not long enough to allow students to mature as responsible adults, as in Germany. It marginalized research and scholarship. In Oxford and

Cambridge, most undergraduates were not serious students until the mid-twentieth century and the single-subject honours degrees (as opposed to multi-subject pass degrees for the less serious) only predominated after 1940 when specialized upper secondary education emerged to cater for this new group of students.

Humanism predominated through its association with one of several strands of nineteenth century higher education and that linked to the preparation of a particular social élite who expected to enter public service. Its survival was made possible also by informal hierarchies both within and between universities which dated from the nineteenth century. These long-standing hierarchies allowed the Oxford-dominated humanist tradition to win ground in the nineteenth century universities such as London but also in those of the mid-twentieth century such as Sussex or York. Humanist education became an easy route to opening access which the research tradition of Germany did not allow.

Teaching styles also reflected nineteenth century Oxford and Cambridge. A pastoral, individual 'tutorial' system focused upon the weekly one-to-one confrontation between teacher and student. A continental lecture style prevailed in London and other nineteenth century large city universities. But the tutorial took over much of the system, outside overcrowded polytechnics and their successors from the 1980s. At its best, students could be encouraged not only to be individual in their choices but also active, imaginative and risk-taking in learning when tutors set only a title and dispensed a few readings and then reacted as critic to the essay produced by the student. It was the heuristic aspect of the inductive English tradition which had its parallel in science conducted through individual student experiments in laboratories where tutors would permit or even encourage students to follow wrong paths of inquiry because of the value of learning from mistakes.

Teaching styles link with differing styles of assessment. The examination – in the form of unseen, timed written papers held at a specific time in a specified year of study – has been an awe-inspiring and health-draining exercise which seems little more than a brutal rite of passage. Its critics argued that it tested no more than stamina and an unshakably elegant and economic style of writing, a coincidence between traditional English and French approaches. Its claims to test quickness of thought depend on an originality of questions and examiner setters with a similar mental agility.

Government policy on expansion from 1966 was to turn previous technical–vocational institutions, which had filled an uncertain place between lower secondary and higher education, either into technological universities or more often into a more strictly government controlled sector of polytechnics and colleges of higher education which were supposed to provide more vocational education. But they themselves suffered academic drift and increasingly turned themselves into imitation humanist universities. Government responded by using the non-university sector as a vehicle for cheap expansion in the early 1980s, rather than maintain a specifically vocational sector as in Germany.

Mass higher education, when it was adopted as policy in 1989, was combined with the institutionalization of hierarchies since the colleges and polytechnics were converted into universities in 1992 but research gradings after 1985 severely distinguished, through funding, between various levels and standings of university. Institutional autonomy was combined with prescriptions designed to maintain efficiency (particularly to ensure the high completion rates were maintained in a mass system) which emphasized shifting hierarchies. But the humanist character of what was taught was not changed. Indeed, it was permitted to continue as the cheapest and most convenient form of general education.

A significant change in course organization came in the 1990s. Courses, as in France and the USA, were broken down into smaller self-contained modules which could be assessed separately. This approach had been advocated in a government statement of 1987 (England and Wales DES, 1987a) but derived from upper secondary vocational education reforms. It was strengthened by the creation of quality assurance mechanisms regulated by quasi-official agencies. In effect the nineteenth century utilitarian philosophy was revived to allow each minute element of activity in higher education to be observed, measured and regulated equally by student customers and external assessors. The source of change was the desire the maintain high completion rates in short time periods associated with the pre-1990 élitist system. Its character was consistent with a revival of English utilitarianism which affected other areas of education and public life.

These changes do not seriously affect élite universities which can follow many of their older traditions in aims, content, teaching and even examining. The major change in the older universities, from the mid-twentieth century, was their embrace of research and graduate teaching. The German tradition invaded Britain as much as it did the USA. Yet the approach to teaching was not essentially changed by this new mission.

The lower-status institutions were marked out by relatively weak research achievements. Yet they were forced by government funding to abandon personalized teaching and by quality assurance mechanisms to move towards modularized courses and continuous assessment. It was the same distinction as applied between state elementary and independent secondary schools in the nineteenth century and was justified by very similar overall conceptions.

Non-european alternatives: the USA and Japan

The USA imported a variety of European approaches to higher education, mixed them with home-grown ingredients and then re-exported them to the rest of the world. The American advantage was that mass higher education was developed earlier than anywhere else. But it also has a richness including an occupational pragmatism, diversity of institutions and community function which Europeans have not achieved. Yet it has become clearer in the 1990s that the USA provides only one model of expansion. A brief consideration of Japan, while not offering the same kind of international challenge as the school system, may put this universalism in a wider context.

The USA

American higher education is comprehensive in content, like the High Schools, but wide in aim and institutionally extremely diverse. Since the late nineteenth century an informal hierarchy has stretched from élite private universities – Stanford, Harvard, Yale, Princeton, Chicago – and the leading campuses and departments of state universities down to local 4-year and 2-year colleges. Local institutions, including 2-year Community Colleges, combine vocational education equivalent to upper secondary schooling in other countries and first-stage higher education which the successful individual student could complete in higher ranking institutions (Ashby, 1971). Unlike Europe, much American higher education is open to all, at least of the locality, so that courses can include remedial English or can require high-entry qualifications including outstanding SAT scores in English/mathematics and special subjects. A further informal selection, accepted in most European countries except Britain, comes through attrition with drop-out rates (temporary or permanent) of around 50%.

The mission of American higher education has become that of the 'multiversity' which Clark Kerr argued in the 1960s should 'be as British as possible for the sake of the undergraduates, as German as possible for the sake of the graduates and research personnel, as American as possible for the sake of the public at large' (Kerr, 1982: 18). This comprehensive role might best be disentangled historically. The English university of Oxford and Cambridge was transplanted to the New England territories and expressed in Harvard, Princeton and other ancient establishments.

Some elements of the humanist mission have been maintained through its prominent advocates – Robert Hutchins in the mid-twentieth century and Allan Bloom at its end were both associated with the mid-west private university of Chicago.

A German research function aspect was introduced in the late nineteenth century and, in the twentieth century, was represented by institutions such as John Hopkins University. Research achievement underpinned the informal hierarchy of institutions even though public funding was not attached to this ranking in the way that occurred in Europe in the 1980s and 1990s.

More significant was the popular and local element of the mission which developed from the 1862 Morrill Act. Land grants from Federal government provided the basis of state universities which were to be concerned with local economic improvement (particularly agriculture and business adminstration), were to be locally accountable and were open in admission to those completing local High Schools. The outcome was a mass, pragmatic university which Flexner later criticized for including journalism, business adminstration, football and corre-spondence courses.

This university had several strands in valuation of knowledge:

- a utilitarian–rationalism with an emphasis on science stressed by the founding fathers, especially Franklin and Jefferson;
- a vocationalism which took in many more occupations than the European institutions;
- a function of service to the community through part-time classes meeting local needs as well as other extension activities;
- the social–recreational aims which were met by formal courses rather than the extra-curricular activity of the European university.

The outcome is an offering in a typical American state university of between 2,500 and 5,000 courses of which a student may follow between 35 and 50 (Ratcliffe, 1992: 1567). The university is comprehensive in the same way that as the High School in offering every level and kind of course across academic, vocational, social and recreational areas, justified by reference to pragmatic principles in institutions which can be massive in size. Specialization of function only occurs through the levels of the informal hierarchy from Community Colleges through to the Ivy League private universities rather than divisions between courses.

The USA had the first mass higher education and inevitably some of its practices were adopted elsewhere. But in important ways it differs from other countries. The naturalist element of higher education – expressed in the rich cultural, social, artistic as well as civic curriculum –

was formalized in teaching programmes in the USA in a style which other countries may have difficulty in replicating. The community origins of American higher education are unique. Yet, also in contrast with most of Europe, private institutions play a major role at every level of the hierarchy and account for 20% of enrolments. It may be this particular combination of localism and privatism which distinguishes the unique political culture surrounding American higher education.

The American higher education system also encourages flexibility and, through lack of state financial support for 80% of students, forces adulthood through engagement in income generation. The pedagogical–didactic uniqueness of the American style has been the enormous diversity of courses both on offer and which are in practice selected by students. Students learn to be adaptable simply by shifting daily or weekly across academic, social, vocational and recreational courses and by having expectations of performing adequately in all. There was also the demand for student self-responsibility in choosing courses from a vast array – which was denied British undergraduates whatever encouragement was given to follow personal choice of interpretation or sometimes topic. Beyond these requirements there has been little remarkable in American higher education teaching and learning apart from the habits of dialogue and joint learning which the High School encouraged. Indeed there were also strong pressures in some areas for uniformity of response. The comprehensive American curriculum may encourage not only adaptability but also a commitment to life-long learning when gaps can be filled in the future. But to have simply growth as the educational aim which Dewey proclaimed can also weaken the fixed targets marked out in time which is one of the incentives of traditional European higher learning.

Japan

On the surface, there is little remarkable about Japanese higher education. The University of Tokyo, its first and premier institution of the western type, was founded in 1877 in response to the international economic challenge. The distinctiveness of Japanese higher education is that it provides a target for schools because it is there. But relatively little is achieved which is unique in the higher education except for lower unit costs which have excited some western governmental interest (England and Wales DES, 1991b).

The structure is closer to that in the USA than in European countries. There is a mixture of 2-year colleges and 4-year university courses as well as private and public institutions. There is a hierarchy of universities so that certain state institutions, notably Tokyo, had the highest prestige while some private universities had a high though not comparable standing. Two-year colleges, both public and private, would not usually have high demands for entry and tended to be finishing schools for wives and mothers as well as preparing for lower level health and social service occupations. About 25% of students are in 2-year colleges, and the proportion is declining with the improvement in the status of women and greater competition in finding jobs. Private institutions take about a fifth of all students (Japan, 1993: 22–23).

Among the universities, the most prestigious held that position because the great corporations recruited from them. But there was little qualitatively different between these universities except the highly selected nature of their students. Nor was there anything particularly different about their selection tests. There are three stages of selection:

- The gaining of a high-school diploma internally assessed and awarded by schools but on the basis of a national curriculum.
- The national examination established by the universities in 1979 following the national curriculum.
- Two- or three-subject examinations of the élite institutions which survive despite the national tests which were supposed to make them redundant (Frost, 1992).

The content and teaching of courses differs little between upper secondary school and higher education. While there are state prescriptions on the number of credits which must be obtained for each qualification and number of years, the content is left largely to universities. The Japanese government has identified the lack of difference between upper secondary and higher education teaching as an area in which change is needed. Proposals suggest both higher levels of specialization and more student choice of courses (Japan, 1993: 78–79).

Yet the international distinctiveness of Japanese higher education is that it allows the student, after years of intense pressure in school, to concentrate on self-development and wider interests in a relatively relaxed atmosphere. There is a return to a European quasi-aristocratic university. Competition and standardized attainment are completed at the age of 18, even though this restricts opportunities. Higher education encourages not only self-development but also co-operation between differentiated segments of the age who will carry this ethos onto working life.

The quid pro quo is that the state is not prepared to pay for this activity. Tuition fees for undergraduate courses in state universities in 1990 averaged almost £3,000 (US$ 4,500) for humanities and social studies courses – about half the rate for only marginally subsidized private institutions. However, the fees for public institution courses in the much more expensive science and medicine fields were only slightly higher (Japan, 1993: 103). The message is that if higher education is for personal development then the consumer should pay. This is the basis of foreign interest in Japanese higher education. Even proposals for reform only change this formula by identifying a small sector of higher education where high intellectual attainment and specialization are needed in the national economic interest.

Conclusion

National diversity in higher education survives. It may also have economic relevance and personal value as internationally mobile students can taste the worth and delights of distinctly different systems. The eighteenth century educational grand tour is reviving among young adults of Europe, North America and East Asia. Unrestrained enthusiasm may not be advised especially of the type of Lord Chesterfield in his advice to his son in 1747 'A Frenchman, who with a fund of virtue, learning and good sense has the manners, learning and good breeding of his country. This perfection you may arrive at, if you please, and I hope you will do so' (Sadler, 1995: 4). But diversity of educational provision itself is a source of personal educational enrichment.

Only a few institutions in each country can take full advantage of national educational distinctiveness. The others serve national or local constituencies. They face outwardly incompatible demands. Higher education continues to provide opportunities to develop basic and general rational, communicative skills either above the level reached in upper secondary education or, in compensation, at the same standard as the highest achievers in the pre-university stage. It allows opportunity to link these aptitudes to general preparation for occupational capacities even though applicable vocational competence is acquired on entering employment. It allows for wider moral, cultural, social and personal capacities to be developed. Three, 4 or 5 years of higher education cannot achieve all of these goals. Choices and priorities have to be established.

Higher education serves different kinds of people. The range of prior educational achievements are greater than in previous generations. Selective institutions for the highest achievers cannot be avoided because of the different occupations for which higher education is a preparation. But differences of students are not only those of previous educational attainment. Higher education is the only phase which is not age specific. Changing individual career paths, produced by a more volatile labour market, mean that many more mature students enter institutions than those who previously took advantage of expansion of provision. Aspirations will differ between age groups.

All higher education systems may need to introduce a phase of acquisition and development of basic, general, communicative skills. Some systems, notably in the French and southern European tradition, already focus on this area. However, the more that this is emphasized the less pressure there is on earlier phases of education to reach basic standards. The maintenance of high standards in German and Japanese High Schools may be attributed in part to the expectation that other kinds of learning will prevail in the higher education stage and so certain levels must be reached at upper secondary level.

Conversely, a higher education which concentrates on personal and individual development – whether through the high culture route of traditional humanism or through local and personal sub-cultures – has dangers of becoming peripheral, of filling years until the student is sufficiently mature to enter working life. There are parallels in the nineteenth century and earlier education of children of aristocratic or mercantile backgrounds. Employers in Japan and in Britain employ graduates not because of the skills and knowledge they acquired at university but because ability to win a place at particular universities indicates a general level of capacity. This peripheral, almost self-indulgent higher education inevitably becomes the target of government attempts to shift costs to student–consumers.

Yet the third option of the vocational route is not entirely viable. The same problem appears in higher education as in the upper secondary level: that the skills needed for the most sophisticated occupations are best learned in the working context of their application. Compromises can be reached whereby students spend alternate periods in work and in study but this does not solve the problem that students need to prepare for entry to a much wider range of jobs than this sandwich allows.

In these conditions of uncertain choices, it is understandable that each country will operate higher education within its own traditions. The alternatives are not easily available. While higher education has an impact on earlier phases, influences also operate in the opposite direction. Higher education depends on capacities students acquired in school. Courses also must develop qualities to which employers, who are also affected by national traditions, give value. And the kinds of thought, morality and taste that higher education can develop relate to the political–administrative cultures in which higher education institutions are situated.

If in many ways educational institutions are both imprisoned and enriched by their national contexts, the free agent is the student who can flit between the static flowers of national education traditions. The imperative for institutions then becomes not so much to depart from their national traditions as to make them accessible to students of other cultures.

8
Conclusion

Educational traditions can be deceptive. Some are old and carved in stone. Others are young and appear immutable because the observer has a short historical memory. Conflicting traditions may compete within a culture. Traditions may be strengthened or weakened by cross-fertilization but the processes by which some imports are welcomed and others rejected are mysterious. Educational traditions are both a source of richness and intransigent obstacles to widely desired change.

It is unlikely, and undesirable, that there should be total global educational convergence. Education diverges because its common values in any culture are imprinted in the minds of all participants and because teaching and learning, despite their future-oriented goals, must always draw principally from the past.

Convergence comes from international economic and social pressures. If one system produces better education more efficiently than another then the disadvantaged have to take measures to compensate. The terms of competition may change rapidly. A few widely adopted technological or organizational developments in production can alter the requirements made of students emerging from educational systems. Globalization only quickens the process of change and discounts the excuse of myopia.

Global economic convergence and the diversity of national educational traditions

Competition between countries focuses upon student achievement and the cost-efficiency of teaching. Relevant student attainment is much more difficult to deduce from occupational changes in the global economy than the likelihood of increasing demands for cost reductions.

Educationists and employers lack clear shared meanings of the achievement of students-turned-employees. Agreed attainment targets are reduced to imprecise epithets such as clever, wise, loyal and resourceful. Yet educational debate across cultures and time centres on such descriptors rather than on more specific cognitive and affective capacities.

Educational cultures have developed in ways that give greater weight to some of these qualities than others. Occupations, in response to global changes in production, give more stress to certain qualities than others at particular times. The contemporary movement is towards expecting all employees (and thus all students) to have communicative competencies in language, number and spatial representation and to be able to think logically and systematically. This emphasis on 'cleverness' is universal and difficult for any student, parent or teacher to neglect.

In comparison, qualities of wisdom, loyalty and resourcefulness are required often only after the basic rational equipment is in place. In countries such as Japan, success in basic education has directed attention to ways of encouraging students to be more individualist and inventive. These qualities may be important for a substantial section of occupational élites in the next wave of global technological–productive change. But they are of secondary importance in countries such as Britain, the USA and France which have had little difficulty in producing talented eccentrics but have more urgent problems of an unemployable underclass.

Some education systems have given more emphasis to the acquisition of communicative competence over a longer period of time than others. Rationality has been more central to overt aims of teaching and learning in France, other southern European countries and, formerly, in eastern Europe than elsewhere. Yet the statement of a widely accepted aim does not necessarily guarantee success. Achievements in Germany and Japan have been greater than those of the countries of south Europe. In Germany an educationally encouraged rationalism in schools is only a prelude to a humanist and individualist investigation of a high culture or a practical training that confers a profession. In Japan rationality has never had a major place in the overall culture and students acquire skills because of an individual moral obligation to learn rather than because of any intrinsic value in what is to be learned.

What is taught, perversely, seems less important than the kind of behaviours that it is hoped that teaching will engender. Routes to rationality have changed over time. Classical languages only lost their pre-eminence in secondary education in the second half of the twentieth century in Europe. Mathematics, science and modern foreign languages replaced them as vehicles for developing rational thought. Britain and the USA lagged in this movement. Yet Japan, while embracing mathematics and science, failed to give foreign languages a central role in schooling.

The organization of content and learning similarly seems to have little relationship with achievement. The subject labels of the elementary and lower secondary school curriculum have much in common across industrial countries. Beyond this superficial communality there is much variation. Central prescription and uniformity are stronger in Japan and France than in the USA. Germany and the Netherlands, with high levels of student achievements in school, do not have powerfully enforced standard curricula. Assessment of students varies considerably between central control and a permissiveness which grants considerable power to individual teachers. Forms of assessment vary between extended pieces of writing at secondary level in Europe to single response examinations in north America and Japan.

The amount of education received, measured by the beginning age of universal participation and the length of school days, hardly seems to affect student achievement. The ways in which children and young people are selected for different kinds of lower and upper secondary schooling do not seem to have any major impact on the achievement of minimum standards. Germany and Japan do not expect their children to start school at an early age. German children do not attend schools in afternoons and are rigidly stratified into different forms of secondary education at the age of 10 while France has universal provision for 3 year olds and, like most countries, common schooling to the age of 15 or 16. These differences seem to have little impact on relative student attainments.

Whether systems are controlled nationally, regionally or locally also has little effect on achievements. Centralization may prevail in Japan and France while regional or local school systems are the norm in Germany, the Netherlands, Scandinavia and the USA. It is difficult to identify any outcomes of school achievement which derive from these differences.

The crucial element is motivation of students which can bridge the gulf between aims and achievements. Yet motivation is a mystery when viewed comparatively. It may have many wide cultural sources. Possibilities of individual economic success, patriotic commitment to collective goals, ingrained cultural beliefs in the worth of individuals and the shame of failing to conform to the general norm can all play a part. Popular motivation can rise and fall in different countries in ways that are amenable neither to understanding nor to control.

In the more specifically educational context, the relationship between motivation and learning is a little clearer. For deeper cultural reasons Germans and Japanese have felt obligations to exert themselves to succeed in education. Educational institutions respond through the expectations teachers have of students and the organization of curriculum and assessment. In France motivations which derive from a state-collectivist ideal have been powerful but have not led to the degree of commitment of the whole nation that was the aim, for instance, in

Communist regimes. An overwhelmingly rationalist education, while consistent with general state-collectivist educational purposes, has failed to capture the freely given loyalties of some sections of their populations.

The major problems are experienced in Britain and the USA which do not have effective means to motivate the whole population. English educational values have dismissed rationalism as a necessary but trivial basis for true humanist education and have retained aristocratic traditions which easily reject a section of the population as unfitted to strenuous public education. In the USA, while traditions support open opportunities for all, motivation is seen to be so personal and individual that a collective expression even of the German and Japanese variety is elusive. As a result, many American students fail by default. They are not denied opportunities but neither is there any deep social obligation upon them to exploit these chances. And American values do not elevate systematic and abstract rational education for its own sake.

Britain and the USA can hope to compensate by the resourcefulness to which their cultures give much worth. Such a quality may be of more use to the highly successful than the average student. But adaptability and individual responsibility for success can perhaps overcome distaste for formal, cumulative, alienating acquisition of skills in languages, mathematics and science. Anglo-Saxon cultures have treated language, mathematics and technology as the systematization of practical experience. As society becomes more suffused with technology – especially information technology – then the stimulus to use these means to acquire logical, systematic skills may be greater especially among students with prior socialization in values of individuality and resourcefulness. Indeed, learning based on games and play, informal competition and co-operation in the right balance may compensate for collective commitment to acquire a rational body of knowledge. While inductionism may recover some of the ground lost over the last half century, this resurgence cannot overcome ineffective national ethics of motivation.

The irony is that cultures that succeed in motivating their young to learn seem to do so as much from historical memory as from current conditions. Obligations to the state, the family and ancient religious values help students to perform well in various societies but against the tide of the disintegration of each of these institutions. Egocentric individualism is not sufficient to help those who have no credible belief in their capacity to win public races. When the problem is not the achievements of the best but the importance for the whole society of the competencies of the worst then more social–collective bases of motivation need to be found to learn what is necessary but cannot always be made attractive in itself.

The crucial relationship is between motivation and the traditional values of each society. Views of the qualities and capacities of an educated person vary between cultures. Conceptions of fair competition and selection also differ. Perceptions of rights and responsibilities in participation in educational decision-making vary between political cultures. Motivation may be high when a consistency is found between these value systems and educational practice. People may be committed because they see that public education gives them what they expect. Yet these expectations differ considerably between cultures. Education may succeed by being unique and faithful to its historical values in each country rather than bowing to transient pressures for international conformity.

The global pressure for cost efficiency is as irresistible as that for uniform standards of student achievement. Any country that devotes a higher proportion of public expenditure to education than the international norm has to reduce expenditure elsewhere or increase taxation both of which may damage competitiveness in a global economy. Cost-efficiency has been sought through a number of common means across countries in recent years including the creation of national measures of student attainment by which to judge individual educational institutions, managerial autonomy for each institution to meet its goals and privatization of various educational services that were previously the responsibility of public authorities. Yet the limits of efficiency are also fixed by historic national values. All systems have major inefficiencies which cannot be removed without threatening the commitment to educational achievement which is of even greater importance.

Efficient teaching and learning would concentrate upon mass, standardized transmission of communicative skills. All other education would become a private affair. This rationale has attraction in the countries of Europe and North America where cultural and personal diversity is so great that the common school can no longer provide education beyond basic rational skills which will meet the whole range of individual aspirations.

In practice, this does not happen. Schooling concentrates upon public knowledge in France and Japan but requires students to spend all day in school to cover as many standard subjects as possible. Northern European countries allow greater space for diversity of cultural attachments alongside a public curriculum but broadly finance these alternatives from public sources. Britain and the USA persist with inefficient schools which attempt to provide a total education through maintenance of a myth that a public school is a complete community or educates the 'whole child'.

Various countries have found ways of cutting public costs which almost fortuitously emerge from different national traditions. State-collectivist traditions in southern Europe seem to be at a disadvantage with an expectation that the state will provide all services including both pre-schooling and post-compulsory vocational education. Yet uniformity and the persistence of an abstract conception of knowledge transmission allows for a cost-efficient standardized teaching with minimum physical resources. In contrast, British individualized teaching and experience-based learning is costly and inefficient while the American comprehensive High School curriculum is wasteful in the extreme.

British and American education, on the other hand, can draw upon a utilitarian tradition that permits regulation of the efficiency of individual institutions by a stipulation of external regulators. Standard measures of student achievement and school efficiency leading to public league tables are much more possible in Anglo-Saxon than other traditions. Yet the British–American efficiency movement only compensates for other inefficiencies which education in state-collectivist traditions does not share.

Other short-cuts to cost-efficiency are also cultural specific. Japanese parents accept that the state will only pay entirely for compulsory schooling. Tuition fees paid by parents for pre-schooling, upper secondary and higher education are unacceptable in other countries despite the reduction in most countries of public financial responsibility for higher education. Employers in Germany and Japan provide (and pay for) vocational training to an extent that their equivalents in other countries would be loathe to accept despite a tradition in some countries, notably the USA, that local businesses may contribute to local schools.

There are many ways to cut public costs. Different levels of education may be taken out of the public financial domain to a varying extent in each country. The questions are what kinds of privatization are politically acceptable in each culture and how far are they compatible with the even more powerful imperative to maintain or raise standards of student achievement?

The educational challenge of globalization is then not to find universal solutions. They can hardly work when some of these solutions suggested in certain countries are addressing problems that are of minor importance elsewhere. If one country succeeds in a strategy which reduces costs and enhances student achievement, the more appropriate response of its competitors is not to copy but to look for others ways to reform. The question then is in what ways the various educational traditions are amenable to change.

**Educational traditions: Intransigent obstacles to necessary reform
or sources of cultural revitalization?**

There is no clear answer to how educational systems must and can
change. A passive response might be to treat the process as one of
serendipity. Every education system has its day. Britain, France and
Germany in different ways used their education to support political and
economic influence throughout the world in the nineteenth century. The
USA and the Soviet Union were able to use different educational
approaches to supplant them in the mid-twentieth century. Japan has
been the latest successful state. China or India may be able to draw upon
different educational traditions as support for global ascendancy in the
twenty-first century.

National governments and their electorates are unlikely to accept such
fatalism. How can they exploit their educational traditions in order to
succeed? There is no one successful strategy. All successful countries
borrow from abroad but in different ways. France and Britain (especially
England) have had a fertile relationship over centuries based on a
delicate balance of mutual admiration and contempt. Each has responded
by digging deeply into its traditions to match the other's advantage by
doing almost the opposite. Germany in the early nineteenth century
adopted some aspects of Bonapartism to give order to an older Germanic
tradition which could then be used to challenge France. The USA openly
drew from Europe in different ways both at the end of the eighteenth
century and the end of the nineteenth yet reconciled borrowing with
powerful indigenous traditions. And Japan carefully separated
indiscriminate educational borrowing in economic areas from a protected
traditional Japanese moralism.

Transfers may occur to fill gaps in the indigenous traditions. But they
may simply reinforce these traditions. England borrowed German child-
centred methods of teaching in the late nineteenth century but to
supplement an older English individualism. Britain exported
inductionism and utilitarianism in the late eighteenth century to North
America and then imported the processed outcomes of the educational
efficiency movement from the mid-twentieth century. On the other hand
there was admiration of American communalism in Britain but a failure
to absorb it while German pragmatic traditions were applied to some
sectors of education almost without recognition of what was happening
across the Atlantic.

Understanding of these processes needs a view of national educational
systems as a whole from the nursery to the graduate school. Some sectors
can survive with little change because they are compensated for by

others. French pre-schooling developed as part of a strategy which reacted to the failings of secondary schools and higher education. German and Japanese higher education, in different ways, can survive as luxuriant indulgences because of the effectiveness of secondary schooling. Yet it may be that secondary education is so efficiently single-minded in these countries because higher education is ineffective or because employers provide such high-quality in-house training.

Different kinds of educational traditions have differing weights. The ethos of primary, secondary or higher education in any of the major countries surveyed has a history of less than 200 years which is a short span in educational history. The obstacles to change are not as great as are sometimes claimed. National traditions of access to education may sometimes derive from views which are a little older. But pressures for change are greater and long-established views have had to respond over the last century to expansion of each level of education in turn. Changes in occupation and economy force modification of these views even though sub-strata of unconscious attitudes survive.

Political cultures affect the ways in which educational institutions are organized. These cultures change little if only because the status quo has so many stakeholders. Collectivist and pluralist cultures are always likely to differ in educational provision. The saviour is that no political culture is totally monolithic. So pluralist tendencies exist in collectivist traditions and vice versa. Within broader, traditional frameworks there are possibilities of change in educational politics even though change usually means resurrecting half-forgotten practices of the past.

While views of who should get education and who should control it can change within broad parameters of traditions of nations and civilizations, values about what should be taught and learned change far less. Educational aims are still, as they were for Socrates, about interpretations of the good, the true and the beautiful. The reference points, in the countries surveyed, are still Plato and Confucius. Everything else constitutes footnotes. Yet Plato and Confucius are rich enough to be interpreted in different ways as variously Erasmus, Comenius and Rousseau for Plato did in the European tradition.

The crucial issue is not about changing the unchangeable traditions of 2000 years but to find spaces for diversity within them. Plato's conundrum about the relationship between learning to be clever and learning to be good may have different national solutions but there is some leeway for negotiation within each. Perhaps more significant in the contemporary world is Rousseau's distinction between citizen and the private person. While the education of the citizen may have a limited range of nationally acceptable interpretations there are many and varied educational concepts of a private person within and across nations. Some need to be further unearthed and explained. They provide enormous educational possibilities though they may need to be separated from citizen education to be developed.

Wider perspectives

This survey has concentrated on a few countries with contemporary or recent political and economic global dominance. Others are also important not only because educational history is more than the story of the big battalions but because today's losers can be tomorrow's winners.

There is much to be explored in Hindu and Islamic traditions as well as variants of Confucianism beyond Japan. Analysis in the past focused on dysfunctional traditionalism of these cultures. Yet a similar archaicism not long ago was held to apply to Japan. Capacities for educational adaptation to a modern economy may be much stronger than has been assumed. A number of Asian countries that are currently undergoing economic transformation have stronger traditions of accommodation of diverse educational cultures such as Korea and Taiwan, with histories of Japanese colonial control, as well as Malaysia and Indonesia which have heritages which include European imperialism.

In Europe the challenge has been to reconcile a historic continental tradition with local diversity and non-dominant cultures. In contrast in the USA, a melting-pot strategy has prevailed despite lip-service to cultural diversity. Other countries – including Australia, New Zealand and much of Latin America – have faced a choice between the two approaches. The melting-pot ideology may now have a limited function. Private cultures, rather than competing, can powerfully complement attenuated public educational domains. In some countries there is a great separation between the two as in Africa and notably South Africa. Elsewhere, a dominant tradition can take on a minority status, as with French education in Canada.

These various traditions are important not only in the context of global competition. Because of the international movement of people carrying with them the expectations of their educational cultures, all the differences described in this book can be found in one school or other educational institution. Indeed, one school classroom or higher education lecture theatre in any industrial country can contain within it students who have all the educational expectations – both of past experience and anticipated futures – which have been described in the previous chapters. This may be the ultimate global educational challenge to everyday teaching and learning.

References

Aamodt, P.O., Svein, K. and Skoie, H. (1991) 'Norway: towards a more indirect model of governance', in *Prometheus Unbound: the Changing Relationship between Government and Higher Education in Western Europe* (eds Neave, G. and Van Vught, F.). Oxford: Pergamon, pp. 129–44.

Aldrich, R. (1988) 'The National Curriculum: an historical perspective', in *The National Curriculum* (eds Lawton, D. and Chitty, C.). London: Institute of Education, pp. 21–33.

Almond, G.A. and Verba, S. (1963) *The Civic Culture*. Princeton, N.J.: Princeton University Press.

Alston, P.L.(1969) *Education and the State in Tsarist Russia*. Stanford: Stanford University Press.

Altbach, P.G. and Kelly, G. (eds) (1986) *New Approaches to Comparative Education*. Chicago: University of Chicago Press.

Ardagh, J. (1973) *The New France*. Harmondsworth: Penguin.

Arnold, M. (1984) *Schools and Universities on the Continent*. Ann Arbor: University of Michigan Press.

Aron, R. (1965) *Main Currents of Sociological Thought*, Vol. 1. Harmondsworth: Penguin.

Ashby, E. (1971) *Any Student, Any Study*. New York: McGraw-Hill.

Bagley, C. (1973) *The Dutch Plural Society*. London: Oxford University Press.

Bamford, T.W. (1967) *The Rise of the Public Schools*. London: Nelson.

Bamford, T.W. (1970) *Thomas Arnold on Education*. London: Cambridge University Press.

Bantock, G.H. (1968) *Culture, Industrialization and Education*. London: Routledge.

Banton, M. (1977) *The Idea of Race*. London: Tavistock.

Barnard, H.C. (1969) *Education and the French Revolution*. Cambridge: Cambridge University Press.

Beattie, N. (1978) 'Parent participation in French education 1968–1975', *British Journal of Educational Studies*, 26(1), 40–53.

Bedarida, C. (1991) *L'ecole qui decolle*. Paris: Editions du Seuil.

Bell, D. (1976) *The Cultural Contradictions of Capitalism*. New York: Basic Books.

Bell, D. (1993) *Communitarianism and its Critics*. Oxford: Clarendon Press.

Benedict, R. (1967) *The Chrysanthemum and the Sword: Patterns of Japanese Culture*. London: Routledge.

Bereday, G.Z.F, et al.(eds)(1960) *The Changing Soviet School*. London: Constable.

Bernbaum, G. (1973) 'Countesthorpe College', in *Case Studies in Educational Innovation*, Vol. 3. CESE/OECD, pp. 7–88.

Bernstein, B. and Davies, B. (1969) 'Some sociological comments on Plowden', in *Perspectives on Plowden* (ed. Peters, R.S.). London: Routledge, pp. 55–83.

Bieroof, H. and Prais, S.J. (1993) 'Britain's industrial skills and the school-teaching of practical subjects: comparisons with Germany, the Netherlands and Switzerland', *Compare*, **23(3)**, 219–45.

Blaug, M. (1970) *An Introduction to the Economics of Education*. Harmondsworth: Penguin.

Blondel, D. (1991) 'A new type of teacher training in France', *European Journal of Education*, **26(3)**, 197–205.

Blondel, J. (1990) *Comparative Government*. London: Philip Allan.

Bloom, A. (1987) *The Closing of the American Mind*. Harmondsworth: Penguin.

Bourdieu, P. (1990) 'Principles for reflecting on the curriculum', *The Curriculum Journal*, **1(3)**, 307–314.

Bourdieu, P. and Passeron, J.C. (1970) *La Reproduction*. Paris: Editions de Minuit.

Bowen, J. (1981) *A History of Western Education*, Vol. 3. London: Methuen.

Bowles, S. and Gintis, H. (1976) *Schooling in Capitalist America*. London: Routledge.

Boyd-Barrett, O. (1990) 'Structural change and curriculum reform in democratic Spain', *The Curriculum Journal*, **1(3)**, 291–306.

Boyer, E. L. (1983) *High School*. New York: Harper Row.

Brandt, V. S.R. (1987) in *Ideology and National Competitiveness: an analysis of nine countries* (eds Lodge, G.C. and Vogel, E.F.). Boston, Ma.: Harvard Business School Press, pp. 207–240.

Braudel, F. (1972) *The Mediterranean and the Mediterranean World in the age of Phillip II*. London: Collins.

Braverman, H. (1974) *Labour and Monopoly Capital*. New York: Monthly Review Press.

Briggs, A. (1965) *Victorian People*. Harmondsworth: Penguin.

Briggs, A. (1968) *Victorian Cities*. Harmondsworth: Penguin.

Brink, G. Van Den and Bruggen, J. Van (1990) 'Dutch Curriculum Reforms in the 1980s', *The Curriculum Journal*, **1(3)**, 275–89.

Broadfoot, P. (1985) 'Towards conformity: educational control and the growth of corporate management in England and France', in *The Control of Education: International Perspectives on the Centralization–Decentralization Debate* (eds Lauglo, J. and McLean, M.). London: Heinemann, pp. 105–18.

Broadfoot, P. and Osbourn, M. (1992) 'French lessons: comparative perspectives on what it means to be a teacher', in *Oxford Studies in Comparative Education*, Vol. 1 (ed. Philips, D.). Wallingford: Triangle, pp. 69–88.

Bromley, Yu V. (1979) 'Towards a typology of ethnic processes', *British Journal of Sociology*, **30(3)**, 341–48.

Bronfenbrenner, U. (1970) *Two Worlds of Childhood: US and USSR*. London: Allen and Unwin.

Bruner, J. (1960) *The Process of Education*. Cambridge, Ma.: Harvard University Press.

Busch, F. W. (1982) 'The one-phase approach to teacher education in West Germany', *European Journal of Teacher Education*, **5(3)**, 169–77.

Carnoy, M. (1974) *Education as Cultural Imperialism*. New York: McKay.

Carnoy, M., Levin H.H. and King, K. (1980) *Education, Work and Employment*, Vol.2. Paris: Unesco.

Castles, S. and Kosack, G. (1973) *Immigrant Workers and Class Structure in Western Europe*. London: Oxford University Press.

Charmasson, T. (1987) *L'Enseignement Technique de la Revolution a nos Jours*, Vol.1. Paris: Economica.

Chen, J. (1990) *Confucius as a Teacher*. Foreign Languages Press: Beijing.

Chesnais, F. (1993) 'Globalization, world oligopoly and some of their implications', in *The Impact of Globalization on Europe's Firms and Industries* (ed. Humbert, M.).

London: Pinter, pp. 11–21.

Chubb, J.E. and Moe, T.M.(1990) *Politics, Markets and America's Schools*. Washington, D.C.: Brookings Institute.

Clapham, J.H. (1961) *The Economic Development of France and Germany 1815–1914*. Cambridge: Cambridge University Press.

Clark, B. R. (1984) 'The organizational conception', in *Perspectives on Higher Education: Eight Disciplinary and Comparative Views* (ed. Clark, B. R.). Berkeley: University of California Press, pp. 106–131.

Coleman, J.S. and Hoffer, T. (1987) *Public and Private High Schools*. New York: Basic Books.

Coleman, J.S., *et al.* (1966) *Equality of Educational Opportunity*. Washington, D.C.: US Government Printing Office.

Comenius, J.A. (1967) 'The Pampaedia', in *John Amos Comenius on Education* (ed. Piaget, J.). New York: Teachers College Press, pp. 116–199.

Conant, J.B. (1959) *The American High School Today*. New York: McGraw-Hill.

Connerton, P. (ed.)(1976) *Critical Sociology*. Harmondsworth: Penguin.

Coombs, F.S. (1978) 'The politics of educational change in France', *Comparative Education Review*, **22(3)**, 480–503.

Council of Europe (1968) *European Curriculum Studies Project*. Strasbourg: Council of Europe.

Cox, O.C.(1943) *Caste, Class and Race*. New York: Doubleday.

Creel, H.G. (1951) *Confucius: The Man and The Myth*. London: Routledge.

Cremin, L. A. (1962) *The Transformation of the School*. New York: Knopf.

Crozier, M. (1964) *The Bureaucratic Phenomenon*. Chicago: University of Chicago Press.

Cummings, W. K. (1985) 'Japan', in *The School and the University* (ed. Clark, B.R.). Berkeley: University of California Press, pp. 131–59.

Dahl, R. (1982) *The Dilemmas of Pluralist Democracy*. New Haven, CT: Yale University Press.

Davie, G. (1950) *The Democratic Intellect: Scotland and Her Universities in the Nineteenth Century*. Edinburgh: Edinburgh University Press.

Dessinger, T. (1994) 'The evolution of the modern vocational training systems in England and Germany', *Compare*, **24(1)**, 17–36.

Dewey, J. (1961) *Democracy and Education*. New York: Macmillan.

Dobson, R. B. (1977) 'Social status and inequality of access to higher education in the USSR', in *Power and Ideology in Education* (eds Karabel, J. and Halsey, A.H.). New York: Oxford University Press, pp. 254–275.

Dore, R. P. (1984) *Education in Tokuguwa Japan*. London: Athlone.

Dore, R. (1985) 'Technical change and cultural adaptation', *Compare*, **15(2)**, 109–20.

Dore, R. and Sako, M. (1989) *How the Japanese Learn to Work*. London: Routledge.

Drucker, P. F. (1993) *Post-Capitalist Society*. Oxford: Butterworth-Heinemann.

Dubreucq-Choprix, F.L. (1985) 'The Decroly Method', in *International Encyclopaedia of Education*, Vol. 3. Oxford: Pergamon, pp. 1335–1337.

Dunning, J. H.(1993) *The Globalization of Business*. London: Routledge.

Dunstan, J. (1985) 'Soviet Education Beyond 1984', *Compare*, **15(2)**, 161–87.

Durkheim, E. (1938) *The Rules of Sociological Method* (ed. Catlin, G.E.G). New York: Free Press.

Durkheim, E. (1977) *The Evolution of Educational Thought*. London: Routledge.

Ekholm, M. (1985) 'Sweden', in *The School and the University* (ed. Clark, B.R.). Berke-

184

ley: University of California Press.

Ekholm, M. (1987) 'School reforms and local response: reviews in 35 school management areas in Sweden', *Compare*, **17(2)**, 107–18.

Eliot, T.S. (1948) *Notes Towards the Definition of Culture*. London: Faber and Faber.

England and Wales, Board of Education (1931) *The Primary School*. Report of the Consultative Committee. London: HMSO.

England and Wales Board of Education (1943) *Curriculum and Examinations in Secondary Schools* (Norwood Report). London: HMSO.

England and Wales Department of Education and Science (DES)(1967) *Children and their Primary Schools* (Plowden Report). London: HMSO.

England and Wales Board of Education (1968) 'Elementary Code 1904', in *Educational Documents: England and Wales 1816–1968* (ed. Maclure, J.S.). London: Methuen.

England and Wales DES (1977) *Education in Schools: A Consultative Document*. London: HMSO.

England and Wales DES (1981) *West Indian Children in Our Schools* (Rampton Report). London: HMSO.

England and Wales, DES (1982) *Mathematics Counts* (Cockcroft Report). London: HMSO.

England and Wales DES/ Her Majesty's Inspectors (HMI) (1986) *Education in the Federal Republic of Germany: Aspects of Curriculum and Assessment*. London: HMSO.

England and Wales, DES (1987a) *Higher Education: A Framework for Expansion*. London: HMSO.

England and Wales, DES/ HMI (1987b) *Aspects of Primary Education in the Netherlands*. London: HMSO.

England and Wales, DES (1989) *National Curriculum: From Policy to Practice*. London: DES.

England and Wales, DES/HMI (1990) *Aspects of Education in the USA: Teaching and:Learning in New York City Schools*. London: HMSO.

England and Wales DES/HMI (1991a) *Aspects of Upper Secondary and Higher Education in Japan*. London: HMSO.

England and Wales, DES (1991b) *Education and Training for the 21st Century*. London: HMSO.

England and Wales, DES/ HMI (1991c) *Aspects of Primary Education in France*. London: HMSO.

England and Wales, DES/HMI (1992a) *Education in England 1990–91: The Annual Report of HM Senior Chief Inspector Schools*. London: HMSO.

England and Wales, Department for Education (DFE) (1992b) *Teaching and Learning in Japanese Elementary Schools*. London: HMSO.

England and Wales, DFE/HMI (1993) *Aspects of Full-time Vocational Education in the Federal Republic of Germany*. London: HMSO.

Esturla, A.R. and Bragado, J.F. (1994) 'Spain', in *Education in a Single Europe* (eds Brock, C. and Tulasiewicz, W.). London: Routledge, pp. 256–276.

Fagerlind, I. (1992) 'Beyond examinations: the Swedish Experience and lessons for other nations', in *Examinations: Comparative and International Studies* (eds Eckstein, M. A. and Noah, H. J.). Oxford: Pergamon, pp. 79–87.

Feldman, M. (1985) 'The workplace as education', in *Education in School and Non-School Settings* (eds Fantini, M. O. and Sinclair, R. L.). Chicago: University of Chicago Press, pp. 102–133.

Faist, T. (1994) 'How to define a foreigner? The symbolic politics of immigration in German partisan discourse', *West European Politics*, **17(2)**, 51–71.

Flexner, A. (1968) *Universities: American, English, German*. London: Oxford University Press.

Fortes, M. (1938) *The Social and Psychological Aspects of Education in Talaliland*. Oxford: Oxford University Press.

Foxman, D. (1992) *Learning Mathematics and Science*. Slough: National Foundation for Educational Research.

Frackmann, E. (1990) 'Resistance to change or no need for change? The survival of German higher education in the 1990s', *European Journal of Education*, **25(2)**, 195–98.

France, Ministere de l'Education Nationale (1982) *La Formation des Personnels de l'Education Nationale*. Paris: Ministere de l'Education Nationale.

France, Ministere de l'Education National (1993a) *Primary Education in France*. Paris: Ministere de l'Education Nationale.

France, Ministere de l'Education Nationale (1993b) *Rapport de l'Inspection Generale de l'Education Nationale*. Paris: Documentation Francaise.

France, Ministere de l'Education Nationale (1993c) *L'Enseignement Secondaire en France*. Paris: Ministere de l'Education Nationale.

Freire, P. (1972) *The Pedagogy of the Oppressed*. Harmondsworth: Penguin.

Friedman, M. and Friedman, R. (1980) *Free to Choose*. London: Secker and Warbourg.

Frost, P. (1992) 'Tinkering with hell', in *Examinations: Comparative and International Studies* (eds Eckstein, M. A. and Noah, H. J.). Oxford: Pergamon, pp. 25–32.

Fuhr, C. (1989) *Schools and Institutions of Higher Education in the Federal Republic of Germany*. Bonn: Internationes.

Furnivall, J.S. (1948) *Colonial Policy and Practice*. London: Cambridge University Press.

Galton, M. and Blyth, A. (1989) *Handbook of Primary Education in Europe*. London: David Fulton.

Gawthrop, R. L. (1987) 'Literacy drives in pre-industrial Germany', in *National Literacy Campaigns: Historical and Comparative Perspectives* (eds Arnove, R. L. and Graff, H. J.). New York: Plenum Press, pp. 29–48.

Gellert, C. (1993) 'The German model of research and advanced education', in *The Research Foundations of Graduate Education: Germany, Britain, France, United States, Japan* (ed. Clark, B. R.). Berkeley: University of California Press, pp. 5–44.

Gellner, E. (1983) *Nations and Nationalism*. Oxford: Basil Blackwell.

Gellner, E. (1994) *Conditions of Liberty: Civil Society and its Rivals*. London: Hamish Hamilton.

Genovese, E. D. (1971) *In Red and Black*. London: Allen Lane.

Girod de l'Ain, B. (1994) 'Modular or General Certification', *European Journal of Education*, **29(4)**, 399–413.

Gonon, P. (1993) *The Work of Georg Kerschensteiner*. Paper presented at London Institute of Education, June.

Goodman, R. (1990) *Japan's International Youth*. Oxford: Clarendon.

Goodson, I. and Medway, P. (eds) (1990) *Bringing English to Order: The History and Politics of a School Subject*. London: Falmer.

Gordon, P. and Lawton, D. (1978) *Curriculum Change in the Nineteenth and Twentieth Centuries*. Sevenoaks: Hodder and Stoughton.

Habermas, J. (1976) *Legitimation Crisis*. London: Heinemann.

Habermas, J. (1984) The Theory of Communicative Action, Vol. 1. *Reason and the Rationalization of Society*. London: Heinemann.

Halls, W.D. (1976) *Education, Culture and Politics in Modern France*. Oxford: Perga-

186

mon.

Halls, W.D. (ed.) (1990) *Comparative Education: Contemporary Issues and Trends.* London: Jessica Kingsley.

Halsey, A.H. (1993) 'Trends in access and equity in higher education: Britain in international perspective', *Oxford Review of Education*, **19(2)**, 129–40.

Hans, N. (1931) *History of Russian Education Policy 1701–1917.* London: P.S. Smith.

Hans, N. (1958) *Comparative Education.* London: Routledge.

Harbison, F.H. and Myers, C.A. (1964) *Education, Manpower and Economic Growth.* New York: McGraw-Hill.

Hargreaves, D. (1967) *Social Relations in a Secondary School.* London: Routledge.

Hatcham, T. E. (1992) *A Quoi Sert le Plan? Un regard sur le System Educatif.* Paris: Economica.

Hearnden, A. (1976) *Education, Culture and Politics in West Germany.* Oxford: Pergamon.

Hiroike, C. (1966) *The Characteristics of Moralogy and Supreme Morality.* Kashiwa-shi: Institute of Moralogy.

Hobbes, T. (1914) *Leviathan.* London: Dent.

Hodolidou, E. (1994) *Literature in English and Greek Secondary Curriculum: A Comparative Study.* Paper presented at the Comparative Education Society in Europe, Copenhagen.

Hollen, L. L. (1994) 'Educational inequality and academic achievement in England and France', *Comparative Education Review*, **38(1)**, 65–87.

Hollifield, J. F. (1992) *Immigrants, Markets and States: The Political Economy of Post-War Europe.* Cambridge, Ma.: Harvard University Press.

Holmes, B. and McLean, M. (1989) *The Curriculum: A Comparative Perspective.* London: Unwin Hyman.

Hopper, E. (1971) 'A typology for the classification of Educational Systems', in *Readings in the Theory of Educational Systems* (ed. Hopper, E.). London: Hutchinson pp. 91–110.

Houston, R. (1987) 'The Literacy Campaign in Scotland 1560–1803', in *National Literacy Campaigns: Historical and Comparative Perspectives* (eds Arnove, R. L. and Graff, H. J.). New York: Plenum Press, pp. 49–64.

Hoyle, E. (1969) *The Role of the Teacher.* London: Routledge.

Huberman, M. (1993) *The Lives of Teachers.* London: Cassell.

Huizinga, J.(1952) *Erasmus of Rotterdam.* London: Phaidon.

Husen, T. (1967) *International Study of Achievement in Mathematics* (2 vols.). New York: John Wiley.

Illich, I. (1973a) *Deschooling Society.* Harmondsworth: Penguin.

Illich, I. (1973b) *Tools for Conviviality.* Glasgow: Fontana/Collins.

Inkeles, A. (1979) 'National differences in scholastic performance', *Comparative Education*, **23(3)**, 386–407.

Inkeles, A. and Smith, D. H. (1975) *Becoming Modern.* London: Heinemann.

Inui, A. and Hosogane, T. (1995) 'Education as a foundation for work? The efficiency and problems of the Japanese upper secondary school', in *Youth, Education and Work* (eds Bash, L. and Green, A.). London: Kogan Page, pp. 162–72.

Ishida H. (1993) *Social Mobility in Contemporary Japan.* London: Macmillan.

Ivic, I. (1989) 'Profiles of educators: Lev S. Vygotsky', *Prospects*, **29(3)**, 427–35.

Jackson, B. (1964) *Streaming: An Education System in Miniature.* London: Routledge.

Jackson, B. and Marsden, D. (1966) *Education and the Working Class.* Harmondsworth: Penguin.

Japan, Ministry of Education, Science and Culture (1983a) *Course of Study for Elementary Schools in Japan*. Printing Bureau, Ministry of Finance.

Japan, Ministry of Education, Science and Culture (1983b) *Course of Study for Lower Secondary Schools*. Printing Bureau, Ministry of Finance.

Japan, Ministry of Education, Science and Culture (1993) *Education in Japan 1994*. Tokyo: Gyosei Corporation.

Jay, M. (1973) *The Dialectical Imagination*. London: Heinemann.

Jones, A. (1994) 'The educational legacy of the Soviet Period', in *Education and Society in the New Russia* (ed. Jones, A.). London: Sharpe, pp. 3–23.

Jullien, M.-A. (1962) *Esquisse d'un Ouvrage sur l'Education Comparee*. Geneva: International Bureau of Education.

Kandel, I. (1933) *Comparative Education*. New York: Houghton Mifflin.

Karadovsky, V.A. (1993) 'The school in Russia today and tomorrow', *Compare*, **23(3)**, 277–88.

Kennedy, P. (1988) *The Rise and Fall of the Great Powers*. London: Unwin Hyman.

Kennedy, P. (1993) *Preparing for the Twenty-First Century*. London: Harper Collins.

Kerr, C. (1982) *The Uses of the University*, 3rd edn. Cambridge, Ma.: Harvard University Press.

Kerr, D. (1983) 'Teacher competence and teacher education in the United States', *Teachers College Record*, **84(3)**, 525–52.

King Hall, R. (1953) 'The social position of teachers', in *The Yearbook of Education* (eds King Hall, R. and Hans, N.). London: Evan Brothers, pp. 1–29.

Kledsvik, U. J. (1989) 'Arbeitslehre – a new field in lower secondary education', *Education Today*, **39(2)**, 9–17.

Kleibard, H. M. (1987) *The Struggle for the American Curriculum 1893–1958*. London: Routledge.

Kogan, M. (1975) *Educational Policy-Making: A Study of Interest Groups and Parliament*. London: Allen and Unwin.

Landes, D. S.(1969) *The Unbound Promeutheus: Technological Change and Industrial Development in Western Europe from 1750 to the Present Day*. London: Cambridge University Press.

Lane, J. E. (1991) 'Sweden in the aftermath of educational reform', in *Prometheus Unbound: The Changing Relationship Between Government and Higher Education in Western Europe* (eds Neave, G. and Van Vught, F.). Oxford: Pergamon, pp. 160–162.

Lapointe, A.E., Mead, N.A. and Philips G.W. (1989) *A World of Differences*. Princeton, N.J.: Educational Testing Services.

Lauglo, J. (1990) 'Factors behind decentralization in Education Systems', *Compare*, **20(1)**, 21–39.

Lauglo, J. (1994) *The Populist Trait in the Nowergian Education Tradition*. Paper presented at the Comparative and International Education Society Conference, Kingston, Jamaica.

Lawson, T. (1992) 'Core Skills 16–19', in *16–19 Changes in Education and Training* (eds Whiteside, T. *et al.*). London: David Fulton.

Lauterbach, R. and Frey, K. (1987) 'Primary science education in the Federal Republic of Germany', in *Science, Society and Science Education Vol. 1 Basic Science at Elementary Education Level* (eds Lauterbach, R., *et al.*). Frankfurt: Johann Wolfgang Goethe University, pp. 17–63.

Lawton, D. and Gordon, P. (1987) *HMI*. London: Routledge.

Lauwerys, J. A. (1959) 'The philosophical approach to Education', *International Review*

188

of Education, **5(3)**, 281–98.

Lauwerys, J. A. (1965) *An Opening Address, General Education in a Changing World.* Max Plan Institute/CESE, Berlin.

Legg, K.(1973) 'Political change in a clientist policy: the failure of democracy in Greece', *Journal of Political and Military Sociology*, **1(2)**, 237–42.

Legrand, L. (1969) 'France', in *Examinations* (eds Lauwerys, J. A. and Scanlon, D. G.). (World Year Book of Education 1969). London: Evans, pp. 123–129.

Le Guen, M. (1994) 'Evaluating School Performance in France', in *Making Education Count.* Paris: OECD, pp. 173–197.

Le Monde de l'Education (1993) September, 30–47.

Le Monde de l'Education (1995) January.

Lieberman, A. (1956) *Education as a Profession.* New York: Prentice-Hall.

Lieberman, M. (1993) *Public Education: An Autopsy.* Cambridge, Ma.: Harvard University Press.

Liebrand, C.G.M. (1991) 'Recent developments in the Dutch system of vocational qualifications', *European Journal of Education*, **26(1)**, 55–61.

Liebschner, J. (1991) *Foundations of Progressive Education: the history of the National Froebel Society.* Cambridge: Lutterworth.

Lijphart, A. (1968) *The Politics of Accommodation: Pluralism and Democracy in the Netherlands.* Berkeley: University of California Press.

Lipset, S. M.(1994) 'Binary Comparisons – American Exceptionalism – Japanese Uniqueness', in *Comparing Nations* (eds Mattei, D. and Ali, K.). Oxford: Blackwell, pp. 153-212.

Locke, J. (1968) 'Some thoughts concerning education', in *The Educational Writings of John Locke* (ed. Axtell, J. L.). Cambridge: Cambridge University Press, pp. 114–325.

Lockheed, M. E. and Hanushek, E. (1988) 'Improving educational efficiency in developing countries', *Compare*, **18(1)**, 21–38.

Lombardi, F. V. (1987) *I programmi par la scuola elementare dal 1860 al 1985.* Brescia: Editrice La Scuola.

McClelland, D. C. (1961) *The Achieving Society.* Princeton N. J.: Nostrand.

McClelland, D. C. (1987) *Human Motivation.* Cambridge: Cambridge University Press.

Machiavelli, N. (1961) *The Prince.* Harmondsworth: Penguin.

McLean, M. (1985a) 'Education in France', in *Equality and Freedom in Education* (ed. Holmes, B.). London: Allen and Unwin, pp. 63–95.

McLean, M. (1985b) Private supplementary schools and the ethnic challenge to state education in Britain', in *Cultural Identity and Educational Policy* (eds Brock, C. and Tulasiewicz, W.). London: Croom Helm, pp. 326–45.

McLean, M. (1988) 'The Conservative education policy in comparative Perspective', *British Journal of Educational Studies*, **36(3)**, 200–217.

McLean, M. (1990a) *Britain and a Single Market Europe: Prospects for a Common School Curriculum.* London: Kogan Page.

McLean, M. (1990b) 'Higher education in the United Kingdom into the 1990s', *European Journal of Education*, **25(2)**, 157–70.

McLean, M. (1992) *The Promise and Perils of Educational Comparison.* London: Tufnell Press/ Institute of Education.

McLean, M. and Lauglo, J. (1985) 'Introduction: rationales for decentralization and a perspective from organization theory', in *The Control of Education: International Perspectives on the Centralization–Decentralization Debate.* London: Heinemann, pp. 1–27.

McLean, M. and Voskresenskaya, N. (1992) 'Educational revolution from above:Thatcher's Britain and Gorbachev's Soviet Union', *Comparative Education Review*, **36(1)**, 71–90.

McNair, J. M. (1984) *Education for a Changing Spain*. Manchester: Manchester University Press.

McQuail, D. (1994) *Mass Communications Theory*. London: Sage.

Madariaga, S. de (1970) *English, Frenchmen, Spaniards*, 2nd edn. London: Pitman.

Maeroff, G. I. (1991) *Teaching and Learning in English Urban Schools*. Washington, D.C.: Council of Great City Schools.

Mahar, J.M.(ed.) (1972) *The Untouchables in Contemporary India*. Tuscon, Az. University of Arizona Press.

Makiguchi, T. (1989) *Education for a Creative Living*. Ames: Iowa State University.

Manzer, R.A. (1970) *Teachers and Politics*. Manchester: Manchester University Press.

Marklund, S. and Soderberg, P. (1967) *The Swedish Comprehensive School*. London: Longmans.

Marsden, B. (1991) '"The Structure of Omission": British curriculum predicaments and false charts of American experience', *Compare*, **21(1)**, 5–26.

Marsden, D. and Ryan, P. (1991) 'Initial training, labour market structure and public policy: intermediate skills in British and German industry', in *International Comparisons of Vocational Education and Training for Intermediate Skills* (ed. Ryan, P.). London: Falmer, pp. 251–85.

Marx, K. (1963) *Selected Writings* (eds Bottomore,T.B. and Rubel, M.). Harmondsworth: Penguin.

Mayhew, A. (1926) *The Education of India*. London: Faber.

Mehran, G. (1990) 'Ideology and education in the Islamic Republic of Iran', *Compare*, **20(1)**, 53–66.

Meijer, K. (1991) 'Reforms in vocational education and training in Italy, Spain and Portugal', *European Journal of Education*, **26(1)**, 13–27.

Meyer, J. W., Kamens D. H. and Benavot, A. (1992) *School Knowledge for the Masses*. London: Falmer.

Mill, J. S. (1956) 'On liberty', in *The Liberal Tradition* (eds Bullock, A. and Shock, M.). Oxford: Clarendon, pp.114–116.

Monasta, A. (1994) 'Italy', in *Education in a Single Europe* (eds Brock, C. and Tulasiewicz, W.). London: Routledge, pp. 162–182.

Montaigne, M. de (1958) 'On the education of children', in *Essays*. Harmondsworth: Penguin, pp. 49–86.

Muckle, J. (1988) *A Guide to the Soviet Curriculum*. London: Croom Helm.

Myrdal, G. (1944) *The American Dilemma*. New York: Harper Row.

Nagy, J. and Szebenyi, P. (1990) 'Hungarian Reform: towards a curriculum for the 1990s', *The Curriculum Journal*, **1(3)**, 247–54.

Neave, G. (1985) 'France', in *The School and the University* (ed. Clark, B. R.). Berkeley: University of California Press, pp. 10–44.

Neave, G. (1992) *The Teaching Nation: Prospects for Teachers in the European Community*. Oxford: Pergamon.

Neave, G. (1993) 'Separation de Corps: the training of advanced students and the organization of research in France', in *The Research Foundations of Graduate Education: Germany, Britain, France, United States, Japan* (ed. Clark, B. R.). Berkeley: University of California Press, pp. 159-191.

Nettl, J.P. (1967) *The Soviet Achievement*. London: Thames and Hudson.

Newman, J.H. (1931) *Selected Discourses from the Idea of a University* (ed. Yardley,

M.). Cambridge: Cambridge University Press.

Nikandrov, N.D. (1989) 'What to compare, when and why: a Soviet perspective', *Comparative Education*, **25(3)**, 275–82.

O'Connor, J.(1973) *The Fiscal Crisis of the State*. New York: St.Martin's Press.

Olmedilla, J. M.M. (1992) 'Tradition and change in national examination systems', *Examinations: Comparative and International Studies* (eds Eckstein, M. A. and Noah, H. J.).Oxford: Pergamon, pp. 135–146.

Organization of Economic Cooperation and Development (OECD) (1974–) *Educational Statistics Yearbook*. Paris: OECD (annual).

OECD (1992a) *Education at a Glance*. Paris: OECD.

OECD (1992b) *Educational Statistics Yearbook*. Paris: OECD.

Ortega y Gasset, J. (1946) *The Mission of the University*. London: Kegan Paul.

Orwin, C. S. and Whetham, E. H. (1964) *A History of British Agriculture 1846–1914*. London: Longman.

Ouzof, J. and Ouzof M. (1992) *La Republique des Instituteurs*. Paris: Gallimard.

Pachocinski, R. (1994) 'Poland', in *Education in East Central Europe* (eds Karsten, S. and Majoor, D.). Munster: Waxmann, pp. 119–155.

Panitch, I.(1980) 'Recent theorizations on corporatism', *British Journal of Sociology*, **31(2)**, 159–87.

Parsons, T. (1958) 'Some ingredients in a general theory of formal organizations', *Administrative Theory in Education* (ed. Halpin, A.). New York: Macmillan, pp. 40–72.

Paul, J-J. (1985) 'Basic concepts and methods used in forecasting skilled manpower requirements in France', *Forecasting Skilled Manpower Needs: The Experience of Eleven Countries* (eds Youdi, R.V. and Hinchcliffe, K.). Paris: Unesco, pp. 35–56.

Paulston, R. (1990) 'Towards a reflective comparative education', *Comparative Education Review*, **34(2)**, 248–55.

Pelling, H. (1963) *A History of British Trade Unionism*. Harmondsworth: Penguin.

Petch, J. A. (1953) *Fifty Years of Examining*. London: George Harrap.

Piaget, J. (1967) 'The Significance of John Amos Comenius at the present time', *John Amos Comenius on Education*. New York: Teachers College Press, pp. 1–31.

Pieron, H. (1969) *Examens et Docimologie*. Paris: Presses Universitaires de France.

Pinson, K. S. (1966) *Modern Germany*. New York: Macmillan.

Plato (1953) *The Republic*. Harmondsworth: Penguin.

Prais, S.J. (1986) 'Educating for productivity: comparisons of Japanese and English schooling and vocational preparation', *Compare*, **16(2)**, 121–47.

Premfors, R. (1991) 'Knowledge, power and democracy', in *Studies in Higher Education and Research*, No.2, pp. 1–18.

Prost, A. (1968) *Histoire de l'Engseignement en France 1800–1967*. Paris: Armand Colin.

Prost, A. (1990) 'Schooling and stratification', in *The Comprehensive School Revisited* (eds Leschinsky,A. and Mayer, K.). Frankfurt: Peter Lang, pp. 38–61.

Ratcliff, J.L. (1992) 'Curriculum: undergraduate', in *International Encyclopedia of Higher Education* (eds Clark, B. R. and Neave, G.). Oxford: Pergamon, pp. 1566–1579.

Rau, E. (1993) 'Inertia and resistance to change in the Humboldtian University', in *Higher Education in Europe* (ed. Gellert, C.). London: Jessica Kingsley, pp. 37–45.

Raum, O. (1940) *Chaga Childhood*. Oxford: Oxford University Press.

Rawls, J. (1972) *A Theory of Justice*. Oxford: Oxford University Press.

Raynor, J. and Grant, N. (eds) (1972) *Patterns of Curriculum. Course E283, Unit 3*.

Bletchley: Open University Press.

Ree, H. (1973) *Educator Extraordinary: The Life and Achievement of Henry Morris.* Harlow: Longman.

Ringer, F. K. (1979) *Education and Society in Modern Europe.* Bloomington: Indiana University Press.

Rodwell, S. (1985) 'A world communications crisis', *Compare*, **15(1)**, pp. 53–66.

Robert, A. (1993) *Systeme Educatif et Reformes.* Paris: Nathan.

Robitaille, D.F. and Garden, R.A. (1989) *The IEA Study of Mathematics, II.* Oxford: Pergamon.

Rohlen, T. P.(1983) *Japan's High Schools.* London: University of California Press.

Rossello, P. (1960) *La Teoria de las Corrientes Educativas.* Havana: Unesco.

Rousseau, J.-J. (1993) *Emile.* London: Dent.

Rudman, H.C. (1967) *The School and the State in the USSR.* New York: Macmillan.

Ruiter, D.W.P. and Van Vught, F. (1990) 'Neo-functionalism in recent Dutch higher education legislation', *European Journal of Education*, **25(2)**, 219–30.

Rust, V. D.(1989) *The Democratic Tradition and the Evolution of Schooling in Norway.* New York: Greenwood Press.

Sadler, M.E.(1898) 'Problems in Prussian secondary education for boys', in *Special Reports in Educational Subjects* Vol. 3. London: HMSO, pp.83–252.

Sadler, M.E. (1995) *French Influences on English Education.* Liverpool: Northern Design Unit.

Sansom, G.B. (1987) *Japan: A Short Cultural History.* London: Cresset.

Schmitter, P. (1974) 'Still a century of corporatism', *Review of Politics*, **36(1)**, 93–98.

Schoppa, L.J.(1991) *Education Reform in Japan.* London: Routledge.

Schulz, T. W. (1977) 'Investment in human capital', in *Power and Ideology in Education* (eds Karabel, J. and Halsey, A.H.). New York: Oxford University Press, pp. 313–324.

Shapovalenko, S.G. (1963) *Polytechnical Education in the USSR.* Paris: Unesco.

Sharpe, K. (1993) 'An Inspector calls; an analysis of inspection procedures in French primary education', *Compare*, **23(3)**, 263–75.

Shavit, Y. and Blossfield, H.-P. (1993) *Persistent Inequality: Changing Educational Attainment in Thirteen Countries.* Boulder, Col.: Westview Press.

Shepard, L. A. and Smith, M. L. (1989) 'Introduction and Overview' in *Flunking Grades: Research and Policies on Retention.* London: Falmer, pp. 1–15.

Simon, B. and Simon J. (eds) (1963) *Educational Psychology in the USSR.* London: Routledge.

Simons, D. (1966) *Georg Kerschensteiner.* London: Methuen.

Singer, B. (1983) *Village Notables in Nineteenth Century France: Priests, Mayors, Schoolmasters.* Albany, N.Y.: State University of New York Press.

Smith, A. (1956) 'The Wealth of Nations', in *The Liberal Tradition* (eds Bullock, A. and Shock, M.). Oxford: Clarendon, pp. 25–28.

Smith, A. (1991) *The Age of Behemoths – The Globalization of Mass Media Firms.* New York: Priority Press Publications.

Sorensen, C. W. (1994) 'Success and education in South Korea', *Comparative Education Review*, **38(1)**, 10–35.

Spring, J. (1978) *American Education.* New York: Longman.

Stenhouse, L. (ed.) (1980) *Curriculum Research and Development in Action.* London: Heinemann.

Stepan, A. (1978) *The State and Society: Peru in Comparative Perspective.* Princeton, N.J.: Princeton University Press.

192

Stocking, C. (1985) 'The United States', in *The School and the University* (ed. Clark, B. R.). Berkeley,: University of California Press, pp. 239–263.

Stone, L. (1970) 'Japan and England', in *Sociology, History and Education* (ed. Musgrave, P.W.). London: Methuen, pp. 101–114.

Suddaby, A. (1989) 'An evaluation of the contribution of the teacher educators to Soviet educational reform', *Comparative Education*, **25(2)**, 245–56.

Sunday Times (1995) January 22

Svingby, G. (1990) 'Comprehensive school curriculum reform: the Swedish experience', *The Curriculum Journal*, **1(3)**, 323–31.

Tanguy, L. (1991) *L'Enseignement Professionel en France: des ouvriers aux techniciens*. Paris: Presse Universitaires de France.

Tawney, R.H. (1964) *Equality*. London: Unwin.

Teichler, U. (1985) 'The Federal Republic of Germany', in *The School and The University: An International Perspective* (ed. Clark, Burton R.). Berkeley: University of California Press, pp. 45–76.

Thelot, C. (1993) 'Les evaluations de masses dans le systeme educatif francais: enjeux, conduite, effect', in *Evaluating Education and Training: Comparative Approaches*, Vol. 2. (eds Cacouault, M. and Orivel, F.). Dijon: IREDU-CNRS, pp. 35–46.

Thompson, E. P.(1968) *The Making of the English Working Class*. Harmondsworth: Penguin.

Thomson, D. (1958) *Democracy in France*. London: Oxford University Press.

Tocqueville, A. de (1956) *Democracy in America*. New York: Mentor.

Toffler, A. (1980) *The Third Wave*. London: Collins.

Tomiak, J.J. (1995) 'Education, Work and the restructuring of central-eastern and eastern Europe', *Youth, Education and Work* (eds Bash, L. and Green, A.). London: Kogan Page, pp. 49–61.

Turner, R. (1971) 'Sponsored and contest mobility in the school system', in *Readings in the Theory of Educational Systems* (ed. Hopper, Earl.). London: Hutchinson, pp. 71–90.

Unesco (1963-) *Statistical Yearbook*. Paris: Unesco (annual).

Vanderhoven, J. (1991) *Education in Belgium: The Diverging Paths*. Brussels: OECD.

Vogel, E. F. (1987) 'Japan: adaptive communitarianism', in *Ideology and National Competitiveness: An Analysis of Nine Countries* (eds Lodge, G. C. and Vogel, E. F.). Boston Ma.: Harvard Business School Press, pp. 141–171.

Vonken, E. and Onstenk, J. (1995) 'Youth training in a changing Economy in Holland', *Youth Education and Work* (eds Bash, L. and Green, A.). London: Kogan Page, pp. 109–118.

Walicki, A. (1980) *A History of Russian Thought*. Oxford: Clarendon Press.

Walsh, W. (1966) *The Use of the Imagination*. Harmondsworth: Penguin.

Weber, M. (1964) in *The Theory of Economic and Social Organization* (ed. Parsons, T.). New York: Free Press.

Weber, M. (1970a) 'The Chinese Literati', *From Max Weber: Essays in Sociology* (eds Gerth, H.H. and Mills, C.W.) London: Routledge, pp. 416–444.

Weber, M. (1970b) 'Bureaucracy', in *From Max Weber* (eds Gerth, H.H. and Mills, C.W.). London: Routledge, pp. 196–264.

Weiler, H. (1989) 'Education and Power', *Educational Policy*, **3(1)**, 32–43.

Weiss, M. (1986) 'The financing of private schools in the Federal Republic of Germany', *Compare*, **16(2)**, 149–65.

White, M. (1987) *The Japanese Educational Challenge*. New York: Free Press.

Whitehead, A.N. (1962) *The Aims of Education*. London: Benn.

Wilkinson, R. (1964) *The Prefects: British Leadership and the Public School Tradition.* Oxford: Oxford University Press.

Willis, P. (1977) *Learning to Labour.* Farnborough: Saxon House.

Wilson, P.S. (1976) 'Plowden children', in *Schooling and Capitalism* (eds Dale, R. *et al.*). London: Routledge, pp. 158–162.

Winckler, E. A. (1987) 'Statism and Familism in Taiwan', in *Ideology and National Competitiveness: An Analysis of Nine Countries* (eds Lodge, G. C. and Vogel, E. F.). Boston, Ma.: Harvard Business School Press, pp. 173–206.

Winther-Jensen, T. (1994) Denmark', in *Education in a Single Europe* (eds Brock, C. and Tulasiewicz, W.). London: Routledge, pp. 45–65.

Wolf, A. and Rapiau, M. T. (1993) 'The academic achievement of craft apprentices in France and England: contrasting systems and common dilemmas', *Comparative Education*, **29(1)**, 29–43.

Woodhead, M. (1979) *Preschool Education in Western Europe.* London: Longman.

Woodward, L. (1962) *The Age of Reform 1815–1870.* Oxford: Clarendon.

Wong, L. (1992) *Education of Chinese Children in Britain and the USA.* Clevedon: Multilingual Matters.

World Bank (1991) *The Challenge of Development.* Oxford: Oxford University Press.

Yagodin, G. (1989) *Towards Higher Standards in Education through its Humanization and Democratization.* Moscow: Novosti.

Youdi, R.V. and Hinchliffe, K. (eds) (1985) *Forecasting Skilled Manpower Needs: The Experience of Eleven Countries.* Paris: Unesco.

Zeldin, T. (1979) *France 1848–1945* (2 vols). Oxford: Clarendon.

Index